AS ICT for AQA

Sharon Yull & Tracey Stump

Series Editor – Jackie Rogers

Heinemann

Inspiring generations

Heinemann Educational Publishers
Halley Court, Jordan Hill, Oxford OX2 8EJ
Part of Harcourt Education

Heinemann is the registered trademark of
Harcourt Education Limited

© Jackie Rogers, Tracey Stump, Sharon Yull 2003

First published 2003

07 06 05 04 03
10 9 8 7 6 5 4 3 2 1

British Library Cataloguing in Publication Data is available
from the British Library on request.

ISBN 0 435 45487 0

Edited by Jan Doorly
Typeset and illustrated by Techtype, Abingdon

Original illustrations © Harcourt Education Limited, 2003

Cover design by Tony Richardson at Wooden Ark Ltd

Cover photo: © Alamy

Printed in the UK by Scotprint.

Acknowledgements
Every effort has been made to contact copyright holders of material reproduced in this book. Any omissions
will be rectified in subsequent printings if notice is given to the publishers.

Tel: 01865 888058 www.heinemann.co.uk

CONTENTS

ACKNOWLEDGEMENTS

The authors and publisher would like to thank the following for permission to reproduce copyright material.

checkmyfile.com, page 39

upmystreet.com, page 45

Eastern Daily Press, page 46

The Guardian, Nic Paton, page 57

Telegraph Group Limited, page 62

The Times, page 63

Computer Weekly, page 70

Computing Canada, page 71

Norfolk Police Headquarters, Norwich, page 71

The Register (www.theregister.com) page 75

Federation Against Software Theft, page 79

UK Web Design Association, page 128

Brainhat, Inc., page 177

google.com, page 178

Screen shots reprinted by permission from Microsoft Corporation

Crown copyright material is reproduced under Class License No. C01W0000141 with the permission of the Controller of HMSO and the Queen's Printer for Scotland

AQA (NEAB)/AQA examination questions are reproduced by permission of the Assessment and Qualifications Alliance

Every effort has been made to contact copyright holders of material published in this book. We would be glad to hear from any unacknowledged sources at the first opportunity. Any omissions will be rectified in subsequent printings if notice is given to the publishers.

INTRODUCTION

Students embarking on an Advanced Subsidiary (AS) course in any subject normally already know something about that subject – they may have studied it for GCSE, or they may have read leaflets describing the AS and A Level courses at their school or college. Something grabs their interest. Certainly they feel an interest in learning something new.

Studying for AS Information and Communication Technology is **different**.

Studying for AS Information and Communication Technology is **special.**

Information and Communication Technology (ICT) is in everything we do. It is all around us in the modern world. Everyone thinks they know about ICT – after all they use it every day, don't they? They can produce a word-processed letter; they can set up a Christmas card list or catalogue their CD collection; they may even be able to set up a web page.

These things are **not** AS Information and Communication Technology.

AS ICT is the study of how ICT is used in the world of business; how data is collected and turned into information; how that information is used and misused, kept and passed on, controlled and kept secure, stored and displayed. It provides an opportunity to study the phenomenal rise in the amount of information that exists in the twenty-first-century world; how this has arisen, what facilities there are to hold and control the flow, and to what purposes this information can be put.

This book is aimed at students following the AQA Advanced Subsidiary 5521 course (and the AS portion of the 6521 Advanced course). The AQA exam board has published a specification, labelled '2004 onwards', that is expected to last the lifetime of the qualification. This book has four separate sections, covering:

- AS Unit 1 (theory module) – Information: Nature, role and context
- AS Unit 2 (theory module) – Information: Management and manipulation
- AS Unit 3 (practical module) – Coursework: The use of generic application software for task solution
- Revision unit – for the two theory papers.

The first two units will follow the AQA specification closely, giving basic facts, ideas for practical exercises to apply your knowledge, quick self-test questions, and pointers on answering exam questions.

Unit 3 will explain exactly what is required in the coursework, and show how to produce the evidence required, giving examples at each stage.

The final revision unit will give pointers on how to read examination papers and questions; some frequently asked definitions; and lists of topic points to remember.

Unit 1 covers the topics:

- Knowledge, information and data
  - The basic definitions; the nature of data; how data arises and the quality of the data source; encoding data and coding value judgements
- The value and importance of data
  - Information as a commodity; the importance of accuracy and of its being up to date; who uses the information
- The control of information
  - Legal aspects of holding data; legal rights of data subjects; value of non-disclosable information
- The capabilities and limitations of ICT
  - Storage and processing capacities and capabilities; speed and response times; limitations of data held; information produced; hardware, software, etc.
- The social impact of information and communication technology
  - Benefits and drawbacks of using ICT in manufacturing, commerce, medicine, the home, education and teleworking
- The role of communication systems
  - Global communications between single and multiple users; Internet hardware, software and services; other communication systems; Internet capabilities and applications
- Information and the professional
  - Qualities and characteristics of ICT professionals and ICT teams
- Information systems, malpractice and crime
  - The consequences of malpractice and crime on information systems (IS); weak points; measures to protect IS; Internet access issues related to malpractice/crime
- The legal framework
  - The Computer Misuse Act; copyright legislation; data protection legislation; Health and Safety legislation as it pertains to ICT, including the design of new software.

Unit 2 covers the topics:

- Data capture
  - Methods; data encoding
- Verification and validation
  - Accuracy and validity of data; sources of errors and methods of preventing them; validation techniques
- The organisation of data for effective retrieval
  - Relational databases; data organisation and retrieval; advantages of relational databases over flat files; structure selection
- Software: Its nature, capabilities and limitations
  - Peripherals: All types of software; systems software, application software, operating systems – their features and functions, what they can do and what they can't do; bespoke versus package software; generic versus specialist packages; upgradability and reliability, including testing aspects
- The manipulation and processing of data
  - Modes of operation/processing; processing of different forms of data
- The dissemination and distribution of information
  - How to output information from an Information system

- Hardware: Its nature, capabilities and limitations
  - Input, output, storage, processing and communication devices, and where they are used
- The security of data
  - Security versus privacy; processes to protect integrity of data; back-up and recovery procedures
- Network environments
  - Network versus stand-alone; LANs and WANs, client-server versus peer-to-peer; hardware, software, communications and topology elements
- The human/computer interface
  - Right level for right person; effective dialogue; design aspects; design of common user interfaces; natural language interface.

Unit 3 covers choosing a suitable task for use as coursework, and gives guidelines on how to produce the solution. Notes and examples are given to help with:

- specification
- implementation
- testing
- evaluation
- producing the user guide.

This section also gives pointers as to the accepted 'advanced' features to use in some of the more popular generic packages. It does not, however, try to provide a package training manual.

The **Revision** unit covers:

- Exam vocabulary: question words and what they are asking for
- Exam technique: how to read the question and interpret what is required
- Some frequently asked definitions (essential technical vocabulary)
- Contrasts and differences, including benefits and limitations, for popular topics
- Lists of examples with short descriptions.

Group activity

Before you begin your study, complete the following activity.

Preparation

Individually, write down a list of information and communication technology systems that are in everyday use, stating what the system is used for, and which business or organisation is using it. Find inspiration from your daily life – a part-time job, perhaps; your parents' work/business; the shopping you do; your school or college; borrowing or buying books, videos, CDs; paying for items or getting cash out of an ATM, and so on. Try to list at least five systems.

Work in groups

Ask the questions below to find as much information about each system as you can. In small groups, brainstorm your ideas and produce, in tabular form (using a package or as a paper exercise) answers to the following questions:

- What is the context/business?
- What is the system called/what does it do (its title)?
- What kind of machine (computer) is used?
- What hardware is used for:

- data collection
- storage
- processing
- output?

■ What are the sources of data?
■ What are the methods of entering data into the system?
■ What happens to data in the system?
■ What is the immediate output, and who sees it?
■ What else might happen?

Other questions that would be useful to ask in certain circumstances are:

■ Who wrote the system, or where did it come from?
■ What software was used to write the system (generic or specialist)?
■ Is it part of a larger system?
■ Where is information sent? How?
■ Is it part of a network?
■ What security is used?
■ Who controls the system?
■ Who operates the system?

Find out this information for as many systems as you can, covering a variety of contexts (commerce, education, home, medicine, manufacturing) and system sizes, from small to large.

Whole class evaluation

Review the tables produced by other groups and suggest improvements. Amalgamate the best information and, using some form of presentation or DTP software, format it so that it makes a useful reference for later study.

After you study each topic in the AS modules, review and improve this reference work where necessary. It will form an invaluable revision aid.

UNIT 1 – INFORMATION:
NATURE, ROLE AND CONTEXT

This unit will focus on data and information, and their use and application as knowledge. A range of material will be used to examine the roles of data and information, the value and qualities of information, and how this can be communicated between different users.

ICT and communication systems have changed the way in which people capture, store, manipulate and output data and information. This unit will also identify the role that ICT plays in organisations, and how this has contributed to better dissemination of information and knowledge. In addition, the social implications of using ICT in certain domains (e.g. education, industry and commerce) will be examined.

Finally this unit will identify the ways in which information can be controlled both internally and externally, through the use of legislation and other measures to protect users of information systems.

1 Knowledge, information and data

1.0 Understanding data

This section will provide coverage of the following key areas:

- Understand the distinction between knowledge, information and data
- Understand the nature of data: recorded facts, events or transactions
- Understand the different ways in which data can arise: (direct capture or as a by-product of another operation)
- Describe the effect of the quality of the data source on the information produced
- Understand the need to encode information as data
- Understand the problems associated with the coding of value judgements.

Data consists of random (or a set of random) unprocessed facts with little or no intrinsic value. Data can be categorised by type or format, as shown below:

Type or format	Description
Alphanumeric	Numbers, letters and other characters
Numeric	Binary, integer, real, currency
Video data	Moving pictures, graphics or images
Image data	Graphic image and/or pictures
Audio data	Sounds and noises

The following are all data:

- Invoice number   Y300TRE/011
- Date   22/04/2003
- Car registration number   AY03 BTR

The **invoice number** as it stands has little or no meaning. We can identify with the **date** because we know that by convention:

    22   = the day of the month
    04   = the month (April)
    2003   = the year

But in the United States, a different convention is used and this date would appear differently, as 04/22/2003.

The **car registration number** may be completely meaningless to us, or we may know that the '03' refers to the first registration period in 2003, and that certain letters identify the area in which the car was registered.

It is clear that without any background knowledge, a string of numbers or characters is meaningless. Insurance policies may contain what looks to be random data in the form of customer policy numbers, such as the following.

ST/01/L/34849

RB/02/M/74788

LD/89/H/56337

If further data were provided, or we had an understanding of the rationale behind the data set, it would be transformed into meaningful data, or information, as shown:

Policy numbers	Customer initials	Customer since	Insurance type	Unique random code
ST/01/L/34849	ST	2001	L – Life	34849
RB/02/M/74788	RB	2002	M – Motor	74788
LD/89/H/56337	LD	1989	H – Home	56337

A lesson to be learnt is that when you are working with data sets consideration needs to be given to a range of users. What may seem straightforward and clear to one user can be a mystery to others.

Test your knowledge

1 How would you define data?
2 Give four examples of data.
3 Give an example of a meaningful data set.
4 Identify a consideration that needs to be taken into account when working with data sets.

1.1 Processing data

Data can be described as 'raw' until some sort of processing activity has been applied. The processing activity converts raw data into meaningful data, or information, as shown in Figure 1.

Figure 1

Initial conversion process: data into information

A number of stages are involved in turning data into information – see Figure 2. These stages are generic (they remain common regardless of the activity):

Stage 1 Data capture
Stage 2 Data storage
Stage 3 Data processing
Stage 4 Conversion/editing
Stage 5 Output of information

Each will be discussed below. However, some of the stages may occur in a different order. For example, stage 3 may be automatic prior to stage 2. Each stage can be broken down further into individual elements that may be unique to certain activities – the accounts department may capture data in a different way from a sales department.

Figure 2

Stages of the conversion process

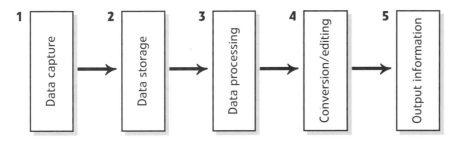

Data capture

Data capture is the process of collecting information from a variety of sources and capturing it by using a manual or electronic resource. The sources from which data can be gathered include the following.

Types of data

Examples of sources

Written	■ Letter
	■ E-mail
	■ Report
	■ Customer order
Verbal	■ Presentation
	■ Discussion
	■ Debate
	■ Conversation
Visual	■ Picture
	■ Graphic
	■ Moving image
Sensory	■ Touch
	■ Smell
	■ Sound
	■ Taste

Direct data capture is completed for a specific purpose and by an automatic process, e.g. the reading of bar codes in a supermarket, or of the magnetic strips on credit cards at a store till.

If an operator is required to input data from, for example, a piece of paper, this is **indirect data capture**. It is more likely to lead to errors. Another type of indirect data capture is where data has already been gathered for another purpose. For example, the bar-code reader at the supermarket checkout is used to compile the customer's bill, but also indirectly captures data which is useful for stock control.

The captured pieces of data must be encoded before they can be stored and manipulated. It would be easy to record the sale of a tin of baked beans, by using the bar code together with any other relevant data such as date, time and the total amount spent by the customer. It is more difficult to encode value judgements, but these are often equally valuable pieces of information. For example, the answer to the question: 'How enjoyable is your ICT course?' will vary from person to person. You could ask respondents to choose from a range of options, such as:

1 Very enjoyable
2 Quite enjoyable
3 Not very enjoyable
4 Not at all enjoyable.

You could then code their responses from 1 to 4. But would your four categories be adequate to cover the range of responses, and give an accurate reflection of opinions? When devising coding systems it is always important to keep in mind the balance between making the coding manageable and making sure it gives an accurate account of the data available.

Data storage

Data storage aims to ensure that captured data is kept secure. The storage of data should allow for ease of access, transference, updating and monitoring. The benefits of electronic storage are that it:

- is permanent (it remains after the system has shut down)
- is easy to access (there can be multi-user access to data stored in a specified location)
- is easy to update (you can access the data, make changes and save)
- can be in a secure format (data can be coded or password mechanisms can be put in place).

Electronic data storage can, however, cause problems if certain security protocols or standard ways of working are not practised.

- If users are not aware of back-up procedures, data can be lost or become corrupt.
- File management procedures, version control and general protocols in terms of saving data in correct formats using appropriate data types and file extensions are necessary.
- With multi-user access, issues of data protection could arise – both confidentiality and security.
- Data must be kept in a secure format, or problems could arise from viruses, hackers, unauthorised users, spamming, or sabotage of data. These dangers will be discussed in Section 8 (page 73).

What does this mean?	
Back-up procedures:	Making an additional copy of data in case the original gets, lost, stolen or corrupted
File management procedures:	Ensuring that files are managed effectively, e.g. given meaningful file names and grouped and structured appropriately
Version control:	The allocation of a code or number each time a piece of data is updated, e.g. V1.0, V1.1
General protocols:	Procedures to ensure that data and information are entered, saved, updated, processed and output correctly

Data processing

Data processing converts data into information.

Figure 3

Data processing

Step 1	Step 2	Step 3

1 Gather the data to be input into the system

2 Input the data to be processed

3 Collect the output information

Some of the more common processing activities include:

- calculating
- merging
- sorting
- selecting and interrogating
- manipulating.

Calculating includes processes such as using a spreadsheet to add up two columns of data automatically and present a final value.

In the example below, columns C and D are being multiplied together to present a total for each week, in column E, and then a total for the month.

A	B	C	D	E
1				
2	**SMY Computing**			
3				
4	Monthly motherboard sales			
5				
6				
7	Month ending March 2003	Total Sold	Unit Price £	Total Price £
8				
9	Week 1	83	79.2	= (C9*D9)
10	Week 2	69	79.2	= (C10*D10)
11	Week 3	78	79.2	= (C11*D11)
12	Week 4	113	79.2	= (C12*D12)
13				
14				**=SUM(E9:E13)**
15				

Merging is where two or more pieces of data are merged together, as in using a mail-merge facility to make a new document. This is a common function in word-processing packages, where a standard letter template can be produced and information such as names and addresses is retrieved from another source and merged with the template to create a customised letter.

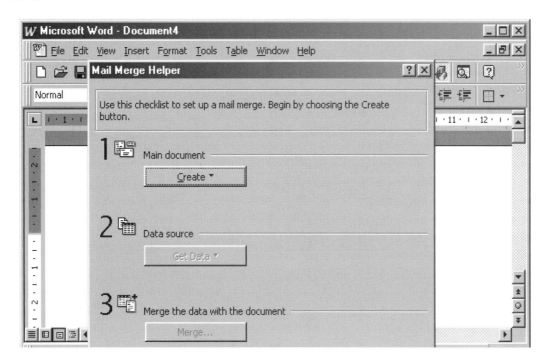

Sorting allows users to sort through information using specific criteria, for example sorting information alphabetically in ascending or descending order.

The following example looks at sorting student enrolment information alphabetically by surname.

1 Unsorted version

Surname	First name	Enrolment number
James	Stewart	SJ/1267OP
Harrison	Charlotte	CH/5374LP
Michaels	John	JM/2900GL
Davids	Rebecca	RD/6729HN
Smyth	Pippa	PS/2773BN
Peterson	Jack	JP/7002LS
Morris	Joan	JM/3544NM
Jacobs	Mary	MJ/1003RT

2 Sorting function

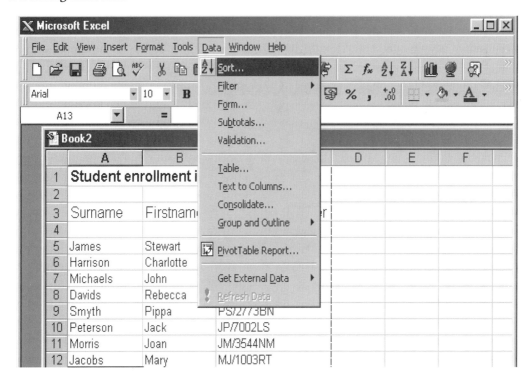

3 Sorted information

Surname	First name	Enrolment number
Davids	Rebecca	RD/6729HN
Harrison	Charlotte	CH/5374LP
Jacobs	Mary	MJ/1003RT
James	Stewart	SJ/1267OP
Michaels	John	JM/2900GL
Morris	Joan	JM/3544NM
Peterson	Jack	JP/7002LS
Smyth	Pippa	PS/2773BN

Selecting and interrogating activities focus on retrieving data and using it for another purpose. An example is using a query to generate a report in a database, retrieving information stored in tables.

Manipulating means using, changing or updating data. An example of this would be applying a filter to a certain data set in order to extract specific data types, e.g. customers living in Norwich.

Individual processing activities will depend on the type of system and the processing requirement. This is evident in the comparison between manual and computerised systems shown in the table below.

Manual activity	Processing method	Computerised activity	Processing method
Complete an assessment	■ Read through tasks ■ Carry out research ■ Produce a draft copy ■ Proof read and make changes ■ Submit final copy	Search for customer information	■ Access a central resource such as a data base ■ Search through information ■ Set up search/sort parameters ■ Select and collate customer details

However, when processing data the same activities are often carried out, regardless of whether the process is manual or computerised. Examples include:

■ **accessing** information: physically from a resource or digitally from a file
■ **sorting** information: physically using files and alphabetical ordering or digitally using a tool or wizard
■ performing a **calculation**: physically using a calculator or digitally using a macro or a program.

Activity 1

A company that sells commercial software has captured data from 2,500 customers using questionnaires and surveys – see Figure 4 on the next page. Facts and statistics on pricing, frequency of purchase, features, competitors and quality of current products have been collected. The company wants to use this information to improve the quality of the service it provides.

Initially, the data has been distributed to the following departments for processing:

■ finance   ■ sales   ■ marketing.

Using Figure 3 (page 10) as guidance and based on your own understanding and knowledge, complete the following tasks:

1 State **three** ways in which each of the departments could use the data.

2 Identify **two** processing activities from the following that could be carried out within each department using the data. Present the information in a table.

■ calculating   ■ merging

■ sorting   ■ selecting and interrogating

■ manipulating.

Figure 4

Sample data capture document – customer survey

Customer survey – software packages

Name:	Age (please tick the appropriate box)
	18 or below ☐ 19–35 ☐ 36–50 ☐
Address:	51–64 ☐ 65+ ☐

Please tick the types of software package purchased new in the last twelve months	Please indicate if you have just upgraded an existing software package in the last twelve months (added to the existing software)
	Upgraded
Word processing ☐	Yes/No
Spreadsheet ☐	Yes/No
Database ☐	Yes/No
Graphics ☐	Yes/No
Presentation ☐	Yes/No
Utility ☐	Yes/No
Multimedia ☐	Yes/No
Specialist ☐	Yes/No
Other ☐	Yes/No
(please specify)	

What is the maximum you would pay for each software package?

Word processing £	Spreadsheet £	Database £
Graphics £	Presentation £	Utility £
Multimedia £	Specialist £	Other £

Where do you purchase your software, e.g. mail order, retail shop, direct from manufacturer, etc. and why?

What features do you look for when purchasing software, e.g. user friendly, compatibility with existing software, etc.?

What has influenced your decision to purchase software from us in the past?

(please rate from 1–5, 1 = lowest 5 = highest)

Competitive prices	☐
Good quality service	☐
Fast despatch	☐
Regular updates and new product information	☐
Friendly staff	☐

How could we improve our service to you?

Conversion/editing

Conversion or editing is the fourth stage in the data-conversion process. After processing, the data may require further refinements in order to become accessible and useful. This could involve transferring the data into documents that already exist in the system.

Output of information

The last stage in the data-conversion process focuses on output of information. It produces evidence of the process, for example a report or other business document. This evidence can be distributed and used to gather feedback. The feedback can then be filtered back into the system to make it more dynamic, efficient and reliable.

The original model in Figure 1 can be extended and updated to reflect these stages, as shown in Figure 5.

Figure 5

Completed conversion process: data into information

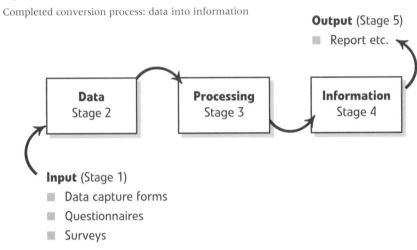

Figure 6 illustrates the fact that with the introduction of feedback, the conversion process can be represented as a continuous loop.

Figure 6

Data conversion as a continuously updating process

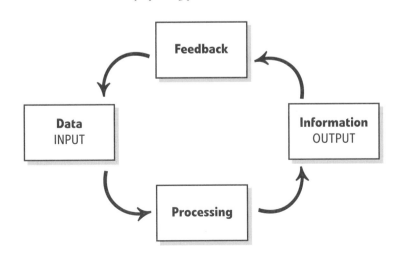

Activity 2

One example of a conversion process is data as input being processed to produce information as output. There are other types of processing systems.

For each of the following activities give the elements in the conversion process.

Example:	**Input**	⟶	**Processing**	⟶	**Output**
Making cider	Apples		Fermentation		Cider

1. Learning to drive
2. Writing an assignment
3. Booking a holiday
4. Making a sandwich
5. Preparing a presentation

Test your knowledge

1. How is information derived from data?
2. How many stages are there in the conversion process, and what are they?
3. In what ways can data be collected, and what are some of the sources of data?
4. What are the benefits of electronic storage?
5. Give two examples of a processing activity.

1.2 What is information?

Information is a set of meaningful, processed data that can be put to a use. Information is exchanged every second of every day, and it provides the infrastructure for society, industry and commerce.

Information can be described according to its:

- categories and formats
- qualities
- value
- function.

Each of these characteristics determines the importance of information as a commodity, in terms of its relevance to individuals. We will examine these criteria below.

1.3 Information categories and formats

Information can be categorised as:

- verbal
- visual
- written
- expressive (body language and gestures).

These categories can further be divided into formats, specifying how the information can be communicated, as shown in Figure 7:

Figure 7

Sample formats for transmitting information

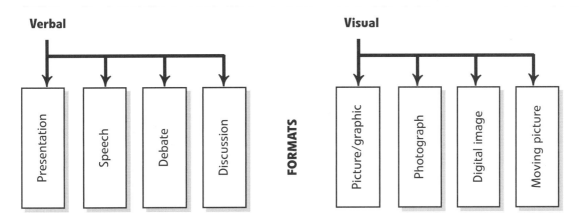

FORMATS

Activity 3

In small groups, discuss different formats of information, including those in Figure 7. From the discussion produce a table similar to the one below, identifying three formats with an example for each category.

For example, 'conversation giving advice' would be a suitable format for verbal information, and the example could be 'providing a recommendation to a friend who wants to buy a PC'.

Category	Format	Example
Verbal	1 Conversation giving advice	Providing a recommendation to a friend who wants to buy a PC
	2	
	3	
Written	1	
	2	
	3	
Visual	1	
	2	
	3	
Expressive	1	
	2	
	3	

Each communication category has a number of advantages and disadvantages, and these will be discussed below.

17

Verbal information

When information is transferred verbally, the communication is usually open, relatively unstructured, and informal. However, this can be a drawback if the purpose is to relay information that is confidential and/or formally structured. Verbal communication includes:

- enquiring
- directing
- informing
- debating
- delegating
- advising
- challenging
- persuading.

Activity 4

1 For each of the verbal formats listed above, identify a situation you have been in which used this format.

2 Choose five formats and identify how you used each in a particular setting.

3 For each of these situations identify another way the information could have been transmitted verbally.

4 Are there any other formats of verbal information that you could add to the list?

Written information

Written information is of great importance because it provides certain assurances. An application form, for example, identifies and provides assurances of the knowledge and skills of the applicant. A receipt is a warranty verifying the sale of an item. Certificates verify an achievement or an event, such as a swimming qualification or a marriage certificate. Birthday cards provide an acknowledgement of a celebration.

Written information can be in a number of formats and serve a range of purposes and audiences. In recent years written forms of communication have become even more popular due to the increasing use of electronic mail (e-mail). E-mail provides the flexibility and convenience which traditional letter writing can lack. Information can be sent instantly and with less expense than by traditional postage methods, and e-mail is available 24 hours a day.

Examples of written information include:

- letters
- reports
- certificates.
- invoices
- memorandums

Letters can be formal or informal documents depending upon the content and the relationship between the sender and the receiver. Many business communications still take place in the form of a letter.

Invoices are written or computer-generated documents that identify amounts owing for the supply of goods and services. They are formal documents that are used within organisations as a record of how much needs to be paid in or out of the company.

Invoice

S.J TRADING

Unit 42
Wendlesham Trading Estate
Oxford OX9 4RZ

Customer: J. Spencer & Co.
23 The Drive
Carhampton
Oxfordshire
OX21 6LU

Invoice Number: ST1234/09OP

Date: 18 February 2003

Item number: W167–34

Quantity: 48

Item description:

4.5" rubber belts (black reinforced)

Unit Price: £0.26

Amount: £12.48

Balance to be paid within 30 days of invoice date

Reports are used to collate information for distribution to other users. A report can bring together ideas, investigations and research. A report may contain a mix of quantitative and qualitative information (see below and page 31). The main focus of a report is to deliver information in a structured format, ending with a conclusion and possible recommendations on action to be taken.

What does this mean?	
Quantitative information:	Information based on numerical facts, figures and statistics. Examples could include financial results presented on a balance sheet, temperature information in a weather report, share prices, etc.
Qualitative information:	Information based on descriptions and judgements. Examples could include reasons why a supermarket performed badly – an increase in competition leading to price wars, and bad weather that affected the availability of fresh produce

Reports normally include the following:

▦ Title page: a front sheet identifying the report's title, the author, date and who the report is commissioned for.

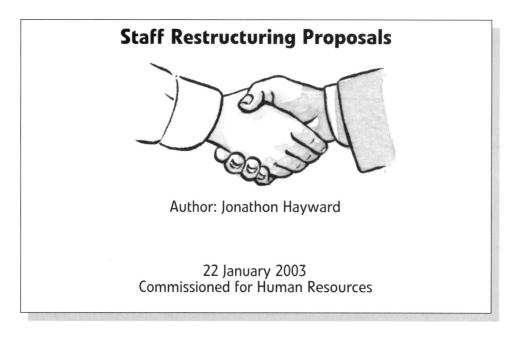

Staff Restructuring Proposals

Author: Jonathon Hayward

22 January 2003
Commissioned for Human Resources

▦ Contents page: showing the information given on each page.

Contents

Introduction	....	Page 1
Statistics on departmental staffing levels	....	Page 2
Marketing resources	....	Page 4
Finance resources	....	Page 7
Staff training	....	Page 10

▦ Introduction: providing a short summary of the overall focus and content of the report.

▦ Procedures: identifying how data was collected, collated, analysed and presented.

▦ Main findings section: where the bulk of the report content is placed. It should be broken down into task, action or research areas. Each argument or statement should be supported by research and analysis. The main findings section can be broken down into sub-sections.

▦ Conclusions: bringing together all the items discussed and providing a summary of the key areas identified.

▦ Recommendations: this section is solution based, offering proposals on how to move forward with the report's objective.

▦ References: this section should identify all information sources used, including books, magazines, journals, reports, and the Internet.

▓ Appendices: supporting documentation, which could include lists of facts and figures, leaflets, information downloaded from the Internet, photocopied material, etc.

Memorandums or memos are used within an organisation as an informal way of communicating and documenting information.

Memorandum

To: Charles Browne

From: Stewart Humphries

CC: Accounts Department

Date: 2 March 2003

Re: Late payments

[Body of text displayed here]

Certificates are used to provide written evidence of an achievement or event.

Examples include:

▓ sports, e.g. swimming
▓ education, recording past grades or achievements in attendance
▓ First Aid or other training course completed
▓ births, marriages and deaths.

Although written forms of information provide the stability and security of documentary evidence, they can be time-consuming and expensive to generate. Also, they may not be the most appropriate form of communication – for example, complex written instructions could be replaced by pictures or graphics.

Visual information

Visual information formats can include pictures, graphics and other design tools. We encounter information in a visual format wherever we go.

Examples of visual information tools are shown in Figure 8. For each of these a further distinction can be made into individual categories. For example, maps provide a visual guide, and contain information that could not easily be presented in a textual format. The category 'maps' can be divided into underground maps, Ordnance Survey maps, street maps, building or site plans, mind maps, etc.

Figure 8

Visual information tools

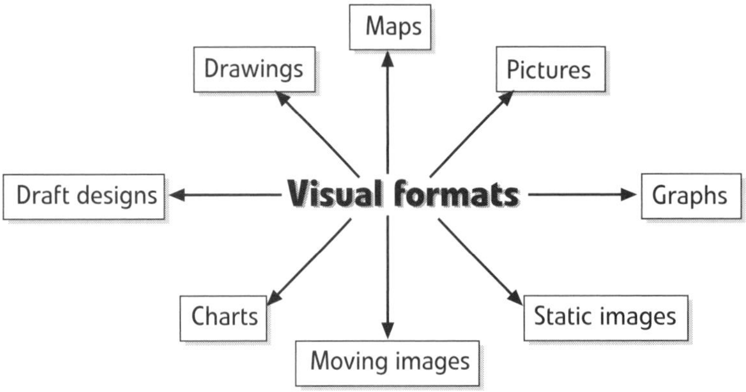
Maps
Drawings
Pictures
Draft designs
Visual formats
Graphs
Charts
Static images
Moving images

Visual information may receive a more positive and motivated response than information presented in a written format. Pictures, graphics, charts and moving images may offer more clarity and aid understanding more readily than lengthy written explanations, but too many visuals may distract an audience from core information.

Group activity

To emphasise the importance of visual information, carry out the following exercise in groups of three.

1. One person in the group should write down a set of instructions on how to get from one familiar location to another.
2. The instructions should be read out to the second team member, to enable him or her to draw a map of the same information.
3. Both team members should present their work to the third team member, and he or she should identify which of the two formats is more appropriate and easier to understand, giving reasons.

Within organisations the most frequently used forms of visual information are graphs and charts. These are used to provide visual support to data and to provide a clear breakdown of key data components. Some of the more popular types in use include the following.

Pie charts

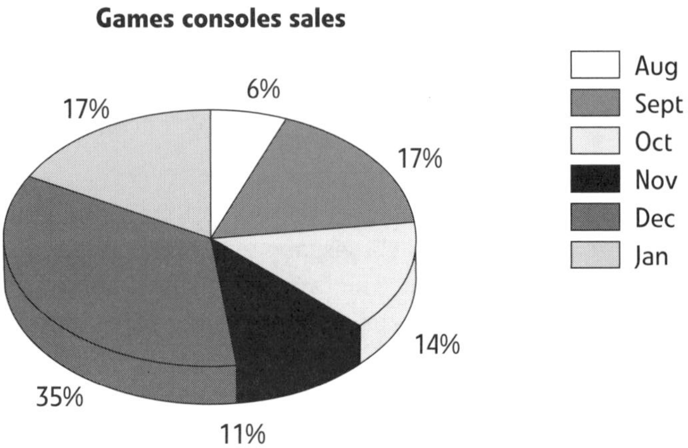
Games consoles sales
6%
17%
17%
14%
11%
35%
Aug
Sept
Oct
Nov
Dec
Jan

Each segment of this pie chart represents the percentage of games consoles sold for each month from August to January. The smallest segment is 6% for August and the largest is 35% for December.

Bar graphs

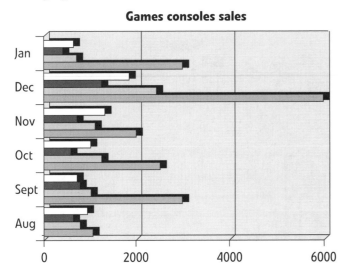

The bars on this graph each represent a type of games console, A, B, C and D. The graph identifies, for each month, how many of each type were sold.

Line graphs

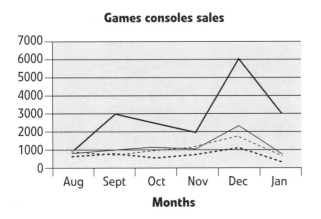

This line graph plots the sales of each type of console from August to January. It is evident that Type A console is the best seller and Type C console is the worst seller. From this graph it is also clear that in August, September and January, sales were very similar for Types B, C and D.

Scatter graphs

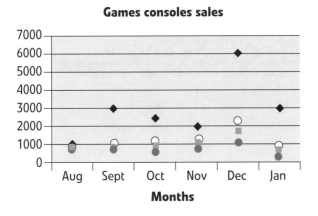

Scatter graphs are best used to plot a lot of numerical data in order to identify a correlation or pattern. This scatter graph illustrates the pattern of sales for each month. In August all four games console types had similar sales figures, whereas in December these were quite diverse.

Activity 5

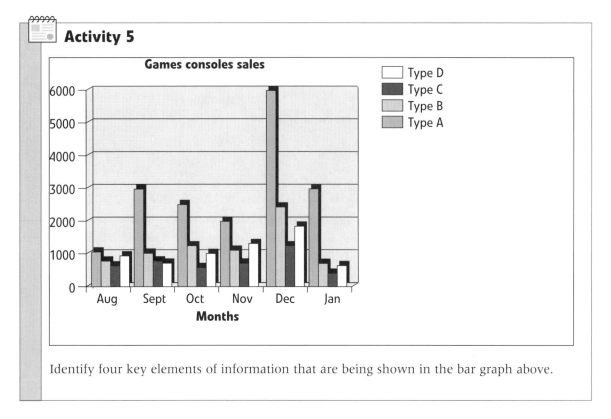

Identify four key elements of information that are being shown in the bar graph above.

Graphs can provide a great deal of information. However, visual formats may not be sufficient for presenting information on their own. For example, to provide a more detailed analysis of games console sales, raw data may need to be included so that more specific information can be gathered, such as average sales over a set period.

Test your knowledge

Sales of games consoles 2002/2003						
	Aug	Sept	Oct	Nov	Dec	Jan
Type A	1000	3000	2500	2000	6000	3000
Type B	800	1000	1200	1100	2400	700
Type C	600	800	550	700	1200	400
Type D	900	700	1000	1300	1800	600

Present the information in the table above in two different visual formats.

Expressive information

Communicating information expressively through the use of body language, sign language and gestures is very appropriate in certain situations, for example a handshake to welcome a delegate to a meeting. However, expressive communication can be misinterpreted or inappropriate, especially facial expressions that reveal thoughts better hidden.

Sign language

Body language and facial expression can communicate a specific thought or mood. For example you might frown to express your discontent at a situation or smile and nod to welcome or to express agreement.

| Discontented | Surprised | Happy | Angry | Secretive |

Test your knowledge

1 What is information?
2 What are the four categories of information?
3 Identify three formats for written information.
4 Identify one benefit of delivering information verbally.
5 Identify whether the types of written communication in the box below are usually formal or informal.

Letter to a friend	Birth certificate	Receipt
Application form	Phone bill	Birthday card
Contract of employment	Booking confirmation for a holiday	
Driving licence	Curriculum vitae	E-mail to a colleague Memo
Agenda for a meeting	Newspaper	Letter of resignation

1.4 Purpose and use of information

Information can also be categorised in terms of its purpose and use. For example, is the information general and generic – common to a number of individuals, users or systems, or is it specialist – unique to individuals, users or systems?

Within an organisation, individual functional departments can produce **generic information,** as shown in Figure 9:

Figure 9

Generic information sources within an organisation

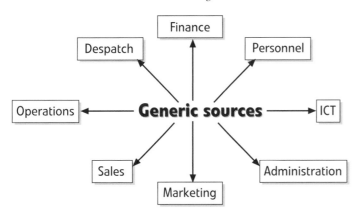

Examples of generic information produced within functional departments include invoices, wage slips, customer orders and despatch notes. These document types are common to a range of organisations.

Specialist information is exclusive to the organisation or organisation type. For example, information required by the marketing department of a bank might be different from that required by a retail organisation's marketing department.

Organisations differ not only in the ways they are structured, the products or services they sell, and their business objectives, but also in the information they use.

Activity 6

For this activity you are required to carry out two tasks. The second one should be carried out in pairs.

1 Identify a piece of specialist information that would be appropriate for the functional department listed for each organisation in the table below.

Organisation type	Functional department	Specialist information
Insurance company	Sales	
Computer shop	Sales	
School/college	ICT	
Hospital	ICT	
Hire car company	Despatch	
Supermarket	Despatch	

2 Work in pairs. Choose two organisations that are involved with very different goods or services, such as a supermarket and a school.

- Find out the functional areas of each organisation.
- Arrange a visit, talk or interview with a person from a functional area within each organisation (it should be the same for each, e.g. finance department) and identify the following:
  – activities normally carried out over a period of one month
  – the information involved with these activities

Activity 6 continued ...

   – the information considered to be specialist to that area
   – how the information is captured, processed and stored
   – who is involved with each information process.

- Discuss your findings and produce a table comparing the results, identifying any similarities in the generic information and differences in the specialist information.
- Feed back the information to the group. If others have selected a similar organisation, examine the variations that exist between similar organisations.

Test your knowledge

1 What is meant by the term 'generic' information?

2 What is meant by the term 'specialist' information?

1.5 Function of information

The function of information will differ depending upon a number of factors, including:

- sender
- environment
- receiver
- format.

Information may be transmitted to meet a specific purpose: for example, the function of a formal letter may be to acknowledge an action. The function of a presentation might be to update customers about a new product line.

Activity 7

Copy the table and fill in the missing variables. Two examples have been completed for you:

Sender	Receiver	Environment	Format	Function
Lecturer	Student	ICT lesson	Verbal	Instructions on how to create a spreadsheet
Employer	Employee	Meeting at work	Written	Agenda given to outline the meeting
Doctor		Ward in a hospital	Written	
You	Employer			Enquiring about job vacancies
You		Cinema		
		Personnel department	Written	

1.6 Knowledge and knowledge systems

In the hierarchy of knowledge, information and data, knowledge is at the top; it involves the application of information and skills.

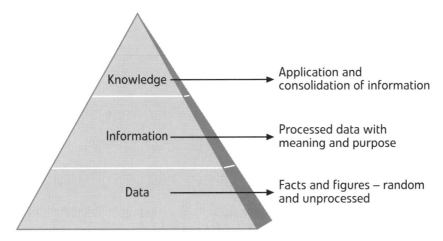

Knowledge can be used to make judgements, to forecast, and to evaluate situations. Knowledge is the experience that allows information to be applied appropriately.

Knowledge systems

Knowledge systems, sometimes called knowledge-based systems, provide support for knowledge users within an organisation.

Their function is to assist an organisation in identifying, analysing and integrating new ideas and information, so that the organisation can be more efficient or profitable, and ensure high standards.

Knowledge system users include engineers, doctors, lawyers and scientists. In a hospital, knowledge systems could include:

- identification of new medicines when they become available and their uses
- identification of patients who are more at risk of certain medical conditions
- the impact of certain drugs upon certain categories of patients
- monitoring of medical histories.

As well as medicine, knowledge systems are used in education, engineering and aviation. Examples include:

- DENRAL – chemical system developed for NASA at Stanford University by Buchanan and Feigenbaum
- MYCIN – medical system developed at Stanford by Shortcliffe
- Drilling Advisor – used in industry and developed in 1983 by Teknowledge for an oil company to replace a human drilling advisor.

Case study – MYCIN

MYCIN is a knowledge system developed in 1970 by Edward Shortcliffe. The system assists physicians who are not expert in the field in the diagnosis and treatment of the infectious diseases meningitis and bacterial septicaemia.

Patient symptoms and any available test results are input as data into MYCIN. The knowledge that is output from the system includes a diagnosis, with an indication of the degree of certainty, and recommended treatment.

Further research

1 Build up a small portfolio on knowledge systems developments. The portfolio should include a range of the following:

- further research on the MYCIN case study
- information on one other knowledge system mentioned or one of your own choosing
- information on recent developments in the field of knowledge systems.

2 Present your findings to your group by giving a short presentation.

Test your knowledge

1 What is the difference between information and knowledge?
2 What is meant by a knowledge-based system?
3 In which types of environments are knowledge-based systems used?

There are a number of ways in which knowledge systems can extract data and information in order to carry out their primary functions of identifying, analysing and integrating facts to create knowledge. These include the use of tools such as expert systems, and data mining.

Expert systems

Expert systems support decision-making. They encapsulate the experience and specialised knowledge of experts and relay this information to non-experts, so that they too can have access to specialist knowledge.

Expert systems are based on a reasoning process that resembles human thought processes. Rules and reasoning processes have been developed by experts in the field. An example of their use is in patient diagnosis.

Data mining

Data mining is a generic term that covers a range of technologies. The 'mining' of data refers to the extraction of information through tests, analysis and sets of rules. Information will be sorted and processed from a data set in order to find new information or data anomalies.

Data mining embraces a wide range of technologies including neural networks. These are programs that operate in a pattern which simulates the operation of the brain. They were first developed in 1943 by the neurophysiologist Warren McCulloch of the University of Illinois and the mathematician Walter Pitts of the University of Chicago.

Exam questions

1   Explain what is meant by Information and Communication Technology.   *(3 marks)*
AQA Jan 2003

2   Three components of an Information Processing System are *input, processing* and *output*. State what is meant by:

- input
- processing
- output

and give an example of each one.   *(6 marks)*
AQA Jan 2001

3   Explain, using examples, the following terms as they are applied within ICT:

(a) data   *(2 marks)*
(b) information   *(2 marks)*
(c) knowledge.   *(2 marks)*
AQA Jan 2002

4   State **three** characteristics of good quality data.   *(3 marks)*
AQA May 2002

5   Data input to an ICT system can take many forms such as pictures, sounds, numbers and letters. In all cases the data has to be encoded.

Using an example, explain why data needs to be encoded.   *(2 marks)*
AQA May 2002

2 Value and importance of information

This section will provide coverage of the following key areas:

- Understand that information is a commodity and as such can have a monetary value, the level of which depends on its accuracy, its potential use and its particular intended use
- Describe the overheads involved in ensuring that information is up to date and of use to an organisation/individual.

It is important to remember that information can be classed as a commodity with a monetary value. Many organisations rely on having up-to-date information in order to plan or make decisions in the short and long term.

The collection, processing and storage of information also carry a price in terms of the overheads involved with keeping it up to date and secure.

This section will examine a range of these issues and provide some useful case studies to illustrate the value and importance of information.

2.0 Qualities of information

A number of quality issues are involved in the transfer of information. Examples of these include:

- appropriateness and relevance of the information
- composition of the information
- timing
- the transmission tool used.

Appropriateness and relevance

Information needs to be appropriate and relevant to the context in which it is being delivered. The quality of information can be measured by the response of its audience, rather than the opinion of its sender.

Composition

The composition of information can affect its overall quality. Some types of information fit better to a certain format, and accuracy is the vital element. Information that has an inaccurate composition or format will not be useful. Two types of composition for information are:

- data-rich – quantitative information
- information/knowledge-rich – qualitative information.

Quantitative information is based on facts and statistics, and it is the key information used for finance, planning and modelling. This type of information includes sales figures, control measurements, and test data for an experiment.

There is a great need for information of this type in mathematical, scientific, medical or logic-orientated environments, where calculations and experimentation play a dominant role in day-to-day tasks.

Information on share prices is regularly presented in a format like this:

Aerospace and automobiles

52 week			Last week		Mkt cap		
High	Low	Close	Chg	%	(£m)	P/E	Yld
386	93	BAE Systems.............127	14	12.4	3,859	-	7.2
1210	898	Cobham...............1029.5	13.5	1.3	1,108	18.4	2.2
360	143	GKN.................... 170.5	-0.5	-0.3	1,249	9.1	6.6
878	602	Inchcape 740	-35	-4.5	573	9.7	3.8
236	153	Meggitt...................175	3.5	2	503	16.1	3.
205	64	Rolls-Royce.............80.5	5.5	7.3	1,301	4.8	10.2
895	553	Smiths.....................676	16	2.4	3,755	15.5	3.8
303	164	VT Group...............206.5	0.5	0.2	351	18	3.9

Qualitative information provides depth and detail. It is knowledge-rich because the qualitative aspect gives insight into its subject matter.

For example, for a group of students taking AS and A2 qualifications in ICT at a college, statistics might be generated to identify retention and achievement rates and compare them with similar groups across the country. This would be quantitative information. A qualitative approach might use a course feedback form to ask which modules students enjoy, how they feel about assessments, support and resource issues, etc.

The best way to extract qualitative information is through interviewing, questionnaires, feedback forms and surveys.

Group activity

1 Design a questionnaire to find out one of the following:
- the types and frequency of magazine purchases, and the reasons for these choices
- cinema attendance and opinions on the best film of the year.

For each questionnaire design 15 questions, using a mix of qualitative and quantitative ones. When the design is complete, print off or e-mail copies to ten people in the group and ask them to complete the questionnaires.

2 From the information gathered, produce two charts and one graph based on the quantitative information, and write a short summary detailing the findings of the qualitative information.

3 Identify which was the easier of the two sets of information to produce. Why do you think this is?

Timing

Ensuring that information is delivered on time is another quality consideration. If information transfer is interrupted, contracts could be cancelled or payments could be delayed, costing organisations thousands or even millions of pounds.

Transmission tool

The tool used to transmit information can have a tremendous impact on how information is received. Some communication tools may be more appropriate than others because of their convenience or flexibility. The type of communication tool that is required to transmit the information will vary depending upon a number of factors, as identified in Figure 10.

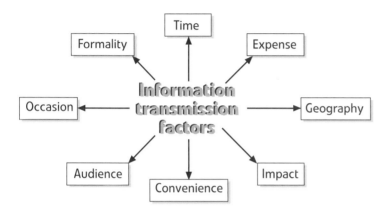

Figure 10

Factors that can affect information transmission

Time: A transmission tool may be selected on the basis of how long its takes to send or receive the information. For example, it might be necessary to send a document by fax rather than post because of the urgency of the information.

Expense: Different transmission tools have different costs. These could include the cost of a stamp or sending a fax or e-mail.

Activity 8

Identify the cost of the following communication services.

- first-class stamp
- second-class stamp
- sending a 1 kg parcel first class
- international phone calls from the UK to Australia, Hong Kong and the United States at peak time
- off-peak tariffs for two mobile phone companies.

Geography: The distance over which information has to travel will influence the choice of tool. To contact someone quickly who is ten miles away, it would be practical to use the telephone, or send an e-mail.

Impact: The impression you need to create for the receiver of your information will influence the choice of transmission tool. You would not enter into a million-pound deal by sending an e-mail; you might deliver a presentation in person, and send written confirmation.

Convenience: Some transmission tools are more convenient to use than others. Writing a letter can be time consuming, and if you have queries a direct conversation either face-to-face or using the telephone may be more appropriate.

Audience: The needs of your audience are a vital consideration in choosing the transmission tool. Within an organisation you might chat informally to a colleague, e-mail a team leader, and send a memorandum to the head of department.

Occasion: The occasion can determine the type of transmission tool, for example a birthday might trigger the sending of a card – a written format.

Formality: There are some instances when a specific transmission tool needs to be used to match the formality of the situation. Written communication is appropriate for certain contracts and legally binding transactions, for example offering someone employment.

 Test your knowledge

1 List the four quality issues that should be considered when information is being transferred.
2 What is meant by the term 'qualitative' information?
3 Give an example of how quantitative information could be communicated.
4 Identify four factors that could affect information transmission.

2.1 Value of information

Information carries different values depending upon the environment and context in which it is to be used. Information is usually generated for a specific need or purpose, and this determines the value that is attached to it.

 Activity 9

Attaching values to information

1 Examine the list of information statements below and order them in terms of importance to you, from 1–10 (10 being the highest and 1 the lowest).

Information statement	Value score (1–10)
■	The amount of money you have left at the end of the month.
■	What your friends are doing at the weekend.
■	What people in your class think of you.
■	How well you are achieving in your course.
■	Where you will go on your next holiday.
■	The release date of the latest film you want to watch.
■	The part-time jobs vacant this week.
■	What to do after your current course is finished.
■	Where to buy the latest fashion item and how much it will cost.
■	What car you would like to buy.

Activity 9 continued ...

2   When you have scored each information statement, discuss them with a partner and identify why your needs are similar and/or different.

3   For each of the following categories of people, identify **two** important pieces of information they would need:

   ▦ a store owner who wants to open a new shop
   ▦ a student who wants to go to university
   ▦ an employer who wants to take on a part-time assistant.

Information as a commodity

Information can be regarded as a commodity with a value. Some information carries a very high price; one of the most valuable forms of information is marketing information. This allows organisations to find out about a range of characteristics in their customers, in order to:

   ▦ sell more products/services
   ▦ judge appropriate price levels
   ▦ target sales
   ▦ change the product or service range
   ▦ introduce a new product or service.

The ways in which organisations gather this information varies, as shown in Figure 11.

Figure 11

Ways of collecting marketing information

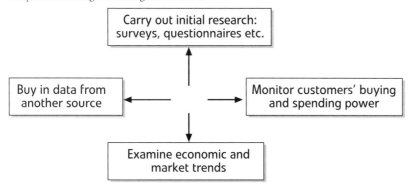

As shown, marketing information can be generated from a number of sources. One of the easiest ways to gather this information is through the use of a loyalty scheme. These schemes, now used by a range of large companies, offer consumers 'loyalty cards' with various benefits, and in return the companies gather large amounts of information. When you use a loyalty card at the point of sale, information is stored that can inform organisations about:

   ▦ how much you spend   ▦ how often you shop
   ▦ what you buy   ▦ trends in your buying patterns
   ▦ aspects of your lifestyle.

Organisation	Scheme	Reward
Tesco	Clubcard	Special deals on a range of leisure pursuits; discount vouchers off shopping
Sainsbury/BP/Debenhams	Nectar	Special deals on flights; holiday vouchers; store discounts
Boots	Advantage card	Discounts; health and well-being products and services
W. H. Smith	Clubcard	Discounts off products in store
Homebase	Spend and Save	Discounts off products in store

2.2 Importance of information

Information is required to maintain everyday processing activities within organisations, providing the mechanics to keep resources working. In an organisation, information is used to:

- plan
- make decisions
- model and control.

- forecast
- structure

Information that is used to plan, forecast and make decisions is based on a combination of quantitative and qualitative data.

What does this mean?

Forecasting: A prediction of the future is made, based on current or historical data and/or information. Examples include forecasting the sale of a particular model of car over the next six months

Planning might involve the collection of qualitative feedback from users or customers in order to improve a facility or service. Planning might also rely on a set of quantitative data to calculate whether a project is financially viable.

Everybody makes plans, from writing down a list of items to buy, to drawing up an action plan in order to prioritise tasks. Working to assignment schedules involves knowing when assignments need to be completed and what you have to do in order to complete them, e.g. carry out research.

In organisations, planning is crucial because it provides for measurable progress. Without planning you would not know where you were going nor recognise when you had got there.

There are a number of ways to plan in an organisation, depending on a number of factors. These factors are known as the TROPIC cycle, as shown in Figure 12.

Figure 12

TROPIC cycle of planning

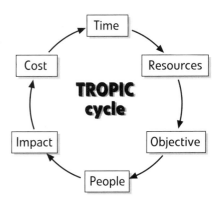

Time – how long is the plan?

Resources – what resources are going to support the plan?

Objective – what is the purpose of the plan?

People – who is involved with plan?

Impact – who and what will the plan affect?

Cost – How much will it cost to implement the plan?

If consideration is not given to all of the factors in the TROPIC cycle, a plan could be incomplete and the chances of successful implementation will be greatly reduced. What would be the point of generating a plan to network an entire department if you didn't have finance for the hardware or software, or if you could not implement the network plan within a certain time period?

Within an organisation, planning can be carried out over different periods of time, which can be recognised as:

- short term
- medium term
- long term.

Figure 13

Examples of planning

Type of planning	Period	Example of plan
Short	1–3 years	Introducing computers into a single department
Medium	3–5 years	Ensuring that all departments within the organisation are computerised and networked
Long	5 years +	Business expansion and acquiring new premises

Forecasting might depend upon qualitative historical data to establish what has been done in the past, analyse whether it was successful, and make forecasts based on previous experiences. It can also be based purely on quantitative data such as the profit and loss account. For example, 'in this period the company made this much profit, so if we increase production by x we should make y amount of profit in the future'.

Decisions are also based on a combination of qualitative and quantitative data and information. For example, the decision to promote a member of staff could be based on his or her ability to meet all sales targets, as well as personal recommendations from a peer.

Information is also used within an organisation to **structure**, **model** and **control**. Quantitative data may be used more than qualitative data because a measurable starting point is needed, and a mechanism for accurate calculation or prediction of the progress made.

Activity 10

Organisations use information for a variety of purposes, as discussed. Copy the table below and complete it by stating the type of information use, and identifying a second example.

Activity 10 continued ...

Scenario	Information use	Another example
A project manager needs to predict the resources needed to support the project	Forecasting	A company wants to gather information in order to predict sales over the next six months
A small health food store wants to expand and acquire new premises		
An organisation uses a set of measurements and calculations to design a new automated system		
Information on staff numbers and roles is used to prepare seating plans in a new office		
Measurements are taken to determine the capacity of machinery loads and adjust them accordingly		
An employer needs to select one candidate from the six interviewed for a job		

Test your knowledge

1 What types of activities can information be used for in organisations?
2 What are decisions based on?
3 What do the initials TROPIC stand for?
4 What periods of time are usually considered to be short, medium and long term when planning?

2.3 Value of information

All information can be deemed to be of value to someone, but some forms of information carry a monetary value.

Credit agency companies are an example of organisations that use information as a commodity.

Credit agencies

Credit agencies are used by a number of retail, banking and financial organisations to check the credit rating of consumers who want to take out a loan, mortgage or credit facilities. To assess a consumer's ability to honour payments, a credit check is carried out. This process is based on a scoring system where historical data and financial stability are assessed. The more points accumulated, that greater the customer's chance of being approved for credit.

Credit agencies gather this information from a variety of sources such as electoral rolls, public surveys, other organisations and agencies. This information is then *sold* to organisations requiring credit check services. Updated information about credit status, approvals and rejections are passed back to the credit agency.

If members of the public want access to their own credit history, the information is available, but they can be asked to pay an administrative charge to gain access. See the checkmyfile.com home page below.

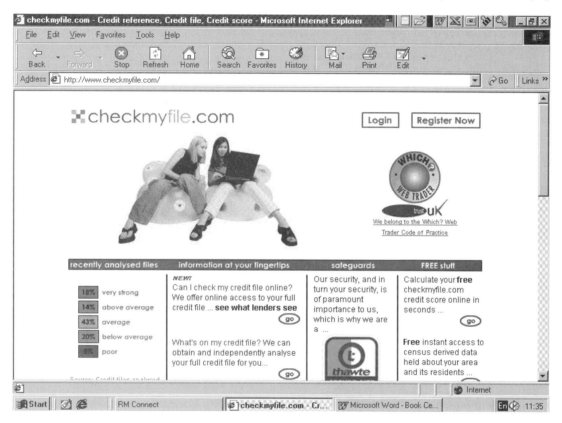

Activity 11

Identify, using a variety of sources, at least three credit agencies. Answer the following:

1 What sort of information is gathered about consumers/applicants?

2 Provide five examples of the types of organisation that might use the services of these agencies.

3 How much does it cost to access your own credit file?

Group activity

Discuss the following in groups of three or four:

1 Do you think information should be bought and sold? If so, under what conditions?

2 Do you think it is ethical for an organisation such as a credit agency to collect information about individuals?

2.4 Overheads involved in ensuring information is up to date

Information needs to be up to date in order to keep processes dynamic and current. Static information resources have little or no use, apart from storing historical data for reference purposes. The cost of updating and maintaining data can be phenomenal for organisations, as consideration has to be given to:

- storage
- updating and transferring
- security
- maintenance.

All of these carry financial implications.

Storage

Storing data and information efficiently may mean continuous investment in technology and the latest resources.

With all ICT resources, storage devices are essential for:

- storing programs
- storing data that is waiting to be processed
- the output of information.

The cost of required storage depends on a number of factors including current resources, current configuration (stand-alone or networked environment), amount of data to be processed, composition of data to be processed (numerical, text or graphics), and amount of historical data to be retained.

Storage requirements differ between user types and organisations. For example, a home user might require 20 gigabytes (Gb), as an entry level, for storing data. A small organisation with three or four stand-alone computers might require a minimum of 40 Gb on each. A small networked organisation with up to ten computers running via a server could have anything up to 500 Gb. A large networked organisation running up to fifty computers without individual local drives could require terabyte (Tb) storage. See the storage measurement tables below.

Bit	Smallest unit of measurement	Single binary digit 0 or 1
Byte	Made up of 8 bits, amount of space required to hold a single character	Value between 0 and 255
Kilobyte (Kb)	Equivalent to 1,000 characters	Approximately 1,000 bytes
Megabyte (Mb)	Equivalent to 1 million characters	Approximately 1,000 kilobytes
Gigabyte (Gb)	Equivalent to 1 billion characters	Approximately 1,000 megabytes
Terabyte (Tb)	Equivalent to 1 thousand billion characters	Approximately 1,000 gigabytes

More recently, larger storage capacities have become available, including:

Petabyte	10^{15} 1 000 000 000 000 000	Approximately 1,000 terabytes
Exabyte	10^{18} 1 000 000 000 000 000 000	Approximately 1,000 petabytes
Zettabyte	10^{21} 1 000 000 000 000 000 000 000	Approximately 1,000 exabytes
Yottabyte	10^{24} 1 000 000 000 000 000 000 000 000	Approximately 1,000 zettabytes

The need to buy more storage can be an ongoing expense for organisations. For some, continuous updates are required almost on a weekly basis, where storage release is granted by suppliers to meet demand. For others, more conventional methods such as purchasing a bigger hard drive are more appropriate.

Vast amounts of storage capacity are needed to support the volumes of data used on a daily basis within certain large organisations. The storage measurement table above provides an indication of how demand by organisations for storage seems to be dictating the advance in technology towards higher storage capacities. Only a short while ago, home computer users were still working with megabytes of data; entry level today is in gigabytes.

Case study

In small groups, carry out the following research tasks:

1   Select two accessible organisations – a place where you or a family member works or your school/college. If this proves difficult, try sourcing organisations through the Internet, magazines, journals or documentary programme footage. For each organisation, identify:
  - the data storage capacities they use
  - whether their storage capacity has changed over the years
  - the cost of updating their storage requirements
  - how they get more storage – is it released by a supplier, or do their systems have a complete storage overhaul and upgrade at set points during the year?
  - other overheads involved with ensuring that information is kept up to date.

2   Produce a table comparing the two organisations and present this to the rest of the group.

3   What conclusions can be drawn from this activity about the storage and updating of information?

Security

Security of data is essential to ensure that sensitive and personal information is confidential. Data security is also paramount in complying with legislation that protects users of data and third parties.

Organisations can face a number of threats to security. These include:

- viruses
- industrial and/or individual sabotage
- accidents by users
- theft.
- unauthorised access – hacking
- natural disasters
- vandalism

These will be further discussed in Section 8, on pages 73–76.

A number of measures can be taken by organisations to protect themselves against these security breaches. Some are enforced within an organisation, whereas others have been introduced externally through legal controls and legislation. See the table below.

Internal security measures	External security measures
Passwords	■ Legislation
Encryption	■ Data Protection Act (1984 and 1998)
Filtering and monitoring software	■ Computer Misuse Act (1990)
Employment of moderators	
Virus checkers and protectors	
Internal security policies and guidelines	
User access levels	
Firewalls	

See pages 77–81 for the Data Protection and Computer Misuse acts.

In order for data to be secure, an investment in time and money has to be made. Further information on security can be found on pages 74–75.

Updating and transferring data

The updating and transferring of data and information raises issues of compatibility between systems, time constraints on users, skill requirements for the process of updating, and what to do with non-current data.

There is a growing requirement for users at all levels to update operating systems, utility and applications software. Updates are required to ensure that more advanced features are installed to comply with changes in legislation, to keep up with currently maintained support levels, and to take advantage of new technologies such as 64-bit operating systems.

Updating software has a direct effect on data. There is a cost involved in ensuring it is transferable and compatible with the new software. This expense could include employing extra staff to assist in the data-transfer process, investment in new systems to manage the process and ensure compatibility, and re-training personnel in the use of new systems to enable them to process and administer the data.

Maintenance

Maintaining systems to ensure the continual and effective processing of data is an ongoing cost. In some cases staffing is required 24 hours a day to oversee the management and maintenance of ICT systems. For some organisations, down-time of even an hour could cost millions.

Test your knowledge

1 What types of costs are involved with updating and transferring data and information?
2 Why do organisations have to invest money in storage?
3 List four possible security breaches.
4 Identify three measures that an organisation can take to protect its data.
5 What considerations need to be taken into account when updating and transferring data?

Exam questions

1 A travel firm arranging package holidays in Spain for the 2001 season uses data obtained from a survey of their customers' favourite holiday resorts in 1997. Explain

(a) why the data from 1997 might not be suitable for use to predict the requirements for 2001

(b) what the effect on the company might be if it used the 1997 data. *(4 marks)*

AQA May 2001

2 State **three** factors that affect the value and importance of information. Give an example that shows clearly how each factor affects the information's value. *(6 marks)*

AQA Jan 2001

3 Control of information

This section will provide coverage of the following key areas:

- Describe the legal rights and obligations on holders of personal data to permit access
- Understand that the sale of entitlement to access to data may mean paying for a more convenient form of access, the right of which already exists
- Understand that files on individuals and on organisations that are non-disclosable have commercial value.

3.0 Information as a commodity

Information has already been described as a commodity with a commercial value. However, in some cases information has more than just a monetary value – it can have a controlling value. An example of this is the results of polls, where members of the public vote at elections for Members of Parliament. The political party with overall majority representation in the House of Commons forms the government.

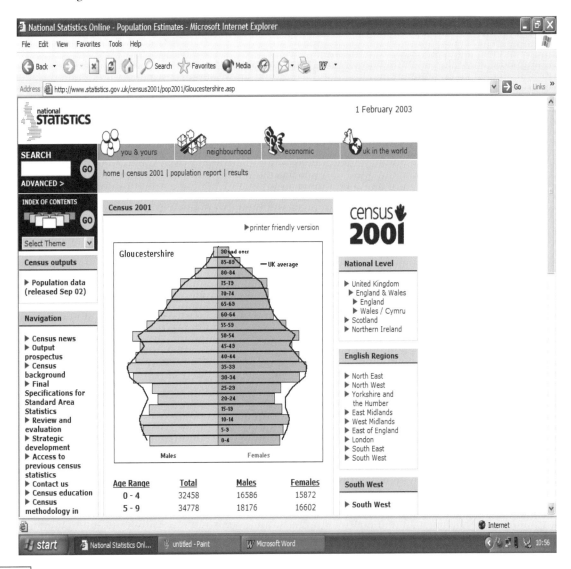

When certain organisations collect public information this does not necessarily give them ownership of the information. Under current legislation, in many cases the information collected by organisations must be accessible to the public. Information about the public can be gathered from a variety of sources, including:

- electoral rolls (local council documents)
- census results (central government documents)
- surveys and polls (by consumer organisations)
- utility documents (electricity, TV licence, gas, water, council tax, etc.)
- existing credit agreements (car loan, personal loan, personal contract plans, etc.)

Some companies make their business in capturing public information and selling this on to other organisations. An example has already been shown in credit check agencies (see pages 38–39).

Electoral rolls, census information (such as that shown on the previous page), surveys and polls are all examples of how information is gathered. Some of this information is readily available at no cost, allowing individuals access to data held about them.

A good example of this is upmystreet.com, a website that provides public information based on each postcode area. The site provides information on typical house prices and types, amenities, schools and public transport. The site builds up a picture of the level of affluence in a postcode area based on the number of cars per household, council tax banding, average age of residents, etc.

This information may well be a deciding factor for people wishing to move into a new area.

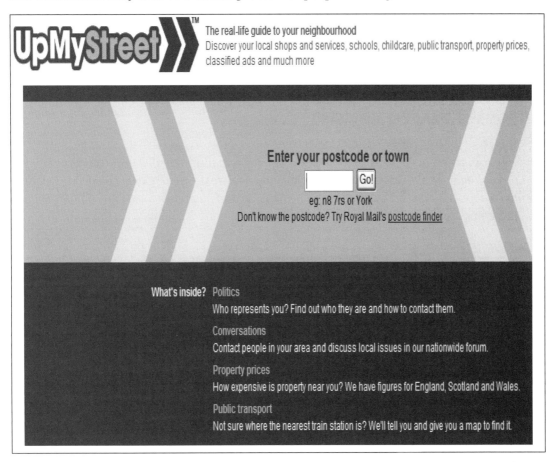

In this particular example, information is used positively to create awareness. Some information collected on individuals may be used more controversially – as shown by this recent article in a local newspaper:

Norwich: The most Godless city in UK

Norwich emerged last night as an island of atheism in Norfolk and the least religious city in England and Wales. According to the census, 27.8% of city residents regard themselves as atheists – almost double the national average (14.8%).

The results were greeted with surprise by the Bishop of Norwich, the Rt Rev Graham James – 'Norwich has higher-than-average levels of church attendance, so if it is the least religious place in the country, it has an odd way of showing it', he said.

Paul Hill
Eastern Daily Press, Friday 14 February 2003

3.1 Legal rights and obligations

The legal framework governing the use of computers and data will be discussed in Section 9 (pages 77–84). The main pieces of legislation to consider are the Computer Misuse Act (1990), the Copyright, Designs and Patent Act (1988), and the Data Protection Act (1984 and 1998).

The Data Protection Act applies to the processing of data and information. The legal rights and obligations on holders of personal data to permit access can be a minefield of legal and ethical issues. When individuals complete forms giving personal information to organisations, there is normally a note at the bottom asking permission to share this information with other organisations. Ticking a box to say 'No' entitles the individual to assurances that the information will remain within the confines of that particular organisation.

In certain situations, however, even though assurances may be given as to maintaining client confidentiality, this can be overruled. A good example of this is in the medical profession. For example, if a midwife strongly suspects that a child is under threat, the personal details of a patient can be passed on to other agencies such as child protection teams. Even if a patient opposes the decision to share personal data, a midwife can refuse to grant confidentiality.

3.2 Control mechanisms

Information can be of great value, and to some it is a commodity with commercial value. It should therefore be protected and kept secure from both internal and external threats. The Data Protection Act states that personal data stored on a computer must be kept secure. However, other measures need to be taken to ensure confidentiality of information, especially information of a sensitive nature.

Within an organisation there are a number of ways in which information can be kept secure, for example setting up passwords, restricting users to certain access levels and providing read-only access, etc. To protect data from external threats, other control mechanisms can be put into place such as firewalls and data encryption.

Exam questions

1 When buying a new house through a large estate agency, customers are asked if they object to the data they are giving to the estate agent being passed on to other companies.

(a) Explain why the estate agent must ask this question. *(2 marks)*

(b) State, with an example, what the estate agent could do with the customers' details if they give permission for them to be passed on. *(2 marks)*

AQA Jan 2001

2 An opticians keeps records in a database of all its customers who have had eye tests. Eye test reminders are sent out to customers when they are due. Customers who do not make appointments after two reminders have been sent out have their details deleted from the database.

Describe **two** possible reasons why these customer details are deleted from the database. *(4 marks)*

AQA Jan 2003

4 Capabilities and limitations of ICT

This section will provide coverage of the following key areas:

- Understand that ICT systems offer fast repetitive processing, vast storage capability, and the facility to search and combine data in many different ways that would otherwise be impossible
- Understand that the response speed of technology within ICT systems facilitates the use of feedback, e.g. maintenance of optimum stock levels, electronic fund/money management systems
- Understand that there are limitations in the use of ICT systems and in the information they produce. Factors could include limitations in hardware, software and communications, in addition to inappropriate data models and data control mechanisms.

4.0 Capabilities

The capabilities of ICT are far reaching, as explored throughout Section 5 (pages 52–58). ICT has been integrated into all areas of industry, commerce and the home, brought improved communications, and a wider distribution of knowledge, resources and development.

ICT has capabilities beyond that of a human, including:

- ✓ fast processing of data and information
- ✓ continuous and constant processing of repetitive tasks
- ✓ vast storage capacity
- ✓ ability to search, query, update, monitor and predict data and information at an optimum level
- ✓ output quality, current and meaningful information.

Computers can process information at great speed. A range of applications can be in operation simultaneously, all performing a multitude of tasks in seconds.

A computer does not become weary of carrying out a repetitive task. If a human had to carry out a very repetitive task with low stimulation and motivation, his or her efficiency would decline after a certain period, as would productivity. With a computer, however, the task can be carried out at the same optimum level continuously.

The vast storage capacities of a computer have already been described in Section 2.4 (page 40). Storage can be upgraded quickly and easily in order to meet an organisation's needs. For a human, however, the time has not yet come when we can pop along to a shop to get a new brain or increase the capacity of our existing one!

The quality of the output from a computer is as good as the software application tools and the expertise of the end user allow. However, it is clear that the use of templates to standardise working procedures has improved the quality of output information. Graphics, specialist drawing packages and desktop publishing tools which produce newspaper and magazine layouts, architectural and prototype drawings, are all vastly superior to human abilities.

ICT has revolutionised the way in which everyday tasks are carried out. In a supermarket, for example, ICT has improved the following operations:

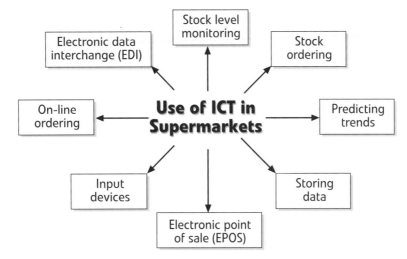

- Stock levels can be continually monitored, keeping each item at an optimum level.
- Stock can be ordered automatically, possibly using the JIT (just-in-time) process; when stock levels fall to a certain point either a warning is issued to alert users that more stock should be ordered, or automatic ordering takes place.
- Supermarkets use a range of tools in order to predict market trends. For example, they may use statistical software to establish how the buying patterns of customers have impacted on the sale of certain food items over a set period of time, and based on this information predict how much stock of that particular item is required in the future. When a promotion is running in store, for example 'buy one get one free', a supermarket could make a prediction based on similar promotions and the popularity of the item in order to judge how much to order.
- Historical data on past promotions and customer buying patterns is a key marketing tool for a number of supermarkets. With the 'loyalty card' system (see page 35) personal information is collected that can assess:
  – which items individual shoppers buy
  – how much they spend on average
  – the make-up of the household (for example, if they buy baby food or nappies frequently, it can be assumed that they have a young child)
  – when people shop
  – their socio-economic status – do they buy own-brand items, branded items, or luxury items?
  – their lifestyle – do they buy organic products and fresh produce or convenience and fast-food items?

  This information can be used to target individuals with direct marketing promotions for certain products.

- At the till EPOS (electronic point of sale) systems have long been used to ensure faster processing of transactions.
- Hand-held scanners and bar-code readers are used to check product details and to update prices and stock levels on the shop floor. Information can then be fed directly to the

warehouse where stock levels can be updated, thus ensuring that shelves are always full and prices are always correct.

■ The Internet can be used to provide customers with on-line ordering, payments and distribution systems.

■ In the warehouse, EDI (electronic data interchange) systems exchange information between stores, suppliers and third parties.

4.1 Limitations

ICT also, of course, has limitations. In the traditional phrase, a worker is only as good as the tools he or she uses; in the same way, ICT is restricted by certain factors.

The limitations of ICT can be attributed to three main components:

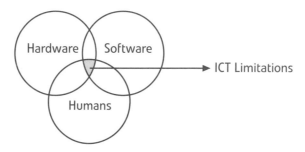

Hardware

Without adequate hardware support, the capabilities of ICT can be restricted. Sharing information with a large number of users may not be feasible without networking hardware, such as sufficient computers, cabling, routers, hubs, etc.

Software

A network would not function without suitable operating system software. Limitations with software can affect the capabilities of an ICT system. Applications software may be adequate to fulfil certain administrative tasks for some functional areas, such as personnel, but the finance department might require bespoke software to assist in payroll and accounts. The use of either applications (generic) or tailored (bespoke) software can limit the processing abilities of an ICT system, as each have their own merits and faults (see the table below).

Bespoke software		Applications software	
Benefits	Limitations	Benefits	Limitations
■ tailored to specific requirements and can carry out specific tasks	■ it can take a long time to develop the software to meet an organisation's needs	■ can be cheaper to purchase, upgrade and maintain	■ may not satisfactorily meet the needs of the organisation
■ can incorporate user needs and requirements for specific ICT tasks	■ it can be more expensive to purchase because of development costs	■ can take less time to implement because of the uniform settings	■ can be of a sub-standard quality

Bespoke software		Applications software	
Benefits	Limitations	Benefits	Limitations
■ software is better quality, because it has been developed for specific tasks	■ it can be complex to use, and might require re-training of staff	■ can be easier to use because of uniformity and standard formatting features	
	■ it may not be compatible with existing ICT systems	■ likely to be compatible with existing systems	

Humans

Human limitations can also limit the capabilities of an ICT system. If a user is unfamiliar with the system, processing tasks may be slower with a greater risk of error. Some ICT systems are not exploited fully because the users do not know their capabilities, or the technology is too advanced for their current knowledge base.

Exam questions

1 When incorrect bills are sent to customers, an organisation often gives the reason as 'the computer got it wrong'. Using an example, give a more likely explanation.   *(4 marks)*
AQA Jan 2001

2 A supermarket chain operates an automatic ordering system between the stores and a central warehouse.

(a) State **two** advantages for the store of using an automatic system.   *(2 marks)*
(b) Explain **one** advantage for the supermarket's customers of the store using an automatic stock control system.   *(2 marks)*
AQA May 2001

3 When ordering goods by telephone many companies ask the purchaser for his or her postcode. They then use this to confirm the address of the purchaser by looking up the postcode in a database of codes.

Explain **two** reasons why companies prefer to buy a database of postcodes rather than to collect the data from purchasers.   *(4 marks)*
AQA Jan 2002

5 Social impact of information and communication technology

This section will provide coverage of the following key areas:

■ explain the benefits and drawbacks of the use of information and communication technology in manufacturing, industry, commerce, medicine, the home, education and teleworking.

ICT has had a tremendous impact on the way in which everyday tasks are carried out, inside and outside organisations. ICT has affected the way in which data is processed, information is transmitted and knowledge is applied. It is a dynamic resource that supports users in a variety of environments, such as:

■ manufacturing and industry
■ retail
■ education
■ home and teleworking.

■ commerce
■ medicine
■ military and government

Each of these has made use of ICT to support both general and specialist tasks, creating a more efficient, supportive and interactive culture based on the sharing of data, information and knowledge.

Social changes have followed from this. There are fewer manual and unskilled jobs, especially in manufacturing, where computer-controlled machines have replaced humans. Other jobs, such as that of a shorthand-typist, have become 'deskilled' in the sense that these traditional skills are no longer needed. Almost anyone can use a word-processing package to produce a document that is well laid out and accurate.

But on the positive side, new and more interesting skilled jobs are continually being created by the introduction of ICT, and many more people now have the opportunity to work at home or become self-employed. Because of the pace of change, workers of all kinds need to constantly update their skills and refresh their training – which can be perceived as either an advantage or a disadvantage, depending on their attitudes and opportunities.

5.0 The role of ICT in manufacturing and industry

Manufacturing companies can be classified as secondary industries, as opposed to primary industries which are concerned with the production of raw materials. In recent years the image of large factories, with blue-collar workers, punch cards and archaic shop-floor procedures has slowly changed. In place of these are teams of highly skilled workers, technical support personnel and specialist engineers, mechanics, technicians and designers.

Procedures that involved multiple personnel on the shop floor working alongside conveyor belts and checking the quality of products have disappeared in many organisations. Mundane and repetitive tasks that could take hours to complete can be done in a matter of minutes, and in many cases a single person or machine can do a job which previously needed many more.

Technology is responsible for all these changes. It has been used in manufacturing in the ways shown in Figure 14.

Figure 14

Technology use in manufacturing

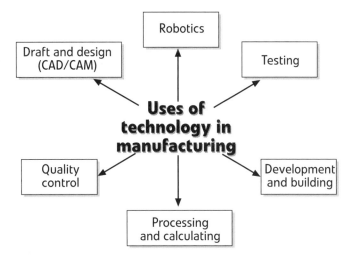

5.1 The role of ICT in commerce and retail

ICT has changed the way in which people bank and shop. Some changes are due to older technology such as ATM machines (cash dispensers) and the move towards electronic data capture at the point of sale in shops. More recent advances in ICT have opened up new opportunities for commerce and retail organisations and their customers. These include:

- on-line banking
- on-line ordering
- on-line payments
- over-the-phone transactions and services such as: setting up mortgages, loans or savings accounts
- automatic stock control and processing systems
- loyalty schemes based on information gathered from bar-coded products and customer data.

The impact of ICT on this sector has been both positive and negative, as shown in the table on the next page.

Positive impact	Negative impact
More streamlined and efficient service (people available at the end of a phone or computer)	Loss of personal one-to-one service – less opportunity to speak to a bank manager, for example, in person
Greater flexibility, e.g. wider payment options, ability to shop around for the best deals and prices, etc.	Could lead to a loss in jobs or unwanted changes in job roles
More choice in products and services available on-line	Not everybody feels comfortable with using ICT facilities to shop or bank and would prefer a personal service
Convenience – not having to leave home for mortgage advice or to transfer funds, etc.	Smaller retail or banking premises may be forced to close, especially ones located in rural areas

The impact of ICT has changed the way in which people use certain services and their expectations of organisations. Customers now expect more choice, greater flexibility and convenience.

Customer demands for e-commerce mean that organisations need to provide on-line payments, ordering and transaction services. Those that fail to deliver these services often suffer in terms of a shift in customer loyalty to more dynamic organisations.

Even specialists such as pensions and financial advisors are being replaced by intelligent systems, and competent operators who can navigate their way through menu systems and decision tables can offer comparable services for customers. The process of applying for a mortgage, which used to involve being assigned your own advisor, and coming into a bank or building society for a personal review, has been replaced by a 15-minute decision process.

Paying by cash or cheque for items is slowly being replaced by debit and credit card transactions.

For some, the changes that ICT has brought are definitely for the better. In an age when 'time is money', the preference for convenience is overriding the wish for personal service.

5.2 The role of ICT in medicine

A prime example of the impact of ICT in the field of medicine can be seen in the use of knowledge systems such as MYCIN (see pages 28–29). Systems like this have been developed to capture the knowledge of specialists and assist with the diagnosis and treatment of infectious diseases.

Cefriel – Education and Research Centre in Information Technology – is an institute that looks specifically at the role of ICT in medicine. The institute conducts research in a number of fields.

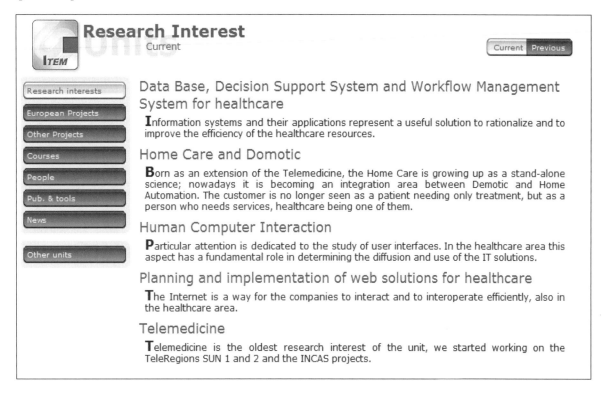

5.3 The role of ICT in education

The expectation now is that children will use computers from an early age and become quite proficient in applications software as they extend into secondary, further and higher education.

To support the teaching of ICT in schools and colleges, a number of initiatives have been set up to provide them with resources. Reduced-price computers are made affordable to teachers and laptops used for teaching have been introduced in an attempt to promote wider access to ICT and encourage new ways of delivering learning material. Support from local councils has ensured that schools are connected to the Internet and provided with the hardware and software that are needed for widening participation.

There is a move towards e-learning in the adult population, with a growing demand for on-line courses and programmes such as ECDL (European Computer Driving Licence), Learn Direct and Webwise.

The impact of ICT in education has been positive, with children and students being taught practical ICT skills that are transferable into the workplace. ICT has also become well established in other academic and training institutions, providing opportunities for all levels and ages of learner.

5.4 The role of ICT in the military and government

ICT has been used to support a number of projects and initiatives in the fields of government and the military. It has been used in areas such as:

- flight and navigation
- defence systems
- security.
- tracking and monitoring systems
- weaponry

Often, large amounts of money are available to support government and military projects, so ICT is used in ways never imagined by other users and industries.

5.5 The role of ICT in the home

ICT in the home has increased dramatically due to the falling costs of the technology, allowing people to own their own computers and access communication tools.

The impact of ICT has been both positive and negative here. The positive aspects include issues of convenience and flexibility. People can now work, shop, bank, learn and socialise from the comfort of their own homes. Items can be ordered and delivered to the door, brochures are no longer a requirement to book a holiday or order goods, and special deals are in abundance on the Internet. People who have restricted time because of work or family commitments can also enjoy the benefits of ICT, with the flexibility of 24-hour shopping and communication.

ICT in the home does, however, have some disadvantages. The popularity of the Internet and of games consoles has changed the way in which many people spend their leisure time. Some may lose social skills or become withdrawn because of devoting more and more time to using ICT resources.

Another problem of ICT, and the Internet especially, is its 'openness'. As the Internet is unregulated, people can publish and view material that may be harmful or offensive. This is a special concern when so many children use the Internet as an exploratory and learning tool.

On the other hand, ICT in the home has opened the door to many opportunities. People can now study and work from home. Distance-learning courses and on-line study material have given people of all ages the opportunity to learn new skills and gain qualifications at home.

The falling cost of ICT provision means that many can now enjoy the flexibility of working from home. Working in this way – teleworking – means that they can work their own hours and fulfil other commitments, such as collecting children from school, alongside work. However, these benefits have to be off-set against the fact that it can be quite an isolating experience to work at home, and sometimes home is even more distracting than the bustle of an office environment.

The growth in teleworking has been supported by the flexibility and portability of ICT provisions, the benefits of which include:

- improved and enhanced communication systems such as the Internet, e-mail and teleconferencing allowing people to send and receive information outside the workplace
- falling costs of hardware such as personal computers and laptops

- compatibility and uniformity of some operating systems and software, enabling teleworkers to use the same formats and systems as they would in an office
- initiatives by employers to supply workers with the necessary hardware and software to encourage greater flexibility in working hours.

Case study – Out of the office, into the unknown
by Nic Paton

Working from home sounds like an ideal solution to the problem of balancing quality of life with a career. A growing number of people are trying it, and next year all employees will be given the 'right to ask' . . .

A month ago Richard Evans swapped the life of a home-worker for the hassle of a 50-minute daily commute to Nottingham . . . He had been working from home since February after spending years travelling extensively for his work.

While he welcomed the flexibility and lack of commuting . . . he missed being in an office.

'You miss out on the social side of it; the coffee machine chats are an important part of working life' he says.

'There is a buzz in the office that isn't at home,' he adds.

. . . More than one in 17 British workers are now estimated to work from home, with the levels rising every year. Next April the government, as part of its employment bill, will introduce a 'right to ask'. Nominally for parents of small children, but expected in practice by some personnel professionals to be applied across the board, it will mean that an employer will need to give serious consideration to a request for flexible working and explain any denial in writing.

The Guardian
Saturday 7 December 2002
© Nic Paton

Working from home can bring a number of benefits depending on personal circumstances. There should be minimal distractions in a home office and a reduction in everyday work pressures. However, some find that working in such an isolated environment can be a disadvantage, with little opportunity to interact and exchange information.

◀ Further debate

1 Identify a range of professions where teleworking would be a viable option.
2 What do you think are the benefits of working from home?
3 Would you choose to work from home in the future? Why or why not?
4 Are there any particular groups of people who would be more vulnerable working at home, or more liable to distractions?

Test your knowledge

What impact has ICT had on the following working environments?

- manufacturing and industry
- retail
- education
- home and teleworking.
- commerce
- medicine
- military and government

Exam questions

1 The use of Information and Communication Technology (ICT) has brought benefits to a number of areas.

For **each** of the following, state a use of ICT, and describe the benefit that can be gained. Your examples must be different in each case.

(a) education

(b) health

(c) the home

(d) offices

(e) manufacturing companies

(f) police. *(12 marks)*

AQA Jan 2001

2 Some transport and distribution companies have now installed information systems on their vehicles that give details of traffic problems across the country.

Explain **one** benefit to the company of installing these systems. *(2 marks)*

AQA May 2002

6 Role of communication systems

This section will provide coverage of the following key areas:

- Explain the use of global communications between single or multiple sources and recipients, including public networks such as the Internet
- Describe the hardware, software and services required to access the Internet
- Describe the facilities offered and the relative merits of telephone, fax, e-mail, teleconferencing, viewdata, teletext, remote databases and other relevant communication systems
- Explain the use of the Internet for a range of activities including communication, information searching and information publication
- Be aware of the recent developments in the area of communication systems.

ICT has generated a number of systems that have created better and cheaper means of communication. One of the most widely available and popular communications systems is the Internet. Others include:

- intranets
- extranets
- e-mail
- newsgroups
- bulletin boards.

Each of these has enabled users of all ages and competency levels to communicate globally at the touch of a button, sharing news, ideas and interests with friends, family, colleagues and strangers.

6.0 The Internet

The Internet was first developed in 1969 as a research and defence network in the United States. ARPAnet was intended to link together servers used by military and academic personnel at the time of the Cold War. Since this time the Internet has grown into a much more advanced and interactive communications system allowing users to navigate between information resources through the use of World Wide Web browsers.

The Internet is a physical network that links computers globally, creating communication links that can store and transfer vast amounts of data and information.

Internet hardware, software and services

Requirements for accessing the Internet fall into three broad categories:

- hardware
- software
- services.

Traditional **hardware** requirements for Internet connection included a computer and a modem with access to a telephone line. However the need for faster and more reliable connections has opened up more advanced ways of accessing the Internet, including:

- cable
- ISDN
- broadband
- ADSL
- T3.

Each of these methods brings a host of benefits, including:

- being able to use the land-line telephone to make calls while surfing on the Internet
- faster connection speeds
- better reliability in terms of instant connection
- permanent connection – no need to continually dial.

For some, especially occasional users, the additional costs associated with upgrading to a faster medium of connection mean this is not a viable option, and others find that they are not yet available in their geographical area.

Over recent years, however, newer and more accessible hardware formats have become widely available, and users do not even need a computer to connect to them. These alternatives include:

- games console machines
- set-top boxes
- e-mail phones (land-line).
- WAP phones
- telephone booths/kiosks

In terms of **software**, the majority of operating systems today have integrated Internet access software that includes dial-up-networking and browsers. If further configuration is required to gain access, one of two procedures can be followed, as shown in Figure 15.

Figure 15

Internet configuration procedures

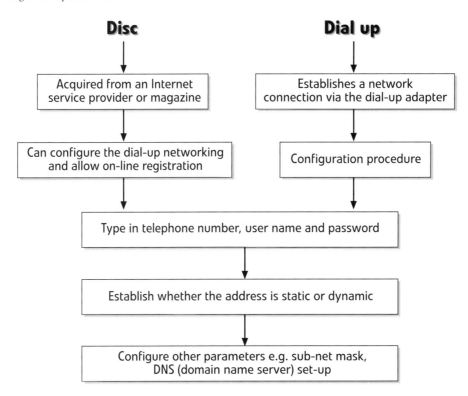

A number of **services** are available to users of the Internet. These include:

- e-mail
- FTP (file transfer protocol)
- IRC (Internet relay chat).
- browsing
- newsgroups

In addition, other services may be available from an ISP (Internet service provider), including:

- web space
- web hosting
- help desk support.

Benefits and limitations of the Internet

The Internet has revolutionised the way in which people bank, shop, learn, socialise and communicate. The Internet has provided greater flexibility and convenience to many sectors of society, including people who are house-bound, or restricted by their work, family or social commitments.

Home users can use the Internet for:

- shopping
- banking
- researching – immense amounts of information on almost any topic can be sourced through search engines, which use programs that use key words to locate relevant websites or pages
- global communication – via e-mail, chat, newsgroups, etc.
- leisure activities – e.g. booking theatre tickets, looking for holidays, checking restaurant reviews, etc.
- learning and education
- gaming
- working.

E-commerce has become popular, and because of lower overheads a majority of Internet companies offer cheaper prices than high-street stores, and also a wider range of stock.

What does this mean?
Overheads: Overheads are the costs associated with a certain project, product, service or organisation. Overheads include wages, cost of hardware, software, distribution and shipping costs, advertising, storage, etc. The lower the overheads, the more profitable the venture because the financial outlay is reduced

Almost anything can now be purchased over the Internet, including books, cars, houses, and even a village (see the next page).

Daily Telegraph Saturday 28 December 2002 © Telegraph Group Limited 2003

Activity 12

Carry out the following tasks to identify the limits of Internet trading and the implications of buying products via the Internet.

1 Using the Internet, identify five unusual products or services that can be purchased on-line. State how easy it is to purchase these items.

2 Do you think that making payments over the Internet is secure?

3 Are there any items that you feel should not be sold over the Internet?

4 Are there any items that you would not buy over the Internet? If so, what are they?

The convenience and flexibility offered by on-line purchasing has meant that there is no need to queue at the theatre, even to collect your pre-ordered tickets – a new system will be coming on line to enable users to print their own e-tickets (see the next page).

Print your own e-tickets to beat theatre queues

By Adam Sherwin
Media Reporter

THEATRE and concert goers will be able to print out their own tickets for big shows when an online ticketing revolution begins next year.

The inconvenience of queuing at the box office or waiting for tickets to arrive through the post will end when Ticketmaster allows customers across Britain to create their own e-tickets at the click of a mouse.

E-tickets are being introduced after this month's Worthington Cup tie between Aston Villa and Liverpool was delayed for 70 minutes when thousands of fans demanded tickets on match-day. Ticketmaster could not post them and fans were forced to queue outside Villa Park.

Premiership football matches, West End shows and rock concerts will all be instantly available, but fans hoping that the technological advances will remove the all-pervasive booking fee are all in for a dissapointment. Although tickets need no longer be posted, Ticketmaster may even increase the fee it charges on top of a ticket's face value to cover the cost of introducing the system.

Consumers are finding that the face value of a ticket is increasingly meaningless. Two tickets for Bon Jovi at Hyde Park, Central London, next June, currently advertised at £70 for the pair, will cost £82.35 through the Ticketmaster website once the company's processing fee and service charges are included. A £3.50 booking fee is charged on each ticket for the West End musical hit *We Will Rock You.*

Ticketmaster, the world's largest ticket distributor, delivers 100 million to buyers around the world each year, and the company believes that customers will be willing to pay more for creating their own instant ticket. In February the "TicketFast" system will be introduced on the Ticketmaster website.

Customers will receive an e-mail containing a unique barcode along with confirmation of the ticket details. The ticket can be printed out immediately via the customer's home computer.

Computerised turnstiles at the venue will confirm that the e-ticket is authentic. Budget airlines use similar technology to provide instant tickets for travellers. Peter Jackson, managing director of Ticketmaster UK, said: "I don't see that there will be any reduction in booking fees. TicketFast is an additional service which is costing us £800,000 to introduce."

This year Clear Channel Entertainment, Britain's largest theatre owner, faced a boycott of its regional venues after the full introduction of Ticketmaster handling charges that added at least £1.50 to the price of each ticket booked. Mr Jackson said that over the past decade, booking fees had been reduced from more than a fifth to an average of a tenth of the ticket price. The company has to pay for box office equipment as well as 800 staff across Britain, who handle ten million phone and post transactions.

Although Ticketmaster argues that the booking fee is justified because it offers a unique service, others argue that the US giant is monopolistic.

The software being introduced by Ticketmaster will also allow football and concert tickts to be traded at the last minute if the buyer cannot attend.

An "internal market" will be created on the website and the bar code will be transferred to a new ticket holder. Football season ticket holders will be able to sell on virtual tickets without meeting the buyer or handing over the season ticket, the aim being to maximise attendances.

What the tickets cost and the extras

☐ **Robbie Williams, Edinburgh**
June 29, 2003

Number of tickets: 1
Face value: £35
Service charge: £3.25
Processing fee: £1.60

Total: £39.85

☐ **Bon Jovi, Hyde Park, London**
June 28, 2003

Number of tickets: 2
Face value: £70
Service charge: £7.50
Processing fee: £4.85

Total: £82.35

☐ *We Will Rock You,* **Dominion Theatre, London**

Number of tickets: 2
Face value: £80
Service charge: £7.50
Processing fee: £1.75

Total: £89.25

☐ *Chicago,* **Adelphi Theatre, Strand, London**

Number of tickets: 2
Face value: £80
Service charge: £2
Processing fee: £1.75

Total: £83.75

The Times Monday 30 December 2002

Business uses of the Internet

The Internet has had a huge impact on businesses and the way in which they trade products and services. Business uses for the Internet include:

- as a marketing tool – e.g. setting up a website to promote and advertise
- to reach a much wider (global) audience
- to improve the corporate image
- to provide on-line facilities for ordering, payments and delivery
- to check competitor markets
- to research new markets and suppliers
- to receive direct feedback from customers via a website
- lowering of overheads.

There are also a number of negative aspects and limitations for business. The costs of setting up on-line facilities and possibly maintaining a website can be a burden, but these are necessary in order to keep up with market demands and with competitors. Employees may find themselves redundant of tasks or even a job as ordering and payment systems become more 'E' focused. Employees may also need to be re-trained in order to work alongside the new technology.

6.1 Intranet systems

Intranet systems originate from the 1990s. An intranet is an internal communications system within an organisation, set up for the benefit of the company and its employees.

Benefits of setting up an intranet system include:

- security – there are minimal external threats (especially if an Internet system is not being used in conjunction with it)
- it is easy to set up as it is web-browser driven
- it is cheap to maintain
- it is easy to use
- it promotes open communication, and breaks down the barriers between levels of employees.

Many organisations have intranets installed because of these benefits, but some companies opt to extend their communications system to third parties such as customers and suppliers, and by doing so they move into the realms of an extranet.

6.2 Extranet systems

An extranet system provides a wider communication system than an intranet, but much less than the Internet. An extranet can include an organisation's customers, suppliers and any other third parties of their choosing. It can allow an organisation to receive comments and feedback from customers, and to order stock on-line from suppliers. See the diagram on the next page.

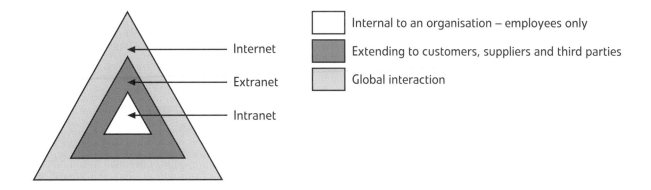

- Internet
- Extranet
- Intranet

☐ Internal to an organisation – employees only

▨ Extending to customers, suppliers and third parties

☐ Global interaction

6.3 E-mail

Electronic mail has become one of the fastest and most widely accessible forms of communication. Now it is not even necessary to sit down in front of a computer terminal and tap on a keyboard. New and more portable tools have become available, including games consoles, WAP phones, digital televisions and set-top boxes.

The advantages of using e-mail include the following.

- **Speed** – the ability to send messages asynchronously at the touch of a button anywhere in the world.
- **Multiple sends and copies** – the ability to communicate the same message to multiple users.
- **Cost** – costs are minimal and, depending upon the environment, possibly there is no cost (within an educational environment, for example).
- **Convenience** – you can communicate 24 hours a day, seven days a week. Messages are stored on the service provider's computer whether or not the recipient's computer is switched on.
- **Sharing data** – because information can be transferred to multiple users, these users can have access to the same shared information, including attached files, graphics and moving images.
- **Ease of use** – once you are familiar with the basic functions of an e-mail package it is very easy (because it is icon driven) to send and receive e-mail.
- **Audit** – you can keep a record (audit) of messages that have been sent and received. Messages can be saved into different formats, updated or printed out if required.

E-mail embraces a range of multimedia elements that allows users to send messages containing graphics, sound, moving images and hyperlinks to Internet pages.

The disadvantages of e-mail mainly concern technical and security issues, such as:

- **Spamming** – the receipt of unwanted messages from advertisers and unknown users who broadcast messages universally to an enormous address book.
- **Routing** – e-mail is not always sent directly from A to B. It can be routed to other destinations before it finally reaches the receiver. Routing can cause a number of problems, including:

– delaying the message

– more opportunities for the message to be intercepted by a third party

– the message can become distorted or lost.

■ **Security –** e-mail can be intercepted easily unless some type of encryption has been applied to it.

■ **Confidentiality** – because e-mail messages can get lost, intercepted or distorted it is not deemed appropriate to send confidential messages using this method.

6.4 Newsgroups

Newsgroups can be described as interactive discussion forums that allow users who share the same interests or research concerns to communicate across the Internet, or an intranet or extranet system. Newsgroups are dynamic in that people post facts and ideas, view current articles and respond to what has been included on the site. Examples of newsgroups include:

■ on-line gaming sites

■ environmental protection groups

■ fan sites for pop singers or sports teams.

6.5 Bulletin boards

Bulletin boards are more static than newsgroups – they are not interactive. People look at a bulletin board for updates and information similar to that in a newspaper or leaflet. Examples of bulletin boards include:

■ staff association notices

■ information on sporting fixtures

■ calendars of events.

6.6 Relative merits of other communication methods

Telephone

Telephones, especially mobile phones, are still an important means of communication. They are easily available and are a quick way to consult another person and receive instant replies to your queries. The disadvantages of using the telephone include the fact that no documents can be communicated, and the difficulty of catching the right person at a convenient time – this is especially problematic with international calls, where time differences have to be taken into consideration.

With **teleconferencing**, several participants can be included in the conversation. **Videoconferencing** is a variant system that includes video cameras and screens, so that participants can see as well as hear each other, with the video usually transmitted over an ISDN (integrated services digital network) line. A videoconference can save the travelling time and expense involved in organising a conventional meeting, but the necessary equipment can itself be expensive.

Fax

Fax is the usual abbreviation for 'facsimile transmission'. Most businesses now use fax machines widely to speed up the sending of documents. With a conventional fax machine, each page – whether text or graphics – is scanned and digitised, then transmitted in analogue form over a telephone line. The receiving fax machine prints out a copy. This process can be slow when many pages are involved. A quicker method of faxing is by computer, where there is no need to scan the document. A fax modem sends and receives documents directly to hard disk, where they can be read or printed out.

Viewdata

Viewdata services send data to your computer terminal or television screen. These are interactive information systems – the user can send information as well as receive it – using a TV or computer, modem and telephone lines. They are paid for by subscription charges, and also involve telephone costs.

Teletext

Most TVs can receive the teletext services provided by the television companies. Pages of information can be accessed using a remote-control keypad. A limited number of pages are available, usually covering topics such as news, weather, sports and traffic information, and they are text only and not interactive. Although teletext is easy to use, moving from page to page can be slow.

Remote databases

An example of everyday use of a remote data base is a travel agent accessing a tour operator's files to book a holiday for a customer, or a ticket agent accessing a theatre's files to reserve seats at a performance. In both cases the organisation gives instant access and interactivity to the agent in order to promote sales and marketing.

 Activity 13

1 A company wants a communication tool and is unsure about using the resources of the Internet, or an intranet or extranet system. Describe the advantages and disadvantages of each system.

2 There are a number of ways in which you can send and receive an e-mail. Research the hardware and other costs involved in sending an e-mail with the following tools:

- WAP phone
- games console machine
- desk-top box.

3 Using the Internet, find two newsgroup sites and:

- identify what the newsgroup is for
- identify if there are any subscription costs
- describe how people interact on the site
- give an evaluation of the newsgroup and grade its usefulness in terms of a score out of 10.

Test your knowledge

1 Give four examples of communication tools.
2 What are the traditional hardware requirements for connection to the Internet?
3 Identify two ways of connecting to the Internet without the use of a computer.
4 What services are available once Internet connection has been established?
5 Identify four benefits each that the Internet has bought to:
   ■ home users
   ■ business.
6 State three advantages and one disadvantage of using e-mail.
7 What are the differences between a newsgroup and a bulletin board?

 Exam questions

1 **(a)** *Browsers* and *search engines* are two items that are associated with the use of the Internet. Explain what is meant by:

   (i) a browser *(2 marks)*
   (ii) a search engine *(2 marks)*

   (b) In order to use the Internet, the owner of a PC at home normally needs to register with an Internet service provider (ISP). State **two** services, in addition to e-mail, that an ISP could provide. *(2 marks)*
   (c) Changes in technology now mean that it is no longer necessary to have a PC to be able to use some Internet services. Give **two** devices that can be used instead. *(2 marks)*
   (d) Explain why it is possible to send e-mail successfully to someone who has not got his or her PC switched on. *(2 marks)*
   AQA May 2001

2 What do the following features, available with most e-mail software, allow the user to do?

   (a) Forward *(2 marks)*
   (b) Reply *(2 marks)*
   (c) Send/receive *(2 marks)*
   (d) Attach *(2 marks)*
   (e) Prioritise *(2 marks)*
   AQA Jan 2002

3 Describe, using examples, **four** ways in which a company could make use of the Internet to benefit its business. *(8 marks)*
   AQA May 2002

4 Many organizations have adopted e-mail as a method of communication only to find that it can have disadvantages.

   Describe **three** disadvantages of the use of e-mail, other than contracting viruses, for business communication. *(6 marks)*
   AQA May 2002

5 A school wishes to allow its students unrestricted access to the Internet for research work during their lunchtimes. The headteacher is concerned that this might cause problems.

   State two problems that the headteacher might be concerned about, and for each one explain a measure that could prevent the problem. *(6 marks)*
   AQA Jan 2001

7 Information and the professional

This section will provide coverage of the following key areas:

- Recall the personal qualities and general characteristics necessary for a person to work effectively within the ICT industry and as part of an ICT team.

ICT has created a new culture in the workplace, at home and in schools and education. Jobs, knowledge and skills are all changing. People are now becoming more ICT literate, and there is an ever-growing necessity to learn and apply these skills.

7.0 ICT skills

For some people, re-training has been required because of changing job roles that now rely on the use of ICT. For the younger generation the need to be taught ICT skills at an early age means the subject is as important as maths or English in preparing them for a competitive and changing job market. Older people who missed earlier ICT opportunities are now looking to update their ICT skills and learn new ones through courses and training.

ICT skills can be summarised as having various levels, as shown in Figure 16.

Figure 16

Levels of ICT skills

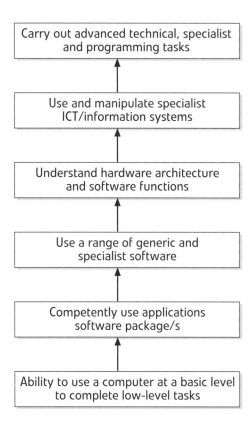

The range of jobs available for people who want to enter the ICT industry is quite diverse, including:

- end user support
- programmer
- help desk operator
- web designer

- network administrator
- applications operator
- ICT administrator
- ICT manager.
- hardware technician
- trainer
- technical support

7.1 Personal qualities

Obviously, technical skills may be necessary to fulfil the requirements of a specific role. But above all, people entering the ICT industry need to display the following qualities:

1   Be a good communicator – able to communicate at all levels, and to end users as well as technical specialists and management. You should be able to communicate well orally and in writing, and be able to listen effectively.

2   Be a good team player – able to work well within a team. Most ICT roles involve working in project teams.

3   Be able to listen well and carry out instructions – if you are working within a team, people may depend on you to complete your task before the project can move forward.

4   Have a friendly disposition – a lot of ICT roles involve mixing with members of the public or supporting colleagues. People will be more willing to discuss their ICT needs with someone who is approachable and friendly.

5   Be willing to work flexible hours – if you are supporting users you may need to keep working until you have solved their problems, and you may have to work unsocial hours if you are involved in installing new software or correcting faults. This work usually has to be done outside normal working hours, when users don't need the equipment.

6   Be well organised and able to work under pressure – you may have several tasks at the same time. You need to be an efficient and determined problem-solver.

7   Be able and willing to learn new skills, as ICT is a constantly changing environment.

The following two articles highlight the need for people entering the field of ICT to display these qualities.

Communication becomes a key skill for techies

The days of the backroom techies are long gone. With IT now integral to all, communication skills have become a necessity for successful IT staff. Many IT professionals spend a substantial part of their working day talking to people outside of their department.

Contacts range from the most junior person in an organisation to the managing director. This means that technical expertise on its own is no longer enough. Employers want ITers to have good communication and business skills.

'Communication skills are probably the single most important skill in a person's working life, irrespective of their level', says Paul Smith, CEO at career management site Firstpersonglobal.com. Many people do have these skills, but don't know how to market them and transfer them to the workplace.

Computer Weekly
Roisin Woolnough 22 March 2001
© Computer Weekly – reprinted with permission

Soft skills key to IT success

Talk may be cheap, but it's worth more than technical knowledge if you want to get ahead in IT, according to a survey of CEOs by an international recruiting firm. 'The single most common requirement (of managers) is to hire individuals with very good interpersonal communication skills and business sense,' said David Tighe, Canadian area manager for RHI Consulting Inc.

In an RHI survey of 1,400 CEOs in the United States, 27% said interpersonal skills are the most important factor for reaching management levels in the IT field.

Computing Canada
Howard Solomon 23 July 1999

Activity 14

Based on the evidence provided in the two articles above and the job advert for Norfolk Constabulary (below):

1 Make a list of ten qualities each that you think a typical person in the following professions would need (some qualities may overlap):
   - IT help desk/support personnel
   - IT manager.

2 Design a table with four columns. Transfer the lists you created for question 1 into the first and third columns. In the other columns, rank each of the qualities you have named from 1–10 (1 = lowest, 10 = highest).

3 Try to locate people who work in help desk support or as IT managers (ask a family member, friend, or somebody within your school or college). Ask them to give their own rankings of each quality in your table.

4 Discuss the findings within your group to see what differences exist between your own interpretations and a professional's view.

Example of job advert for an ICT position

Analyst

Norfolk Constabulary

North Walsham

Analyst
Crime & Disorder Reduction Partnership
Fixed Term Contract until 31 March 2004
£16,896 - £18,453 per annum
Crime and Disorder Partnerships are responsible for developing and implementing strategies to reduce crime and disorder locally, and involve a number of partner agencies, including the police, district and county council. The new post of Analyst will be pivotal in providing accurate information about the nature of crime and disorder problems within each partnership area. Your duties will include dissemination of relevant information, analysing this information for trends and significance and presenting the results. You will develop effective mechanisms for the sharing and analysis of information between key partner agencies.

You must have good written and verbal communication skills, an ability to share and analyse information effectively and possess good IT skills. Previous knowledge of Crime and Disorder Reduction Partnerships and experience of analytical software would be an advantage.

Eastern Daily Press
February 2003

Exam questions

1 Professionals involved with ICT systems often have to work with people with little, or no, understanding of the ICT system that they are using.

State **two** personal qualities that IT professionals should have that will enable them to help such people effectively, and give an example of when each quality would be needed. *(4 marks)*

AQA Jan 2002

2 An advertisement for an IT support worker to join the PC support team in a company specifies that the applicant must be 'willing to work flexible hours, be able to communicate well orally, have good written skills and get on well with a wide variety of people'.

Explain, giving examples, why **each** of these characteristics is important for someone working in such a role. *(8 marks)*

AQA May 2001

3 A company is recruiting a new member of staff for their IT support desk. The head of personnel asks the manager of the support desk what personal qualities the new employee must have in order to carry out the job effectively. State, with reasons, **four** personal qualities that the manager would want a new employee to have. *(8 marks)*

AQA Jan 2001

8 Information systems malpractice and crime

This section will provide coverage of the following key areas:

- Explain the consequences of malpractice and crime on information systems
- Describe the possible weak points within information technology systems
- Describe the measures that can be taken to protect information technology systems against internal and external threats
- Describe the particular issues surrounding access to, and use of, the Internet; e.g. censorship, security, ethics.

A number of problems and issues can arise with IT systems. Here we examine the problem of malpractice and crime to see how measures can be taken to counter internal and external threats to systems, and look at the consequences of unauthorised access to systems. Issues surrounding access to and use of the Internet are all relevant here.

8.0 Malpractice and crime

IT systems can be prey to a range of unauthorised and illegal activities. These activities include:

- hacking into systems (seeking unauthorised access)
- sabotaging systems and data
- creating viruses (programs that damage files) and worms (viruses that can reproduce themselves), and introducing them into systems
- removing, copying or altering data without authorisation.

Legislation which aims to protect systems from potential malpractice and crime is described in Section 9 (pages 77–84).

Consequences of malpractice and crime

Organisations can suffer losses of money, goods or information through computer crime and malpractice. Using a company's IT system, payments could be diverted fraudulently into false accounts; goods could be delivered to an unauthorised destination; files or databases could be misused or copied and sold; and vandalism could destroy or corrupt data.

Internal and external threats

Each organisation confronts both internal and external threats to its security. Internal threats are from an organisation's own staff, and include the types of theft and vandalism described above, as well as unintentional damage such as accidentally introducing viruses or corrupting data.

External threats come from people and events outside an organisation. A natural disaster such as flooding, or a power failure, can have serious consequences, as of course can the damage deliberately caused by people through hacking or the theft of data.

Weak points in IT systems

Hardware, software and human beings can all constitute weak points in an IT system. Portable computers with access to networks can pose a risk, as can lack of security (such as password protection) at user workstations. Data stored off-line can be vulnerable to theft, and viruses can corrupt or destroy files. The human risk element involves not only hackers and other unscrupulous outsiders, but an organisation's own staff – so measures must be taken to protect against fraud and misuse by disgruntled or dishonest employees.

8.1 Measures used to protect IT systems

There are a number of security issues to consider when working with computers and information systems. To protect organisations, users of information systems and the general public (about whom information may be stored), a number of measures and guidelines have been introduced. They fall broadly into two categories:

- data security
- data protection.

These two are closely related. Data security includes physical security issues, and data protection includes measures that have been introduced to protect consumer data from misuse.

Keeping data secure can be difficult because of the environment in which users need to work and the access they require. Businesses have moved towards a totally networked environment promoting a culture of sharing data, so the issue of security is even more important and needs to be addressed at a number of levels, as shown in Figure 17.

Figure 17

Levels of security

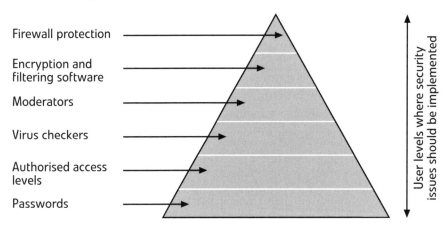

What does this mean?

Firewalls: Intelligent protective devices that can be placed between the network file server and external networks such as the Internet to protect computers from unauthorised access or unwanted data

Encryption: The coding of data before sending along communication lines. Decoding is performed by the receiving machine. Encryption is widely used in e-commerce to protect customers' credit card details.

Moderators: People who monitor and regulate proceedings to ensure that tasks are carried out to an agreed standard

Virus checkers: Widely available pieces of software that detect viruses and repair the damage they do. Regular updates, usually monthly, are required to ensure protection against the latest viruses

Security measures need to be integrated at each user level within an organisation. Protection of data necessitates, at a simple level, good practice such as backing up all data to a secondary storage device. However, data protection is also a wider issue. For example, it involves meeting the requirements of the Data Protection Act 1984 (see page 79).

Internet issues

Currently the Internet is not well regulated – it is controlled or supervised on a partial basis by some institutions. This means that people may stumble innocently across sites that contain offensive, racist, pornographic, propaganda, criminal or other harmful material.

There may also be hidden dangers, such as communicating with strangers in chat rooms who may not be as they portray themselves to be. Disclosing personal information such as your name, address, telephone and e-mail details can lead to harassment.

Case study – Australia goes stark raving mad over Net censorship

The South Australia Parliament is pushing an Internet censorship bill that will make it an offence for anyone to post any information deemed offensive to children anywhere on the Internet. And it's the police that get to decide what is and isn't offensive.

In what is clearly politicians gone barking mad, fines of up to $10,000 can be levied against any individual that posts material seen as unsuitable for minors. The country's film certification system will be used to rate how strong material is – but the police will NOT have to go through an independent adjudicator, they can decide themselves whether the posting breaks the law.

It is expected that the Bill will be pulled into all other Australian states' legislation in the future.

The basic premise of the legislation appears to be that since kids are able to access Internet sites at any time, then everything on the Internet ought to be acceptable to children. This is clearly bonkers thinking seeing as Australia's laws will have no effect on the rest of the world – which contains more than its fair share of 'unsuitable' material. Unless of course Australia is thinking of going China's route and running ISPs through the government and blocking any sites outside the country.

Kieren McCarthy 2 March 2001 © The Register (www.theregister.com)

◀ Further debate

Some might argue that imposing Internet censorship is going a step too far. Complete the following tasks basing your answers on your own feelings about the Internet and censorship.

1   Do you think that there should be some restrictions on information posted on the Internet? Take into consideration the following issues:

- schoolchildren having unlimited access to all sites
- illegal, pornographic, racist, unethical and propaganda material
- there is often no warning of site content, as there is for example with the certification system for films (PG, 12, 15, etc.).

2   Whose job do you think it is to regulate sites viewed by individuals on the Internet?

- the individuals themselves
- ISPs
- government
- parents/guardians
- regulatory authorities
- police.

Test your knowledge

1   Identify four ways in which you can ensure the security of data kept on a computer.
2   What is meant by the following terms?
- virus
- encryption.
3   As a home user, what could you do to ensure that information accessed via the Internet is secure?

Exam questions

1   Information Systems need to be protected from both internal and external threats.

   (a) Explain, using examples, the differences between an internal and an external threat to an Information System.   *(4 marks)*
   (b) For each of the following, describe a measure that a company can take to protect their Information System from:

   (i)   internal threats   *(2 marks)*
   (ii) external threats.   *(2 marks)*

   AQA Jan 2002

2   A company offering security services for ICT systems includes the following quotation in its advertisement: 'You are protected against hackers, viruses and worms, but what about the staff in the sales department?'

   Describe **three** ways in which a company's own staff can be a weak point in its ICT system.

   (6 marks)

   AQA Jan 2002

3   Explain, using examples, the difference between malpractice and crime as applied to Information Systems.   *(4 marks)*

   AQA May 2002

9 The legal framework

This section will provide coverage of the following key areas:

Software and data misuse:
- Describe the provisions of the Computer Misuse Act
- Describe the principles of software copyright and licensing agreements.

Data protection legislation:
- Recall the nature, purpose and provisions of the current data protection legislation of the Public Register
- Recall the type of data covered and various exemptions from the legislation
- Recall the definitions of processing and consent to process
- Explain how the requirements of the legislation impact on data collection and use
- Describe the obligations of data users under the legislation
- Recall the rights of individuals under the legislation
- Recall the role of the Commissioner in encouraging good practice, acting as Ombudsman and enforcing legislation.

Health and safety:
- Describe the provisions of the current health and safety legislation in relation to the use of information systems
- Recognise that health and safety guidelines cover the design and introduction of new software.

9.0 Computer Misuse Act 1990

The Computer Misuse Act was passed to address the increased threat of hackers – people trying to gain unauthorised access to computer systems. Prior to this act there was minimal protection, and it was difficult to prosecute because theft of data by hacking was not considered as deprivation to the owner.

The offences defined, and the penalties established, under this act include:

Offences
- unauthorised access: an attempt by a hacker to gain unauthorised access to a computer system
- unauthorised access with the intention of committing another offence: on gaining access a hacker proceeds with the intent of committing a further crime
- unauthorised modification of data or programs: introducing viruses to a computer system. Guilt is assessed by the level of intent to cause disruption, or to impair the processes of a computer system.

Penalties
- unauthorised access: imprisonment for up to six months and/or a fine of up to £2,000
- unauthorised access with the intention of committing another offence: imprisonment for up to five years and/or an unlimited fine
- unauthorised modification: imprisonment for up to five years and/or an unlimited fine.

9.1 Copyright, Designs and Patent Act (1988)

The Copyright, Designs and Patent Act provides protection to software developers and organisations against unauthorised copying of their software, designs, printed material and any other product. Under copyright legislation, an organisation or developer can ensure that its Intellectual Property Rights have been safeguarded against third parties who may wish to exploit and make gains from the originator's research and development.

What does this mean?

Intellectual Property Rights: Patents, registered designs and design rights, registered trade marks and copyright

---

Copyright

Copyright is awarded to a product or brand following its completion. No further action is required in order to activate it. Copyright is transferable if the originator/author grants a transfer and it can exist for up to fifty years following the death of the originator/author.

A number of copyright issues exist in connection with software. The first is software piracy – the unauthorised copying of software, or its use on more machines than permitted by the licences that have been paid for. A software licensing agreement between the software producer and the user sets out how software may be used, and on how many machines. The second is the question of ownership. If a bespoke piece of software has been developed for an organisation, the copyright remains with the developer unless other conditions have been written into a contract. An employee who has developed a piece of software for an organisation can take the ownership and copyright to another organisation unless this is addressed in the employee's contract.

Software piracy

Software piracy can be broken down into a number of key areas:

- recordable CD ROMs – pirates compile large amounts of software onto one recordable CD-ROM and make multiple copies of it
- professional counterfeits – professionally made copies of software including media, packages, licences and even security holograms made to resemble the genuine article
- Internet piracy – the downloading or distribution of software on the Internet, infringing copyright
- corporate overuse – organisations install software packages onto more machines than they have licences for
- hard-disk loaders – retail outlets or dealers who load copyright-infringing versions of software onto a computer system to encourage customers to buy their hardware. These customers will not have the appropriate licences or be entitled to technical support or upgrades.

The Federation Against Software Theft (FAST) was set up in 1984 by the software industry with the aim of preventing software piracy. Anyone caught breaching the copyright law would be prosecuted under the procedures established by this federation.

9.2 Data Protection Act 1984 and 1998

The Data Protection Act applies to the processing of data and information by a computer. The act places obligations on people and organisations who collect, process and store personal records and data about consumers or customers. The act is based upon a set of principles that binds a user to following a set of procedures offering assurances that data is kept secure. The main principles include the following:

- Personal data should be processed fairly and lawfully.
- Personal data should be held only for one or more specified and lawful purposes.
- Personal data held should not be disclosed in any way that is incompatible to the specified and lawful purpose.
- Personal data held should be adequate and relevant, not excessive to the purpose or purposes.
- Personal data kept should be accurate and up to date.

- Personal data should not be retained for any longer than necessary.
- Individuals should be informed about personal data stored, and should be entitled to have access to it, and if appropriate to have such data corrected or erased.
- Security measures should ensure that no unauthorised access to, alteration, disclosure or destruction of personal data is permitted, and protection should be provided against accidental loss or destruction.

Useful definitions from the 1984 Act

Personal data:	Information about living, identifiable individuals. Personal data does not have to be particularly sensitive information, and can be as little as a name and address.
Data users:	Those who control the contents, and use, of a collection of personal data. They can be any type of company or organisation, large or small, within the public or private sector. A data user can also be a sole trader, partnership, or an individual. A data user need not necessarily own a computer.
Data subjects:	The individuals to whom the personal data relates.
Automatically processed:	Processed by computer or other technology, such as image-processing systems.

Consent

Data subjects are deemed to have given permission for their data to be processed only for the purpose for which they provided the data. For example, if you complete an application form for a supermarket loyalty card, you are consenting to the supermarket's use of your information for its own ordinary business purposes. However, there will be a box for you to tick if you do not wish the supermarket to sell this information to other interested parties, who may wish to use it for direct marketing.

Rights of the individual

Any data subject can, under the legislation, ask the holder of the data (the data controller) for a copy of the personal data held about him or her. This can be done either by contacting the particular data controller directly, or by writing to the Information Commissioner. A small charge is often made by data controllers for supplying the information, but when requested they must do so within 40 days. (Not all information held about a person is included in this right of access – see page 81.)

If the data subject discovers inaccuracies in the data held, he or she can ask for these to be corrected or deleted. A data subject can sue for compensation if damage or distress is caused by the actions of a data controller, or the use of inaccurate data.

The role of the Information Commissioner

The Commissioner is an independent supervisory authority and has an international role as well as a national one. Primarily, the Commissioner is responsible for ensuring that data protection legislation is enforced.

In the UK, the Commissioner has a range of duties including:

- promoting good information-handling practices
- encouraging codes of practice for data controllers.

The Commissioner maintains a public register of data controllers. Each register entry contains details about a controller, such as name, address and a description of the processing of the personal data by the controller.

Registering entries

All users, with a few exceptions, must register, giving their name, address and broad descriptions of:

- those about whom personal data are held
- the items of data held
- the purposes for which the data is used
- the sources from which the information may be obtained
- the types of organisations to whom the information may be disclosed, i.e. shown or passed to
- any overseas countries or territories to which the data may be transferred.

In December 2002, Richard Thomas assumed the role of Information Commissioner. His mission statement is:

We shall develop respect for private lives of individuals and encourage the openness and accountability of public authorities

- by promoting good information-handling practice and enforcing data protection and freedom of information legislation, and
- by seeking to influence national and international thinking about privacy and information access issues.

See the website www.dataprotection.gov.uk/commissioner.htm for more information.

Data protection overview

The act does not apply to:

- payroll, pensions and accounts data, or names and addresses held for distribution purposes
- data for personal, family, household or recreational use.

Subjects do not have a right to access data:

- if the sole aim of collecting it is statistical or research purposes
- if it is for back-up purposes.

Data can be disclosed to:

- the data subject's agent (e.g. lawyer or accountant)
- persons working for the data user
- any persons in urgent need to prevent injury or damage to health.

Additionally, there are exemptions for special categories, including data held:

- in connection with national security
- for prevention of crime
- for the collection of tax and duty.

9.3 Health and safety

The working environment of users of computer and information systems is vitally important. The issues involved include environmental, social and practical aspects of the working conditions, as shown in Figure 18.

Users should be working in an environment that has adequate ventilation and natural lighting. The temperature should also be controlled, especially as computers give out large amounts of heat.

Filters to minimise glare from screens and height-adjustable chairs should be provided. Wires should always be packed away in appropriate conduits and not left trailing across the floor.

Staff should be reminded that when working at a computer no food or drink should be consumed in case liquid or crumbs fall onto the keyboard or into the case. They should also ensure they have regular breaks or changes in activity.

Figure 18

Health and safety considerations

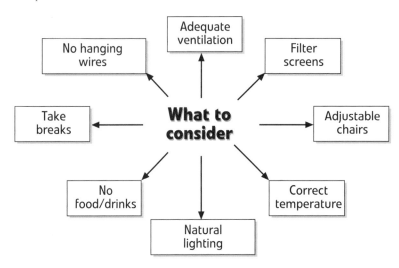

The best way to ensure health and safety in the workplace is to use common sense and adhere to standard ways of working. Most organisations offer guidelines and procedures for maintaining good working practice.

Display Screen Equipment (VDU) Regulations 1992

The Display Screen Equipment (VDU) Regulations 1992 aim to protect users of information systems and general ICT.

Under these regulations an employer has six main obligations. For every user and operator working in an undertaking, the employer must do the following:

1 Assess the risks arising from their use of display screen workstations and take steps to reduce any risks identified to the 'lowest extent reasonably practicable'.

2 Ensure that new workstations ('first put into service after 1st January 1993') meet minimum ergonomics standards set out in a schedule to the Regulations. Existing workstations have a further four years to meet the minimum requirements, provided that they are not posing a risk to their users.

3 Inform users about the results of the assessments, the actions the employer is taking and the users' entitlements under the Regulations.

For each user, whether working for the employer or another employer (but not each operator):

4 Plan display screen work to provide regular breaks or changes of activity.

In addition, for employees who are users:

5 Offer eye tests before display screen use, at regular intervals and if they experience visual problems. If the tests show that glasses are necessary and normal glasses cannot be used, then special glasses must be provided.

6 Provide appropriate health and safety training for users before display screen use or whenever the workstation is 'substantially modified'.

Such legislation benefits all users and helps to protect them against computer-related injuries such as:

- repetitive strain injury (RSI)
- eye strain
- epilepsy
- back and upper-joint problems
- exposure to radiation and ozone
- stress-related illnesses.

Test your knowledge

1 What penalties can be imposed on people who hack into systems and gain unauthorised access?

2 What does the Data Protection Act do, and who does it protect?

3 Identify at least one piece of legislation that protects users and enforces health and safety at work.

4 Identify four measures that can improve general health and safety within an office environment.

5 If you were working at a computer workstation all day every day, what should you do to ensure your own health and safety?

Exam questions

1 Data protection legislation was introduced into the UK in 1984; it has since been superseded by the 1998 Act.

(a) State why the legislation was originally introduced. *(1 mark)*

(b) State what type of data is the subject of the Data Protection Act 1998. *(2 marks)*

(c) A company wishes to collect data from order forms submitted by its customers to sell to other companies. State **two** actions that the company must take so that it can legally collect and sell that data. *(2 marks)*

(d) The Data Protection Act gives individuals the right to see what data is being held about them.

    (i) State how an individual must ask to do this. *(1 mark)*

    (ii) Could an individual have to pay to receive a copy of his or her data? *(1 mark)*

        AQA Jan 2002

2 **(a)** State **five** of the principles of the 1998 Data Protection Act. *(5 marks)*

    (b) Describe **two** exemptions to the 1998 Data Protection Act. *(4 marks)*

        AQA Jan 2001

Exam questions continued ...

3 **(a)** State why an organisation must apply for entry on to the Data Protection Register. *(1 mark)*

(b) State **three** items of information that must be provided by the data user about the data that is to be stored. *(3 marks)*

AQA May 2001

4 A company provides all new employees with an induction booklet including guidelines for working with ICT.

State, giving a reason for each one:

(a) **three** health and safety guidelines. *(6 marks)*

(b) **two** guidelines to protect the company's data. *(4 marks)*

AQA Jan 2003

MANAGEMENT AND MANIPULATION

This unit will focus on the management and manipulation of data and information, looking in detail at devices, processing functions, and formats that are used during the input-process-output cycle. A range of material will be used to examine the way in which data is input and processed into information, and the different ways in which information and data can be output.

Newer technologies have affected the way in which information and data is captured, processed and presented to users, and this unit will identify key aspects of this. The study of the human/computer interface is affecting user interaction, and the unit considers different users and target audiences in relation to this.

Security is vital to most organisations, and the unit will look at the different ways in which data can be kept both secure and private, looking at the different hardware and software options that can help.

Most organisations use networked computer systems and this unit looks at the different topologies available for setting up a networked system, taking into account the environment of an organisation, the hardware required, and benefits or disadvantages that the organisation would need to consider.

This unit can be mapped to the AQA specification as follows:

11.1	Data capture	Section 1
11.2	Verification and validation	Sections 1 and 2
11.3	Organisation of data for effective retrieval	Section 3
11.4	Software: Nature, capabilities and limitations	Section 8
11.4	Nature and types of software	Sections 8 and 9
11.4	Capabilities of software	Section 9
11.4	Upgradability	Section 9
11.4	Reliability	Section 9
11.5	Manipulation and/or processing	Sections 4 and 5
11.6	Dissemination/distribution	Section 6
11.7	Hardware: Nature, capabilities and limitations	Sections 1, 7, 10 and 11
11.8	Security of data	Section 7
11.8	Back-up systems	Section 7
11.9	Network environments	Section 11
11.10	Human/computer interface	Section 12

Each section is clearly signposted to show which areas of the specification are referred to.

1 **Data capture**

This section will provide coverage of the following key areas:

- Describe methods of data capture and identify appropriate contexts for their use

- Understand the concept of data encoding

- Understand the distinction between accuracy of information and validity of data

- Explain possible sources and types of error in data capture, transcription, transmission and processing

- Describe methods of preventing and reducing such errors

- Describe the broad characteristics, capabilities and limitations of current input devices.

Data capture is an essential part of the processing of information. It concerns the 'input' stage of the 'input – process – output' cycle described in Unit 1.

The initial stage of data capture concerns the way the data is originally gathered. This can be done using different techniques, including surveys, interviews and questionnaires. Once the data has been gathered, it needs to be converted into a format that is readable by the computer. All computers use the **binary** method of storing data, where each character is represented by a series of 0s and 1s (in most personal computers the code is called ASCII code, American Standard Code for Information Interchange). This is known as **encoding** the data.

1.0 **Data capture methods**

The most common ways of inputting data into the computer are via the keyboard and/or mouse.

- **Keyboard** data entry can be a slow process, especially for those who are not trained keyboard users. When keys are pressed, corresponding symbols appear on the computer screen and data that is entered is represented in a true format, meaning that what you type in will be what the computer reads. The most widely used type of keyboard is a **peripheral** that will be included in the computer package as purchased. Its layout is based on the old-fashioned typewriter 'QWERTY' keyboard.

  Other types of keyboard include:

  - **Touch-screen keyboards** presented on the monitor screen. The user touches the character or command required and the computer reads the data and presents it on screen or carries out the command. A common use of touch-screen keyboards is in tourist information kiosks.

  - **Ergonomic keyboards** developed for health and safety reasons to prevent injuries such as RSI (repetitive strain injury).

  - **Concept keyboards**, which are specially designed keyboards where the keys represent a collection of data rather than individual characters. Concept keyboards can be developed to speed up the input of data, as well as to help individuals with physical disabilities or learning difficulties. A common example of the use of concept keyboards is at the ordering points in fast food restaurants, where the keys represent items of food.

■ **Mouse** data entry is used to give commands to the computer by clicking the mouse to select actions. An arrow (or other specified icon) will appear on the screen so that the user knows where the mouse is as it moves around. The mouse can be used to click and drag to highlight blocks of text or graphics and advances in mouse technology, alongside developments in software, mean that double clicking and right clicking can also be used to give commands.

Other types of data entry that use pointing devices include:

■ **Joysticks**, which are hand-held devices normally used as pointing devices for games. They usually have extra buttons that enable the user to perform extra tasks, e.g. 'shooting'.

■ **Trackballs**, which are commonly used as part of a laptop computer. A trackball is like a mouse upside down. It is the ball that has to be manipulated by the user, which in turn moves the pointer on screen.

■ **Light pens** are light-sensitive, pen-shaped devices used to draw directly onto a screen. The patterns are read by the computer and presented on screen. **Interactive whiteboards** use a light pen to select commands and write on a screen. The technology is not yet perfect, as the user often has to write very slowly to enable the computer to keep up.

■ **Graphics tablet/pads** are flat surface devices that use a pen or stylus to draw on a tablet or pad. The lines are then presented on the monitor screen via an electronic sensor read by the computer.

Activity 1

Research the different methods of data capture using keyboards and pointer devices. What other devices can you find, not listed above? Find out more so that you can present your findings to the class.

Find out what type of person would typically use each device, or what type of job would involve using them.

Some forms of data gathering use processes whereby the data can be immediately transferred to a computer, without any conversion process. This is known as **automatic data capture**. Examples of input via automatic data capture, which uses input devices, include:

■ **OMR (optical mark reading)**: On a pre-printed sheet, a pencil is used to place marks in special grids, and the data is fed directly into a computer via a special input device.

When you fill in a lottery ticket, the machine into which it is fed is a special input device, directly connected to the main lottery computer. The machine reads the marks you have made on the ticket and sends the information to the central computer (see Figure 1).

When your examination scripts are marked, the examiner uses a form to record your marks, which can then be fed into a central computer.

Figure 1

Lottery form

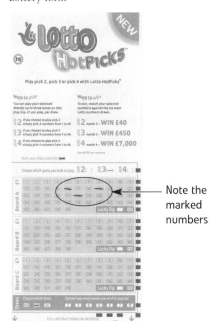

Note the marked numbers

Figure 2

Marking form

Note the
marked
numbers

- **OCR (optical character recognition)**: A scanner is used to read letters and numbers from the sheet being scanned. With the use of special software, these can be recognised by the computer and presented on screen as a copy of the sheet scanned in. Without the special software, the computer would read the sheet as a graphics file and you would not be able to edit the document. It must be noted that the conversion software currently available is not always 100% accurate; some of the most common errors are an 'S' read as a '5' and a 'Q' read as a '0' or 'O'.

- **MICR (magnetic ink character recognition)**: This is used by the banks to help prevent fraud. Numbers are printed on the bottom of each cheque in magnetic ink (see Figure 3) and the banks' computers can read these numbers using a special character recognition program. As well as helping to prevent fraud, the processing time is much quicker using this method, and the computer can still read the cheques even if they are not in good condition.

Figure 3

Cheque

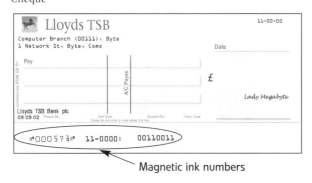

Magnetic ink numbers

- **Magnetic strip recognition**: A magnetic strip placed on a card contains information about the holder of the card. The card is swiped through a machine that reads the information encoded. The type of information held in the magnetic strip will typically include the card holder's account number, and it could include a credit limit, how many loyalty points the holder has earned, etc.

The card you use to take money out of your bank account through an ATM (automatic teller machine) is an example of this. A library card for your school/college will probably have a magnetic strip, so that when it is swiped through a machine your details can be brought up on screen for the librarian to check, for example, whether you have any overdue books.

Figure 4

Customer loyalty card

Magnetic strip from a loyalty
card with data held on it

Customer loyalty cards are another example of this type of data collection.

- **Bar codes**: These are used in supermarkets, and are another example of the scanning input of data. The scanning machine reads the bar codes printed on the labels of products by interpreting reflected light patterns. The data contained in the bar code includes the product description and price, and this information is transferred to the till. Most supermarkets also use the bar-code reader as a form of stock control – it is directly linked to a central computer and products are subtracted from the stock level as the bar-code reader scans them. Many other organisations use bar codes. For example, in many hospitals each patient is allocated a number and any tests taken are identified using bar codes.

- **Voice recognition**: This software uses a type of voice data entry to input speech directly into a word-processing package. Commands spoken to a computer, such as 'open file', can also be carried out using this type of software. It must be noted that voice recognition software is not 100% reliable and the user will have to 'train' the software to recognise his or her speech patterns and any dialect/accent used. A microphone is used to input the data.

Other data capture devices include the following.

- **Scanners**: These are used in many of the above capture methods. They are either hand-held or desktop peripherals which can read in information in graphic or text format. Advances in technology have meant that recently a wider variety of scanners have become available, including text-reader pens.

- **Portable automatic data entry devices**: These are used by utility companies, such as electricity, gas, or water companies, to read customer meters. The data can be downloaded to the central billing computer.

- **Sensors**: These are used to log data such as traffic flow, river levels, etc. Sensors are connected to computers and the data is directly downloaded. Sensors are also used in most real-time systems (see page 110), for example in temperature-controlled greenhouses.

- **Digital cameras**: These can input pictures via a cable linking the camera and computer. Digital cameras can also save pictures onto disk, either floppy disk, for smaller pictures, or, more commonly, CD. These can then be downloaded onto the computer via the disk drive.

- **Key-to-disk**: This system is used where large amounts of data need to be entered in one batch. A keyboard operator enters the data, which is read and stored directly by a disk or tape. The data is then sent through a validation process to check for errors. This type of input is used by utility companies for customer bills, and payments are processed in large batches.

1.1 Checking input data for errors

Once the data has been captured, it will usually need to be checked. Several different errors can occur during data entry.

As an example, let us take an application form for a college, which could look like this:

Figure 5

College application form

- When filling in the application form, the student might enter the wrong details. For example, he or she might enter an incorrect course code. Once the form is processed, the course title will not match the course code.

- The person keying in the data could key it wrongly. For example, the form may give the student's name as 'Achmed', but the name keyed onto the computer could be 'Ahmed'. This is known as a **transcription error.**

- The person keying in the data could key a number the wrong way round. For example, the course code 099345 on the form could be keyed in as 099354. This is known as a **transposition error.**

Once data has been entered, **processing errors** can occur:

- If data that is being entered requires a calculation to be performed, the outcome will only be correct if the calculation formula has been correctly entered.

- If the wrong validation criteria have been set, this can lead to real problems. The 'Y2K' problem is a good example of this. In the 1970s when memory in computers was still very limited, memory bytes were precious. To save space, some computers were programmed with a two-digit coding for the year, rather than four digits. This meant that instead of a year being represented as, for example, 1974, it was represented as 74. As the year 2000 approached, computers that were operating this two-digit system could not cope with transactions that required accurately computing calculations based on these dates, unless their programming was updated.

- The wrong transaction file or master file might be used, resulting in an out-of-date set of data being used.

- More than one person might use a transaction file at a time during transaction processing. This could result in a person reading out-of-date information without realising it. The most common example of this is when booking flights. Travel agents all use the same central computer to look up the availability of flights. If a travel agent in Cornwall and a travel agent in London were able to book the same seats on a flight at the same time, there would be some very unhappy customers. To prevent this, once one travel agent has opened a record to check availability, it can be **locked** to prevent anyone else using it at the same time. The record is unavailable to other travel agents until the transaction is completed.

If the data needs to be transmitted to another computer, **transmission errors** can occur. There might be a fault in the connection between the two computers, or a problem with the communication line over which data is being sent. When data is being sent along a communication line, it can be corrupted or fail to arrive at its destination. It is important to have a checking procedure which notifies users of any such errors.

A **parity check** can be used to check whether the data has been transmitted correctly. A **parity bit** is an extra bit that can be added on to the data code to give either an even or odd total. Even parity is where the number of 1s in the data code total an even number, for example 110011. Odd parity is where the number of 1s in a data code total an odd number, for example 111011.

The modem sending the data keeps a record of the parity bit and the receiving computer will send a response to state whether there was odd or even parity. If not all the data has been correctly transmitted, the sender can be notified and resend it.

While parity checks can be useful, they will not, of course, detect all errors. If there is more than one fault, once all the data has been received the parity check might still total the correct odd or even number.

Other errors, such as entering details twice or missing out blocks of information when entering the data, can also result in problems. Most errors that occur when entering data are due to human error, and not all can be avoided or detected. To ensure the quality of data being held in the system, checks should be carried out wherever possible. There are two main methods of trying to prevent or reduce data entry errors:

- **verification**, which checks the data against the source document it has been taken from

- **validation**, a check included in the programming of the software that the data makes sense in the context for which it is being used.

These will be discussed in the next section.

Test your knowledge

1　What is the meaning of the term 'data capture'?

2　List four different data capture devices and give an example of use for each one.

3　What is the difference between a transcription error and a transposition error?

4　Describe two processing errors that might occur.

Exam questions

1　A village store has just installed a computerised point-of-sale system including a bar-code reader.

(a) Describe **two** advantages that the store gains by using a bar-code reader attached to a computerised point-of-sale system. *(4 marks)*

(b) Describe **one** disadvantage to the store of using a bar-code system. *(2 marks)*

AQA Jan 2001

2　The local council wishes to store the contents of documents on a computer system. The documents consist of hand-written and typed text. The documents will be scanned and OCR (optical character recognition) software will be used to interpret the text and export it to files that can be read by word-processing software.

(a) (i)　Describe **two** problems that could occur when scanning and interpreting the text. *(4 marks)*

(ii)　Describe **two** advantages to be gained by using OCR software. *(4 marks)*

(b)　State **three** types of material, other than text, that could also be input using the scanner. *(3 marks)*

AQA May 2001

2 Verification and validation

This section will provide coverage of the following key area:

▓ Describe appropriate validation techniques for various types of data process, from data capture to report generation.

2.0 Verification

Verification involves checking the data as it is being entered, before it is processed. This method is used to check the **accuracy** of data entry. There are two main methods of performing verification checks:

▓ **Visual checking:** the person inputting the data does this. He or she checks what is on the screen against the source document.

▓ **Double entry:** data is entered twice; either by the same person or, when batch processing is taking place, by two people entering the same data. The two entries are then checked to see whether there are any differences between the two sets of data. An example of this way of verifying data is when you change your password on your computer; you are asked to enter the data twice so that the computer can check both versions are the same.

2.1 Validation

Validation involves software checking the data as it is being entered. Depending on the computer system being used, there will be a set of rules to which the data has to conform. It must be noted that validation checks for **validity**, rather than **accuracy** – the data entered could follow the rules, but still be incorrect. Where a transcription error occurs, validation processes will not necessarily pick it up.

The validation rules that are commonly used include the following:

▓ A **presence check** makes sure that data has been entered where required. For example, the college application form could not be processed without a name and address being present.

▓ A **range check** makes sure that the data entered is within a specified range. For example, on the college application form, if a date of birth had been entered as 01/21/1986, the system will not accept it – it is not possible to have a month represented as the number '21', as it has to be within the range of 1 to 12.

▓ A **format check** is used, for example, when entering data into a database. The **field** into which the data is being entered can be preset to contain only certain types of data. For example, on the college application form two letters followed by three digits might be the format for all course codes. If the course code were wrongly entered as three digits followed by two letters, it would not be accepted.

▓ A **length check** makes sure that the correct number of letters or digits has been entered. For example, on the college application form there is a field for entering your age at a certain date. This field could be preset to accept only two digits, as it is unlikely that anyone under the age of 10 or over the age of 99 would be applying for a college course.

■ A **combined or cross-field check** makes sure that any data that is connected to another database or field within the same database is the same as that previously entered. For example, on the college application form the course code that relates to a certain course must be the same for each entry, whichever student is being entered into the system.

■ A **look-up table** or **list** makes sure that the data entered is within the list of acceptable entries. For example, on the college application form you are asked to state your sex. The acceptable entries for this would be male or female, or M or F. If the data entered varied from this, it would not be accepted.

■ A **check digit** is used to make sure that the code being entered is valid. Used for codes such as bar codes on products, a check digit is an extra digit added to the end. Long codes such as these are more likely to attract transcription and transposition errors. The original digits in the code can be used to calculate a check digit. The computer automatically recalculates the check digit, and if the result differs from the digit entered, it will be noted as an error.

The most common method of using check digits is the modulus-11 system. If a college course had the code 7307, the check digit could be worked out in the following way:

Each of the digits has a weighting attached to it which enables a calculation to be performed. The last number in the code has a weighting of 2, so it is easier to start the calculation from the right-hand side and work backwards to find the weighting for each digit.

Once multiplied by their weighting, these numbers are added together. For the code 7307, this gives us the following calculation: $(7 \times 5) + (3 \times 4) + (0 \times 3) + (7 \times 2)$

Put more simply, we have: $35 + 12 + 0 + 14 = 61$

This total is then divided by 11 (hence the title 'modulus-11'):
$61 \div 11 = 5.5454545454545454545454545454545455$

This looks extremely confusing, but it works out at 5×11 with a remainder of 6.
$61 = (5 \times 11)$ remainder 6

It is the remainder of 6 that is important. This is subtracted from 11 to give the check digit:
$11 - 6 = 5$

This means that 5 is our check digit, so the full code will now become: 73075

Sometimes the remainder will work out as either 0 or 1. In these cases you do not subtract them from 11. A remainder of 0 becomes a check digit of 0, and a remainder of 1 becomes a check digit of 1.

Working through this calculation is a long process, but remember that computers can perform such calculations in seconds. Using the modulus-11 method, if a transcription error occurs and two digits are entered the wrong way around, the computer will pick up on this, as the check digit will be wrong.

■ **Hash totals**, used mainly in batch processing, make sure that the correct number of entries has been made. A numeric field can be used to add the digits up and produce a meaningless total for the whole file. When the file is next updated the hash total can be recalled by the computer and compared against the new hash total, to ensure that all records have been processed.

■ **Control totals** are similar to hash totals in that they make sure the correct number of entries has been made, but the control total has some meaning to it. An example would be where a number of invoices are being keyed into the system. The total amount on each invoice could have been calculated for the batch, and once the processing has been completed this total can be recalculated by the computer to ensure that it is the same as the original.

Activity 2

Try working out some more check digits for yourself. Work through some calculations using the one above as a guideline.

Use some of the following numbers:

- Your student ID.
- The ISBN number of a book you are currently reading. Remove the last digit before you start, as this will be the check digit. You can then check whether you are right.
- The barcode from a sweet wrapper, again removing the last digit before you begin.

2.2 Report generators

Another check that should be carried out is when you are using a report generator. Most database software packages have an in-built program to allow the user to design an output format for the information contained in the files. This makes the output of the information much easier to read and understand. The data is taken directly from the records within the file and it is necessary to ensure that the information contained in the report is correct.

Utility companies use report generators to print out customer invoices. To avoid errors occurring, they can check the total of the bill against previous records to see if there are big differences. For example, if a bill totalled £1,000 for three months' electricity supply, the previous records for that customer could be checked, and if previous bills average £80, it becomes obvious that there is either a human error on entry of data, or a computer error on calculation.

Activity 3

Look again at the college application form on page 90.

- Work out any validation checks that could be set up to prevent or reduce errors when entering this data into a system such as a database.
- Are there any fields that could be used for verification checks?
- If the college was batch processing the application forms, are there any special processing validation checks that could be set up?
- Can you see any other problems that might be encountered when entering this data?

Test your knowledge

1 What is the difference between verification and validation?
2 Describe two ways of carrying out verification checks.
3 Describe three ways of carrying out validation checks.
4 Why does data obtained from report generators need to be checked?

Exam questions

1 A video and games rental shop uses a database package to record membership details of customers who wish to borrow videos or games. The following details must be entered for each new member: full name, address, postcode and date of birth.

(a) Name and describe a validation check that could be used when data is first entered into the following fields for a new member. Your validation check must be different in each case.

    (i)   Full_Name   *(2 marks)*
    (ii)   Postcode   *(2 marks)*
    (iii) Date_of_Birth   *(2 marks)*

(b) The database package automatically generates a membership number. Explain why this is required.   *(2 marks)*

AQA Jan 2001

2 A company stores its staff records in a computer file. Examples of records from the file are shown below.

Surname	Forename	Department number	Department name	Extension number
Chan	Dan	132	Accounts	572
	Wendy	123	Training	467
Jones	Sarah	121	Training	468
Chan	Dan	132	Accounts	572
Patel	Paul	132	Accounts	573

(a) The records in this file have been input with the validation checking turned off. Referring to the records above, state **four** problems that have occurred.   *(4 marks)*

(b) Name and describe **three** different validation checks that would have prevented these problems.   *(6 marks)*

AQA Jan 2002

The following question also requires knowledge gained from Section 1:

3 SupaGoods is a home sales company. Catalogues are left at people's homes. A local agent calls two days later to take orders and collect the catalogues. The agent sends the details of the goods ordered to the Head Office where they are processed. The completed order is returned to the agent who distributes the goods and collects payment.

(a) Describe **two** distinct methods of data capture for the agent. State **one** advantage and **one** disadvantage of each method.   *(6 marks)*

(b) The orders are validated at Head Office.

    (i)   Explain what is meant by validation.   *(2 marks)*
    (ii)   Describe briefly **two** validation checks that might be carried out on an agent's order.

        (4 marks)

AQA Specimen question

3 Storing and using data

This section will provide coverage of the following key areas:

- Describe the nature and purpose of a database and how they work

- Understand that data needs to be organised in a database to allow for effective updating and retrieval

- Understand how data can be retrieved to produce meaningful information.

- Recall the relevant advantages of databases over flat-file information storage and retrieval systems

- Select and justify appropriate file and database structures for particular applications.

The way in which data is stored is an essential factor in how easily it can be retrieved and used. Ways of storing data without the use of a computer include the following:

- A notebook that lists what is currently on your videos. This might be divided into numerical or alphabetical sections that relate to labels placed on your videos. If you keep this up to date, you will always know what is on each video. This would represent a 'set' of data.

- An address book containing names, addresses and telephone numbers of your friends and relatives. This is usually arranged in alphabetical order, with the details of each person appearing under the first letter of the surname. Again, this is a 'set' of data.

- Contact details of customers or suppliers kept on an index-card system. A record is created for each customer/supplier, containing all essential information. It is kept in alphabetical order, so this can sometimes create problems. For example, if the cards are kept in the order of the name of the company, you might be able to remember the name of the person you normally talk to within that company, but not the company name. In this instance, the whole index-card system would need to be searched manually to find the contact name and therefore the company name. If the information were kept on a computerised database, this problem would be solved easily.

3.0 What is a file?

A file is a collection (or 'set') of related data. A file is often sorted into some kind of order, to make it easier to use. The examples given above are types of non-computerised files.

Computerised data storage systems enable the quick and efficient retrieval of data, without manual searching. There are two main types of computerised data storage systems: flat files and relational databases.

3.1 Flat-file data storage

Flat files are a computerised version of the index-card system mentioned above. All the data is still held on one **record**, which is a computerised version of the individual cards within the index system. Within some computerised systems, the record is even represented by a drawing of an index card on screen. On each record the individual pieces of information are split into **fields.**

Figure 6

Computerised record

Flat files are useful for sorting through data quickly and retrieving relevant pieces of information by using the fields within the records as the search basis. There are, however, some drawbacks to using computerised flat files. As each record contains all the information required, in our example for each person/company, there is likely to be some repetition.

For instance, if the business deals with more than one person in a particular company, what would be the best way of storing the information? Should it be stored as a single record with a list of contact names within the record, or should it be stored so that each contact has a record with the company details on it? If the latter, then the company details will be repeated several times within the file. This is known as **data duplication**.

Also, the records are usually not linked in any way, so if the company changes its telephone number, then each record will have to be changed one by one. What if one record was missed out in the change? The next time someone tried to contact this person, the telephone number on the record would be wrong. This is known as **data inconsistency**.

So a flat-file structure can make finding information easier, but it is not easy to stop data duplication. A lot of time can be wasted searching for the right information, or entering data more than once. Flat-file structures are best used if only a small amount of data needs to be stored.

 Activity 4

Think about the errors that could occur when entering the data into each record in a flat-file system. Check back to pages 90–91 for those we highlighted.

Make a list of any errors you think could occur. Against each error type, list the ways in which you think they could be avoided or checked for, and state whether this could be done using a verification or validation technique.

3.2 Relational databases

The main difference between a flat-file system and a relational database is that relational databases can easily link the data between different records. It is known as a relational database because these links are known as 'relationships' between the records. If there is more than one collection of records, relationships can also be built between records contained in different sets. This way, several pieces of data or information can be combined to give relevant information that is required at any time.

The terminology of relational databases is slightly different:

- A collection of *records* is called a **file**.

- Records are stored in **tables**. Tables are made up of columns and rows. A row holds all the fields for one occurrence of the record, e.g. one person or one stock item. A column holds all of one field for every row/record, e.g. all telephone numbers (see the example in Figure 7).

- An individual item of data in a record is called a **field** (the same as in a flat-file system).

Figure 7

Computerised database

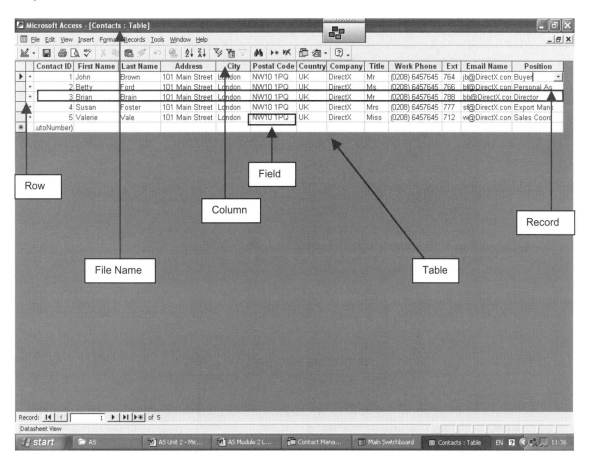

There are industry standard ways of building relational databases, so that data is always organised in a logical format. This facilitates efficient updating and retrieval of data in databases and makes the process of working with data relatively easy. Some of the standards that need to be adhered to are described below.

Format

The **format** of each record within the database must be specified, taking into account the following.

- the order in which the fields are stored in the record

- the name of each field

- the field type.

Field types include:

- **Text** fields, used for all general data where no calculations will need to be performed, for example names, addresses and telephone numbers. Even though telephone numbers are numeric in format, there is no need to perform any calculations on them, so they can be stored as text files.

- **Numeric** fields, used for any numbers where calculations may be necessary. For example, amounts of goods purchased should be stored as numeric so that in the future they can be included in calculations of total product purchases.

- **Date** fields, which are obviously used to enter dates.

- **Yes/no** fields, which usually give a drop-down option between two choices. For example, they can give a choice of male or female. This helps to lower input errors.

- **Memo** fields, used where a greater amount of text is required. Most computerised database programs have a maximum character set for the text field that is too low for much general information. Memo fields can be used where more than just a line or two of information is required.

The field length for some types of field, such as a text field, must be large enough to hold the maximum expected length of data.

If data is to be linked, the **relationships** between the tables must be defined. Computerised database programs can usually do this for you, using a wizard to take you through the steps involved. **Keys** are used to define the relationships between tables. It is keys that enable a link to be made between fields of information/data.

- A **primary key** is a unique identifier for each table. This is set up in its own field. A primary key is necessary so that data can easily and efficiently be retrieved or updated. The basic requirement for a primary key is that it is unique. Because all records will need some data to identify them, the use of a primary key is important. In the example database above, the company name cannot be used a unique identifier, as all the entries within that table are for the same company. Even a surname cannot be used as a primary key, because there is a possibility that two people might have the same surname. Most databases use numeric combinations for unique identifiers. The database program can usually enter these automatically, and they make it much easier to avoid duplication.

The 'Contact ID' field in the sample database in Figure 7 would be our primary key.

- A **secondary key** can be used to identify more than one record. This is another way to identify a field to be used as the main search field, when it is not a primary key. For example, in the Figure 7 database the 'Last name' field could be set as a secondary key. If someone required a listing of all people on the database who worked for DirectX, in alphabetical order by surname, this could be compiled quickly. The basic difference between a primary key and a secondary key is that a primary key is a unique identifier for each record, while a secondary key can be an identifier for more than one record.

- **Foreign keys** are used to link a field containing primary key data from one table to a primary key field in another table. For example, in our sample database, we might have another table containing a record of telephone calls made to people within DirectX. The column headings for this might include the 'Contact ID' number. This can be linked to the main contact table so that a set of information can be retrieved relevant to user needs.

Let us assume that Dave Dupont is the Sales Director for our company. He needs a report on the latest situation regarding a large order that DirectX might place with us. He wants to be able to talk to Brian Brain to try to push the order through. If he looks only at the contact information, he will not know about the latest contacts and discussions between the two companies. By combining information from both tables (see Figure 8) he can see the up-to-date situation, and have the contact details available. Running a **query** that involves using the 'Contact ID' fields to link the two tables together can give Dave Dupont a report that contains all the information he requires at once.

Figure 8

Relationships between tables with the screen for editing/building relationships. Also shows primary and secondary keys.

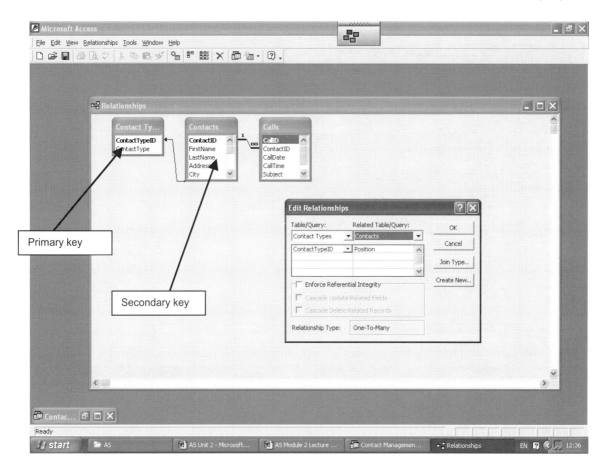

There are several ways in which data can be sorted and searched, and you will learn more about these techniques in the A2 units, if you progress to A2 level. We will now look at some of the ways in which data can be retrieved and used.

Forms, **queries** and **reports** are three other basic components of computerised databases.

Forms

Forms are used so that entering and viewing data is a simple process. If you wanted to look at all the details for a record at once, it might be difficult without scrolling through the table. People also usually find it quite difficult to enter data directly into the table. When you first build your database, you can create a form that has all the same headings as the table, but is presented in user-friendly format. A form is a little like an individual index card. Each record is represented by one form, and a collection of forms then makes up the file. You can still view the information in table format, if required. The example in Figure 9 below shows how much easier it is to view all the information than it was in table format.

Figure 9

Contacts table shown in form view

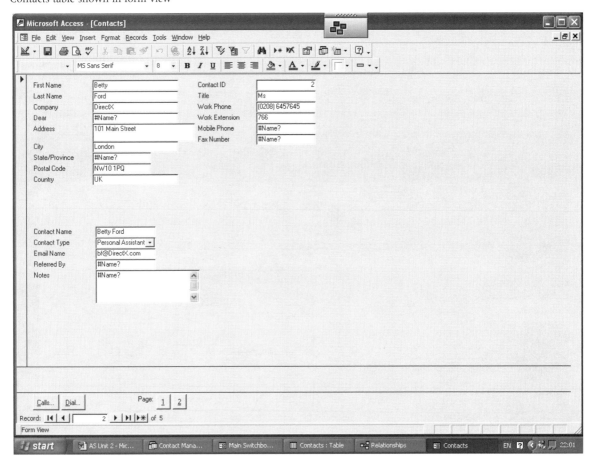

Queries

Queries are used to view, change or analyse subsets of data. If you have multiple tables in your database, information can be taken from one or any number of them and combined to create new forms or reports. Queries can also be used to summarise data, delete or update all records, append data from one table to another, or create a new table.

The form in Figure 9 has been created by using a query. All the information from the 'Contacts' table (Figure 7) is placed into the query. This is then saved, using a meaningful name so that it will be easy to identify. When you create a form, you can select this query as its basis and the form can then be used to enter data. The query format used is shown in Figure 10.

Figure 10

A simple query used to create the Contacts form

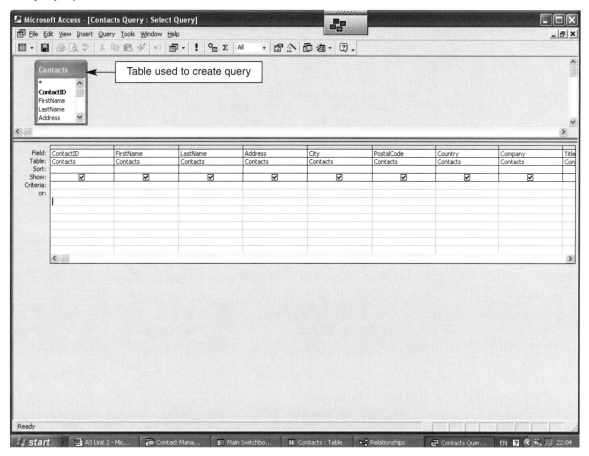

A more complex query might involve taking information from more than one table. Let us create the query that will form the basis of the report that Dave Dupont required in our earlier scenario. We need the contact details for Brian Brain, together with up-to-date information on calls and discussions that have recently taken place. By selecting only the fields from each table that contain this specific information, we can produce a query without any unnecessary data. This will mean that when we produce the report it will have all the information Dave Dupont requires and none that he does not.

The query in Figure 11 shows that relevant fields from both tables have been selected. Figure 12 shows the information within the query.

Figure 11

Query selection for Dave Dupont to use to contact Brian Brain

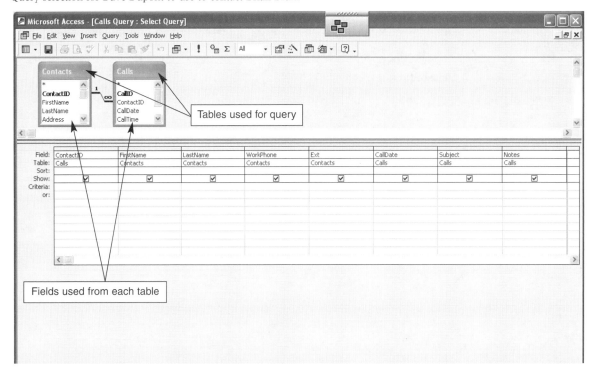

Figure 12

Information from each field that has been used in the query

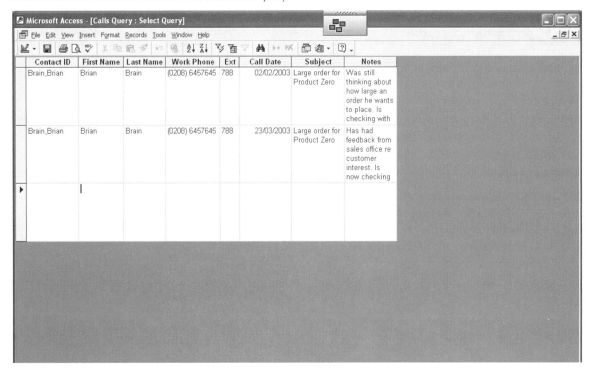

Reports

Reports are used to present information from the database in a user-friendly format.
Computerised database programs usually have an automatic feature, through the use of wizards, to

generate reports. Reports are created from queries where either information is combined from different tables and fields, or the information is taken from a single table, using all the fields or selecting just those that are required.

If we produce the report based on the above query for Dave Dupont, it will look like the one in Figure 13:

Figure 13

Report for Dave Dupont to contact Brian Brain

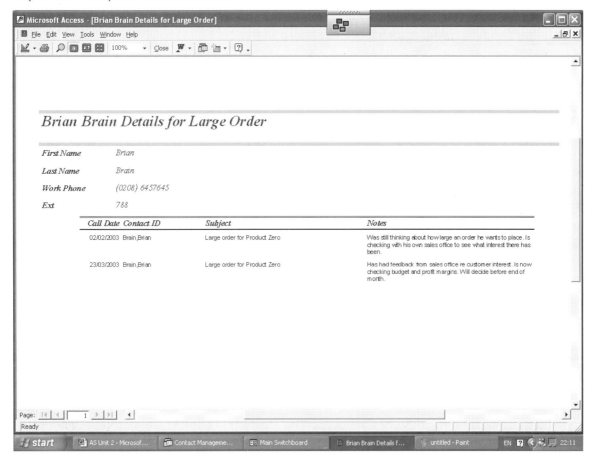

3.3 Why use relational databases?

Now that we have looked at the use of relational databases for effective retrieval and updating of information, let us look again at the reasons for using relational databases as opposed to flat-file information storage and retrieval systems.

Advantages

The main advantages of using relational databases are:

- You need to enter data only once. Because relational databases are organised logically, data repetition can be avoided. With flat-file systems it is difficult to avoid data repetition, as it is difficult to link data.

- There is better accuracy of data. Because information is entered only once, fewer mistakes are made.

- Accuracy is also improved through the validation checks performed on data as it is entered. When you set up your database, because different formats can be set for the fields, you can ensure that someone does not enter a name in the field for amount of money owing. Once the basic formats have been set, it is also possible to set up other validation techniques. For example, you can set the format of a postcode field to ensure that a code is the right length and format, or you could have drop-down lists for products and their codes. All of these techniques will ensure accuracy of data.

- Files, tables, records and fields can all be linked. This means that it is easy and quick to collate information using queries.

- Access to information is quick. Using the different sort, filtering and search techniques, you can quickly find what you need, in the order that you need it. Detailed, and sometimes complex, search criteria can be used. With flat-file systems, information is difficult to separate and it is often necessary to view a lot of irrelevant information.

Disadvantages

Despite all the advantages of using relational databases, there are also some disadvantages that need to be taken into account when deciding how to store and use data. Computerised databases are often widely accessible within a company through a local area network. This saves repetition of the database, and means that those employees who need regular access to the information do not have to ensure they have an up-to-date copy on their hard drive. All the information is held centrally, but this presents its own set of problems to a company.

- If the file server that holds the database crashes, or becomes unavailable for other reasons, no one will be able to access the required information. This could result in the company not being able to do business until the database is accessible again.

- Security will need to be considered. Confidential information might be held on the database, such as the pay rates for some employees. The setting up of authorisation levels, different views of information, and passworded files need to be considered.

- If a company is looking at setting up a large database that needs to be accessed by many employees, it could prove expensive to train employees to use the system properly. Because a relational database is more complex than a flat-file method of holding data, it usually requires specialist technical staff to manage the database.

Activity 5

Study the following scenarios, and select appropriate file and database structures for them. Justify your selection.

- A company that manufactures Christmas crackers has been holding both customer and employee details on a card index system. Most employees work from home, putting the crackers together out of components sent by the company and then sending back the finished product. There are 70 employees, 50 of whom work from home and 20 in the factory/office. Currently the product is supplied to only three different purchasers.

Activity 5 continued ...

■ A new company is being set up to offer advice over the telephone about health insurance. It has one main office, where currently 30 people are employed. It is forecast that by the end of the current financial year the company will need to employ over 100 people. It already has a small number of enquiries from potential customers but expects to have a customer base of about 2,000 people by the end of the financial year. It needs a good, easy-to-use system to hold all details on both customers and employees.

Test your knowledge

1 What are the differences between a flat-file information system and a relational database?
2 Name three types of fields for relational database structures and state when they should be used.
3 Name two other standards that should be considered when building relational databases.
4 What is a primary key?
5 What is a foreign key?

Exam questions

1 A company is experiencing difficulties with its computerised flat-file information storage and retrieval system. Describe **three** benefits that the company would gain by converting to a relational database system. *(6 marks)*
AQA Jan 2001

2 Give **four** advantages of using a relational database rather than a flat-file system. *(4 marks)*
AQA May 2001

3 A company makes use of a computerised flat-file information storage and retrieval system. The company is experiencing problems due to the use of this flat-file system.

(a) Describe **three** benefits that the company would gain by using a relational database as opposed to a flat-file system. *(6 marks)*

(b) The company currently has three files in use; customer, stock and orders. During conversion to a relational database system these files would need to be changed.

Suggest appropriate field names for the three files used. *(8 marks)*
AQA Specimen question

4 A database has been used to replace a flat-file information storage and retrieval system.

List **four** advantages of using a database. *(4 marks)*
AQA Jan 2002

4 Processing of data

This section will provide coverage of the following key area:

- Describe the different modes of operation: batch, interactive, transaction, real-time, and identify appropriate contexts for their use.

Once the methods of storing and retrieving data are selected, the next step is to consider how data is processed. Processing of data is the middle part of the 'input – process – output' cycle that you looked at in Unit 1. The role of processing is to convert data into a readable format that makes sense – to turn data into information.

There are many different ways of processing data, depending on how it is stored and how it needs to be used. The term for how data is processed is the 'mode of operation', and different factors need to be considered before the system is set up. The two main modes of operation are **batch processing** and **interactive processing**. We will look at each mode of operation and consider the advantages and disadvantages for each, using examples to highlight the factors for consideration.

What does this mean?

The main terms used when talking about processing are:

Transaction: The input of data to a system, including changes/amendments and the addition/deletion of data

Master file: The term used for the main file that holds all the data in the system. The master file is the file that gets updated when transactions are entered

Transaction file: A file that holds the individual records of transactions. For systems which process more than one record at a time, such as batch-processing systems, it is the transaction file that will be entered to update the master file

4.0 Batch processing

Batch processing is the term used when groups of similar transactions that have been gathered over a given time period are collected and processed during one processing run.

The main disadvantage of using batch processing is that the only time the system is truly up to date is immediately after the batch process has been run. The longer the time lapse between each batch process, the longer the system will be holding out-of-date data. Batch processing is therefore only suitable for applications where the currency of data is not vitally important.

Another disadvantage is the fact that if an up-to-date overview of the system is required, it is not immediately available. Personnel who require such information would usually have to order it in advance and wait until the batch process has been run.

The main advantage of batch processing is that it can be run automatically, on a given day and at a given time each week. This enables the process to be run when the system is likely to be less busy, for example overnight, and it will therefore cause less disruption to those using the system. Another advantage is the fact that security can be improved. As the transactions are entered in batches, fewer people have a direct role in updating the system, so fewer errors are likely. It is also possible to set up **audit trails** through the use of **transaction log files**. Transaction log files record each transaction as it is entered and, when used in an audit trail, can record the date, time, changes made and user of the system. If any problems occur with the new data in the system, a trace can be made back to the old data to see where the errors have arisen.

Applications that are suitable for batch processing include:

- payroll systems, where it is not necessary to run the process constantly but only at certain times of the month or week

- utility company bills, where meters are read or estimated once a month and the data is processed in batches, producing bills to be sent out to the customers

- producing company sales figures, where there is a 'run' of the system at a certain time to give an up-to-date overview of the situation.

4.1 Interactive processing

In interactive processing the system responds immediately to the input data from the user while the program is running. This is also known as 'on-line processing'. Data is entered into the system while it is running. The system usually runs constantly, so there is no need to run processes at given times.

Travel agencies use interactive processing systems. If you were to visit the travel agency and ask about the availability of a certain holiday, the agent would log into that part of the system. While the agent is looking for availability, other users anywhere in the world can view the same details and make reservations or bookings. However, if you were to decide to book the holiday, the system dealing with that particular hotel, flight, etc. would become locked. While you were giving your personal details and paying for the holiday, no one else could access the system and take your holiday. Where systems can be locked in this way, and individual transactions have to be completed before another transaction can begin, this is known as **transaction processing**.

Another example you are probably familiar with is player-led computer games or interactive games on digital television. The system will await input from the user or player before processing the command and going to the next stage of the game.

The main advantage of using an interactive processing system is the fact that the data is always up to date. This means that situations should not occur where, for example, seats on aeroplanes are double-booked. Also, because the data is constantly being input and updated, it is easy to produce current reports.

One disadvantage of using interactive processing systems is that because data is usually input directly into the system via face-to-face or telephone communication, very little paper-based documentation is involved. This makes it difficult to set up verification of the system, so people entering the data must be competent with the system; training on individual systems is imperative.

Other applications for interactive processing include:

- most home PC user applications, for example a word-processing program

- ATMs (automatic teller machines) where you input data after placing your card into a reader and give commands, such as withdrawing money or checking your bank balance

- interactive Internet services, for example applying on-line for a loan, or purchasing goods. When purchasing goods, the stock level can be checked to ensure that your order is in stock and the system can advise you of an expected delivery time.

4.2 Real-time and pseudo-real-time systems

If you think back to the 'input – process – output' cycle, you will remember that the final part of the cycle is **feedback**. Real-time and pseudo-real-time systems rely on feedback following any transactions. The difference between real-time and pseudo-real-time systems is that real-time processing has an immediate effect on the master file. With pseudo-real-time there is a short delay before the master file is updated. The two terms are often used interchangeably, as very few systems are truly real-time.

Real-time systems

Air-traffic control in the United Kingdom is now performed by the use of a real-time system. The position of aircraft is tracked on radar, and this data is fed through to screens in the air-traffic control room. As aircraft move constantly, it is imperative that their position is constantly updated and that the data being used is current. If the transactions, in this case tracking the movement of aeroplanes, were not real-time, the results could be disastrous.

Other real-time systems include:

- robotic systems where a program reacts immediately to the flow of input information

- systems that monitor a situation through reading current data, for example a heart monitor in a hospital, where an alarm is sounded immediately no output is detected.

Pseudo-real-time systems

Point-of-sale systems are pseudo-real-time systems. When you purchase goods, say at a large supermarket, the bar codes on the items are scanned into the system. The stock level will then be lowered by the amount of each item bought. Although this appears to happen immediately, there is a few seconds delay between the transaction of the scanning process and the transaction of the stock level being reduced.

Pseudo-real-time systems are those where a transaction process is used, for example concert ticket bookings.

Activity 6

A mail order company is in the process of computerising its customer sales accounts. It needs to make a decision on which type of processing it should implement. The requirements listed are:

- new orders placed need to be recorded
- invoices then need to be produced and sent out
- any payments received against invoices need to be recorded.

Write a short report for the company, detailing the following:

- the main advantages and disadvantages of processing systems that could be used
- which processing system you would recommend
- a justification explaining why this processing system is the most suitable.

Test your knowledge

1. Describe one advantage and one disadvantage of using batch processing.
2. Describe one advantage and one disadvantage of using interactive processing.
3. What is the difference between real-time processing and pseudo-real-time processing?

Exam questions

1. A college uses a computer-based batch-processing system for keeping the students' records. The students provide their details, or changes to their existing records, on pre-printed forms. The completed forms are collected into batches ready to update their master files. These occur every night at certain times of the year, and once a week at other times.

   (a) Explain what the term *batch processing* means. *(3 marks)*

   (b) (i) Give **one** advantage of batch processing to the college. *(1 mark)*

   (ii) Give **two** disadvantages of batch processing to the college. *(2 marks)*

   The college decides to install a transaction-processing system with which student records are keyed in on-line by a clerk.

   (c) Explain what the term *transaction processing* means. *(3 marks)*

   AQA Jan 2001

2. A mail order company is using an interactive processing system for its computerised telephone ordering system.

   Explain what is meant by the terms *interactive processing* and *transaction processing*. *(4 marks)*

   AQA Jan 2002

5 Processing different formats of data

This section will provide coverage of the following key area:

■ Describe the characteristics of processing data in the form of text, pictures, numbers and sound.

When considering the processing of data, you also need to look at how different formats of data are processed. First, we need to understand how data is stored on the computer.

5.0 Internal storage of data

All computer data is stored in what is called **binary code**. Binary code is a system that uses combinations of just two symbols to represent all information, no matter how large or small. A binary coding system can use any two symbols. For example, Morse code is a binary system, where information is represented as dots or dashes. The individual symbol is known as a binary digit.

In a computer system, the binary digits used are 0 and 1. Each binary digit is termed a **bit**, and these bits are usually grouped together eight at a time. A group of eight bits is known as a **byte**.

The way in which the computer binary code works is that each combination of 0s and 1s represents a different character, number or section of a graphic. Each byte can hold 2^8 representations of 0s and 1s, meaning that 256 characters can be determined. Standard tables can be used to convert data to and from binary, and we will look at these for each format of data. It is important to remember that data in binary code could represent any format of data (text, graphic, number, or sound) so the context in which the data is presented must be kept in mind for the correct interpretation to be made.

5.1 Storing and processing text

Most personal computers use what is called ASCII coding (American Standard Code for Information Interchange). This coding is the most widely used today and represents English characters, each with a binary code between 00000000 and 11111111.

As the ASCII system has enough spaces to code only English characters, with a few more commonly used international characters, rapid advances in worldwide communication meant that problems arose when exchanging information between different languages. A new type of coding, Unicode, has been designed. This uses 16 bits per character, instead of eight, and allows easier, more compatible exchange of information worldwide as it has expanded the character availability to 65,536.

The binary representations for numbers, letters and some commonly used characters are shown below in ASCII coding format.

Character	ASCII code	Character	ASCII code	Character	ASCII code
0	00110000	u	01110101	Y	01011001
1	00110001	v	01110110	Z	01011010
2	00110010	w	01110111	ESC (escape)	00011011
3	00110011	x	01111000	SP (space)	00100000
4	00110100	y	01111001	! (exclamation mark)	00100001
5	00110101	z	01111010	" (double quote)	00100010
6	00110110	A	01000001	# (number sign/hash)	00100011
7	00110111	B	01000010	$ (dollar sign)	00100100
8	00111000	C	01000011	% (percent)	00100101
9	00111001	D	01000100	^ (caret/circumflex)	01011110
a	01100001	E	01000101	& (ampersand)	00100110
b	01100010	F	01000110	* (asterisk)	00101010
c	01100011	G	01000111	((left parenthesis)	00101000
d	01100100	H	01001000	) (right parenthesis)	00101001
e	01100101	I	01001001	– (minus or dash)	00101101
f	01100110	J	01001010	_ (underscore)	01011111
g	01100111	K	01001011	= (equal sign)	00111101
h	01101000	L	01001100	+ (plus)	00101011
I	01101001	M	01001101	~ (tilde)	01111110
j	01101010	N	01001110	'(single quote)	00100111
k	01101011	O	01001111	@ (AT symbol)	01000000
l	01101100	P	01010000	; (semi-colon)	00111011
m	01101101	Q	01010001	: (colon)	00111010
n	01101110	R	01010010	/ (forward slash)	00101111
o	01101111	S	01010011	? (question mark)	00111111
p	01110000	T	01010100	. (full stop/dot)	00101110
q	01110001	U	01010101	> (greater than)	00111110
r	01110010	V	01010110	, (comma)	00101100
s	01110011	W	01010111	< (less than)	00111100
t	01110100	X	01011000		

Activity 7

Convert the following words into ASCII coding:

- holiday
- friends
- mobile phone
- networked computer.

Convert the following ASCII codes into words:

- 01010000 01000001 01010010 01010100 01011001
- 01000011 01000001 01001101 01010000 01001001 01001110 01000111
- 01010100 01001000 01000101 01001101 01000101 00100000 01010000 01000001 01010010 01001011
- 01001100 01001111 01000011 01000001 01001100 00100000 01000001 01010010 01000101 01000001 00100000 01001110 01000101 01010100 01010111 01001111 01010010 01001011

5.2 Storing and processing graphics

There are two main ways in which graphics are stored: as a bit-mapped graphic or as a vector-based graphic.

Bit-mapped graphics

A bit-mapped graphic is made up of **pixels.** Each bit in the stored graphic tells the computer whether a pixel is to be switched on or off. This means that the number of bits allowed in each pixel dictates how many colours can be included within that pixel. For example, if a pixel contains only four bits in a black and white graphic, 16 different shades of grey can be stored, whereas eight bits per pixel means that 256 different shades of grey can be stored. Many graphics are stored in colour, and these need to have enough pixels to allow the basic red, green and blue colours as well. When working with and storing colour graphics, an eight-bit pixel will allow more than 16,000,000 different colours to be stored, working on the basis that each colour can use eight bits, giving $256 \times 256 \times 256$.

There are problems associated with using bit-mapped graphics. These include the following:

Figure 14

A bit-mapped image

- Bit-mapped graphics need every detail of every pixel to be stored, so the file size is often large. The number of pixels used gives what is known as the **resolution** of the graphic, and the higher the resolution the better the image, but that also means the image size is larger.

- If the image size is changed, or the graphic is used on a screen with a different resolution, this can lead to the graphic becoming distorted or the overall quality of the graphic being reduced. If you look at the two figures opposite (Figures 14 and 15) you will see how the flowers have become distorted through changing the image size.

Figure 15

A section of the picture exploded to show the pixels

- Bit-mapped graphics are often difficult to edit.

There are several different ways of storing bit-mapped graphics, indicated by the file extension. Some of these include:

- .bmp
- .pcx
- .jpg or .jpeg
- .tif or .tiff

Vector-based graphics

Vector-based graphics are also known as object-oriented graphics, and they work in a different way. Rather than being stored as a graphic, these are stored as geometric-based data. Instead of individual pixels storing the required data, vector graphics work on a linear basis, where drawing starts from a certain point that is central to the image. For example, if you were to draw a line in a vector-based graphics program, the line would have a middle point and two end-points, one on the left of the middle point and one on the right.

With vector-based graphics an image can be altered without resulting in distortion or loss of quality or resolution. It is also possible to scale vector-based graphics, ensuring that different parts of the graphic remain in proportion to the whole graphic.

Vector-based graphics programs are mainly used for design purposes. Architects, CAD designers and garden designers are just some of the people who use vector-based graphics.

File extensions that indicate a graphic is vector-based include:

- .ai
- .cgm
- .wmf
- .cdr
- .mpp

Activity 8

Research the file extensions given above, for both bit-mapped and vector-based graphics.

Produce a table listing the file extensions, examples of software than can be used to save graphics in this format and any advantages and disadvantages you can find for each.

Look for any other file extensions for bit-mapped or vector-based graphics, and add these to your table.

If possible in your school/college or at home, produce some images in both vector-based and bit-mapped formats. Try editing and resizing them so that you can see the difference between the two.

5.3 Storing and processing numbers

Numbers are also stored in binary code on a computer. When numbers are being treated as characters, for example to represent a telephone number, the ASCII code is used to convert the numbers to binary.

A telephone number of 0800 765 4421 would be represented in binary as:

00110000 00111000 00110000 00110000 00110111 00110110 00110101 00110100 00110100 00110010 00110001

If you need to use numbers for any kind of calculation, the ASCII code is not suitable. For example, if you wanted to store a person's age, say 21, the binary code would be 00110010 00110001. If you wanted to include that in a calculation to find out the average age of your friends, using the binary code as a representation of the number 21 would give no meaningful result unless a special program had been written to convert all these ages, covering the calculation formula as well. This would not only take a lot of expertise and time, but storing these numbers in ASCII binary code would also take up a lot of memory.

In order to usefully store numbers to be used for calculations, a binary number system has been developed. This is used for whole numbers only (**integers**). The system uses pre-defined base

'

numbers, starting at 1 on the right-hand side and doubling each time you move left along the scale. Each number still consists of eight bits, so the numbers 1 to 128 commonly represent the system:

| 128 | 64 | 32 | 16 | 8 | 4 | 2 | 1 |

If we wanted to represent the number 21 in binary number format, it would work like this:

128	64	32	16	8	4	2	1
0	0	0	1	0	1	0	1

We have taken one each of the numbers 16, 4 and 1, which when added together equal 21 – so the binary number code is 00010101.

If we look at a larger number, say 201, we would work it out like this:

128	64	32	16	8	4	2	1
1	1	0	0	1	0	0	1

Therefore, the binary number code for 201 is 11001001.

A large number, such as 365, would be impossible to represent under this system, as 128 is the highest number, and you can multiply by only 0 or 1. In order to represent 365 we would need to start with 2×128, and this is not possible. It is common, therefore, for two or four consecutive bytes to be used. This would look like this:

0000000101101101

which is 1×256, 0×128, 1×64, 1×32, 0×16, 1×8, 1×4, 0×2, 1×1

As noted above, this system is suitable only for whole numbers. For fractional numbers (known as **real** numbers), a different system has been defined, which is known as **floating-point notation.** This is a very complex system, and is not one that you will need to be able to use at this point in your studies.

5.4 Storing and processing sound

One of the main problems with storing and processing sound is that all sound travels in analogue waves. An analogue wave is a signal that is continuously changing. Computer systems store and process data digitally, so sound waves need to be converted to a digital format in order for the computer to deal with them. Once a sound wave becomes digitalised it is known as a **discrete** signal. This conversion can be done by using an analogue-to-digital converter, known as a sound card. Once the conversion has taken place, the digital sound waves are stored as binary code.

The quality of sound stored on a computer is determined by the **sampling frequency**. This is the rate at which the analogue data is 'sampled', i.e. how often the sound card records a section of the sound wave, measuring its height and storing this as binary code. The higher the sampling frequency, the more accurate the sound data when compared to the original analogue version.

Test your knowledge

1   How is data stored on a computer?
2   What is ASCII coding used for?
3   Describe two problems associated with storing bit-mapped graphics.
4   Why would vector-based graphics be used instead of bit-mapped graphics?

Exam questions

1 State a suitable medium for transferring sound files, and give a reason for your choice. *(2 marks)*
AQA Jan 2001

2 State **two** types of data, other than alphanumeric, that can be stored in a computer file. *(2 marks)*
AQA May 2001

6 Output and sharing of data

This section will provide coverage of the following key area:

- Describe the need for suitable output formats and orderings to communicate the results of data interrogation and undertake report generation.

We have previously looked at the way data is processed into information and stored on a computer. We now need to consider another important aspect of information – how it is presented. This is known as the 'output format' of the data or information, and is often referred to as the **dissemination and distribution** of data.

The output format for presenting and sharing data and information is important for different reasons:

- data that is shared or presented must be in a logical, easy-to-follow format

- information must be shared or presented in a meaningful way

- data and/or information must be shared or presented within a given context

- the target audience must be considered.

6.0 Output formats for data

When sharing or presenting data, the output format will depend to some extent on the type of software being used. In Unit 1 you learnt that data becomes information only when it has a meaning placed on it. Sometimes it will be necessary to share or present data in its raw format. For this reason, it is extremely important that the people you share the data with or present the data to are aware of the context to which it relates. The data would be totally meaningless otherwise.

An example will highlight this. A class of 10 students record their dates of birth for a project they are working on. This data could be presented in several ways. Look at the examples below and decide which one makes the most sense.

a) 01.01.1987 03.03.1986 09.03.1987 10.05.1986 10.06.1986 13.06.1987 19.08.1986 21.08.1986 25.10.1987 27.11.1987

b) 1st January 1987, 3rd March 1986, 9th March 1987, 10th May 1986, 10th June 1986, 13th June 1987, 19th August 1986, 21st August 1986, 25th October 1987, 27th November 1987

c) 1/1/87 3/3/86 9/3/87 10/5/86 10/6/86 13/6/87 19/8/86 21/8/86 25/10/87 27/11/87

d) See Figure 16 on the next page.

Sometimes you might believe that the best way to represent any kind of data would be via a chart of some kind. As you can see from the examples shown, charts are not always the best presentation style. In fact, none of the examples makes any sense, unless you know the context in which it is set. If you did not know that these were people's birth dates, any of the four examples given would be totally meaningless.

To a person who knows English, example **b)** is probably the easiest to understand.

To ensure that the data is read within the correct context, the best idea would probably be to place the data in a table, as in Figure 17 on the next page.

Figure 16

Area chart showing birth dates

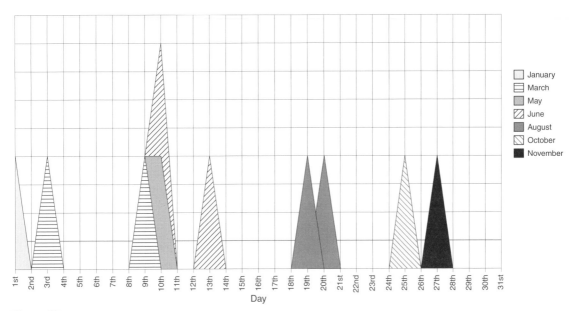

Figure 17

Table showing birth dates

Dates of birth for our class:												
	January	**February**	**March**	**April**	**May**	**June**	**July**	**August**	**September**	**October**	**November**	**December**
1st	✓											
2nd												
3rd			✗									
4th												
5th												
6th												
8th												
9th			✓									
10th												
11th					✗	✗						
12th												
13th						✓						
14th												
15th												
16th												
17th												
18th												
19th								✗				
20th												
21st								✗				
22nd												
23rd												
24th												
25th										✓		
26th												
27th											✓	
28th												
29th												
30th												
31st												

✓ = 1987   ✗ = 1986

Even this is not very helpful, as there is only a small amount of data to present. However, if there were more data, say 100 different birth dates, using a table to present the data would make the most sense.

Charts

Studying data in this way is known as **data interrogation**. Spreadsheets are a common way of entering data, and this can be presented as a data table or a chart. Most spreadsheet packages will allow you to automatically create a chart from data held on a spreadsheet, following the steps through a wizard. This will allow the data to be represented graphically, and it is often easier to make sense of the data in this way. Charts commonly used include:

Bar charts – rectangular bars, usually distinguished by shading or colouring, to show different values and how they relate to each other. Bar charts can be shown in outline, 3D, clustered, or stacked, and the bars can be horizontal or vertical.

Pie charts – a circle, broken into different segments. The values are represented by a segment within the circle and are, again, distinguished by either shading or colours. Pie charts can be shown as outline, 3D, or exploded (where one or all segments are separated out from the circle).

Line charts – a symbol is used to indicate each piece of data, joined together in a chart by lines. Again, shading or colouring can be used to distinguish between the values, or the different lines represented. Line charts are normally used to represent trends of data and can be shown as outline, stacked or 3D.

Scatter charts – 'markers' are used to represent the different values on a chart. Sometimes, the markers can be joined by the use of lines. Again, the markers and/or lines can be distinguished through the use of shading or colouring. Scatter charts are normally used to compare pairs of values.

 Group activity

These are just some of the charts that can be used. Try using these and some other types of charts in this group activity.

Gather some data from members of your class, for example how much they spend on fares to get to school/college. Enter the data into a spreadsheet and produce different types of charts, following the wizard steps, to find which type of chart best represents your data.

Printouts

Figure 18

Computer printout sheets

Other output formats for data include computer printout sheets, printed onto special computer paper. These are normally used to print out, for example, end-of-month sales figures for a company.

6.1 Output formats for information

Many different output formats are available for sharing or presenting information. Remember, information is data that has been given a meaning, so it is important to ensure that information is presented at a level that the user will understand. There would be no point in presenting to a class of nine-year-olds, for example, some research you had carried out on computer games, if it mainly discussed the memory required for the game, the specification of the game, complicated manoeuvres that could be made, and extra programming you could do to make the game more interesting. Most nine-year-olds would not understand this; they would be more interested in how the game worked, what the objective of the game was, and the controls used for certain moves. You must take your target audience into consideration when thinking about the best way of presenting information.

In a business context, it may be that a manager will require an overview of the sales data, for example, in the format of graphs, charts and tables. This will save time and prevent information overload. A sales representative, however, will require the full details of sales data to enable him or her to see a breakdown of sales made in comparison to the other sales representatives within the company.

There are two main ways of presenting information: **hard copy** and **soft copy**. A hard copy presentation means that information is physically given to someone in a printed, written or drawn format – it is a paper-based document. A soft copy is where information is presented through ICT, without a paper-based format being used.

The most common ways of presenting information are still through books, leaflets, brochures, pamphlets and flyers. These are all hard copy examples, although most will be prepared on computers.

Another common hard-copy way of presenting information is a written report, including the use of graphics and/or diagrams where necessary to explain information in more detail. Reports can be shared electronically, by using the attachments feature of e-mail software, but are still commonly shared in hard-copy format.

It is possible to produce reports automatically from data and text held on software. We have already mentioned report generators in Section 3 (page 104). A report generator is normally available as part of accounting, database, and some programming software packages. A wizard can be used to extract data and/or text from one or more files and then present them in a certain format. In your project for Unit 3 it is likely that you will use a report generator.

Some other ways in which information can be presented include:

- An **OHP** (overhead projector) and OHTs (overhead transparencies). This is still commonly used in classrooms and at business meetings. Information must be presented in short bursts, in logical steps, and preferably be broken up by the use of graphics and/or diagrams. OHTs are cheap to produce and the equipment is widely available.

- An **on-screen** or **projected presentation**, for example using Microsoft PowerPoint. As with the use of OHP/OHTs, the information must be presented in short bursts, in logical steps and broken up by the use of graphics and/or diagrams. The main difference between an on-screen presentation of this type and the use of OHP/OHTs is that the on-screen presentation can be dynamic. This means that simple animation (such as moving letters or

121

words), can be included and graphics or diagrams can be built step-by-step in front of the target audience to ensure that the meaning is understood.

Presentation packages are also capable of:

- using sound and video clips to make them more interesting to the audience, or to highlight points within the presentation
- allowing the presenter to use remote control to direct the presentation, so he or she does not have to stand at the front of a room and stay within reach of the computer
- allowing a non-linear presentation, so that the slides do not have to be viewed in a pre-set order – slide views can be changed randomly and slides can be reordered easily
- allowing different formats of print-out of the slides, for example a copy of the slides with space to take notes alongside each one.

■ An **on-screen animation**, for example using Macromedia Director. There are several different ways of presenting information through the use of animation. You could produce a simple animation of the outline for an advertisement, or a more complex animation of an idea for a computer game.

On-screen animation packages are also capable of:

- using sound and video clips to enhance the presentation
- allowing interaction from the users
- combining different animations into one presentation, so that more than one person can prepare the data and it can be put together to run as a single, fluid presentation.

■ An **on-screen interactive quiz**. There are several ways in which on-screen interactive quizzes can be produced. Some programming will normally be involved, such as telling users if they have answered correctly or incorrectly, or to ensure the user can be taken through the quiz in the correct order. On-screen interactive quizzes can be produced using software such as PowerPoint, Director, Flash, Visual Basic, or web-based software such as FrontPage or Dreamweaver for web-based quizzes. On-screen interactive quizzes are also capable of:

- using sound and video clips to enhance the quiz, so songs or nursery rhymes could be used, for example
- allowing non-linear forms of interaction, so that the user does not have to follow the quiz from question 1 to the end, but can move back and forth between questions.

■ A **website**. With the introduction of easy-to-use web design software, such as Microsoft FrontPage and Macromedia Dreamweaver, the use of websites to present information is becoming more popular. Your centre may even have a site on its intranet where you can take part in on-line learning through using links to lecture notes, which is useful if you have missed classes through illness. Website packages are also capable of:

- using sound and video clips to enhance the website
- allowing interaction with the user through the use of, for example, drop-down boxes and forms
- allowing a non-linear form of presentation
- using hotspots and text- or graphic-based links to move between the pages of the website.

■ A **CD-Rom**. CD-Roms can be used to present permanent information. It is common today to find CD-Roms that explain the biology of human beings, for example, through the use of diagrams, animations and text. CD-Rom presentations can include the use of any of the other presentation methods, saved onto CD-Rom, so that the presentation can be specifically built with the target audience in mind. For example, an encyclopaedia for children can be produced that allows a child to use links to see more detail, or find other pages with similar content.

- **Electronic whiteboards**. These allow people in different locations to view simple diagrams or text-based documents at the same time, while holding a videoconference, for example. The people involved in the conference can all view the diagram and make real-time changes to it while the meeting is being held.

- **Interactive whiteboards**. These are a way of projecting information that is linked to a computer. The interactive whiteboard has common features, commands and programs indicated on the whiteboard, which can be accessed through the use of a light pen.

- **Video**. Information presented on video can be as simple as, for example, a recording of a BBC documentary looking at the history of computers.

Activity 9

Look at the list below and decide which output format you think would best suit the purpose and the target audience. Make a list of the different features that would be available to enhance the presentation. List any advantages and disadvantages you think would be specific to the scenario for the output format you choose. Note that some of these scenarios may be suitable for more than one output format, and that not all output formats may be covered.

1 A teacher needs to show a class of young students who have not used the Internet before how to browse Internet sites and use links.
2 A mother would like her child to learn how to count but wants to make it a fun exercise.
3 A business person needs to present an idea for a new product in a meeting.
4 A teacher needs to show a class of students how different data capture methods work.
5 An architect needs to discuss some plans with a colleague in an office in another country, but does not want to have to travel there.
6 A student is preparing a presentation on the dangers of taking drugs.

Test your knowledge

1 What is data interrogation?
2 Describe two different types of chart that can be used for presenting data. For each give an example of the type of data you think would be best represented.
3 Describe three output formats for information. For each, give an example of a situation where they could be used.

Exam questions

1 A large college provides a wide range of courses. The college has three options for distributing information on the courses to potential students.

For **each** of the following options, describe **one** advantage and **one** disadvantage to the college of this method of disseminating the information.

Option 1 Issue a prospectus containing the details of all the courses.

Option 2 Publish course information on the college website.

Option 3 Publish a course information booklet that can be downloaded from the college website.

(12 marks)

AQA Jan 2002

7 Data privacy and security

This section will provide coverage of the following key areas:

- Describe the broad characteristics, capabilities and limitations of storage devices

- Understand the importance of and the mechanisms for maintaining data security

- Describe the distinction between security and privacy

- Understand simple processes that protect the integrity of data against malicious or accidental alteration; standard clerical procedures, passwords, levels of permitted access, write-protect mechanisms, back-up procedures, restoration and recovery procedures

- Understand the need for regular and systematic back-up and procedures for recovery.

Safeguarding data can be looked at in two different ways:

- keeping data private – also known as **data privacy**

- keeping data secure – also known as **data security**.

It is important that you recognise the difference, as the two have distinct meanings. Another aspect of data security is **data integrity**. We will look at each of these factors and examine the measures that can be set up to ensure data held is kept safely.

7.0 Data integrity

If data is altered or deleted, this will affect its integrity. Data integrity means the accuracy and correctness of data, not only on input but also when being transmitted or processed. It is important that data integrity is maintained at all times, so data must be continually checked for accuracy.

Ensuring data integrity on input is discussed in Section 2. It is a good idea to read this before proceeding, if you have not already done so, or to refresh your memory by reading it again. Other measures that can be taken to ensure data integrity include the use of standard clerical procedures to help minimise user error. All systems should have a clearly laid-out set of operational procedures that all staff must adhere to. For example, there should be a standard way of naming files held on the system, with a strict directory structure that cannot be altered.

7.1 Data privacy

Data privacy means that other people cannot look at the data held on the computer, unless they have been given permission to do so – the data cannot be accessed by unauthorised users.

Data privacy is necessary because:

- all employers hold private information about their employees; not only addresses and telephone numbers, but often details such as salary level

- companies need to ensure that information such as new product plans cannot be passed to competitors

■ customer information may be held on the system; a customer ordering goods using a credit card would expect that the credit card number would be kept confidential

■ in a government office, highly confidential budget details, for example, may be held.

Personal and confidential information that is held on computers is usually covered by the Data Protection Act, which is discussed in Unit 1. This is another very important reason to ensure that a system has data privacy.

There are different ways the system and software can be set up to ensure data privacy, including the following.

Using passwords and log-ins

This is probably the most common way of protecting data on a system. All users who are authorised to access the system are given a log-in, which is usually either their name or a random number. They are also given a password. Each time they log onto the system, they have to enter both the log-in and the password. The system checks whether what has been entered matches any log-in and password held in its memory. If it does, the user can access the system. If it does not, the user will be denied access to the system. Most education centres use a system similar to this.

Setting levels of access rights

Access rights can be programmed into a user's log-in code so that once logged onto the system, certain information cannot be viewed. Setting up different levels of access rights also enables an organisation to make sure that information is not altered by unauthorised persons. There are different reasons for using access rights.

■ In your school or college, software might be available for certain courses that is not licensed for everyone to use at one time. Although this software might be available on every workstation in the school/college, it would be breaking the law if more people than the license covered were to access it at the same time. The software could be restricted to those users who needed it and made unavailable for others. For example, someone taking a web-design course would need to access web-design software, but someone taking a carpentry course would not.

■ Not everyone in a company may need to view confidential or personal information about a customer. Also, only a small amount of information may be needed for certain purposes, and information overload could result if all the data had to be read to find the section required. For example, someone in the accounts department would not need to see the complete sales history for a longstanding customer when sending an invoice for goods recently ordered.

■ The management of the system could be made more efficient by the use of access rights. It may be that a company does not want employees to have open access to the Internet, as it is felt that this is not needed in their job roles. However, some employees may need full access, for example researchers.

The different levels of access restrict files of data in different ways.

■ **Read** – the user is allowed to view the information held on the system, but cannot alter it in any way. Users with read-only access cannot delete information. One example would be product information leaflets for a company. Once they have been issued, the company will not want anyone to be able to delete or alter them, unless they are authorised to do so. By making the file a read-only file, the company knows that only someone with the correct access rights can update a leaflet.

- **Write** – the user can alter the information held on the system. A person whose job involved updating product leaflets could call a leaflet onto their workstation, update it, and save it back to the directory or file.

- **Create** – the user is allowed to create new files, folders or directories on the system. Restricting this right can save duplication and confusion.

- **Erase** – the user can erase files, folders or directories on the system. One example would be if a product became obsolete. It would not be wise to keep the product leaflet available to everyone, so the person with the correct access rights could delete it to ensure that no one was recommending that product to a customer.

- **Modify** – the user is allowed to change the names and attributes of files, folders and directories. As an example, a company could have a folder for product leaflets that is named 'Product Leaflets'. When a product becomes obsolete, they might not want to delete the leaflet from the system completely but to keep it for future reference. Someone with the correct access rights could change the name of the existing folder to 'Current Product Leaflets', and create a new folder called 'Obsolete Product Leaflets' to store the old leaflets.

- **Copy** – the user can copy work from one area to another, or from the hard drive to a disk. For example, a person who has been given the task of creating a new product leaflet might want to take a product leaflet template home so that they can work on it over a weekend. If the correct access rights have been set up, the employee can copy the template to a disk.

Defining internal procedures

Companies will have guidelines for employees to ensure they are aware of legal requirements when working with computer systems, their responsibilities and the standards of behaviour that the company expects of them. These guidelines are often known as a code of conduct. This issue is looked at in more detail in the A2 ICT course.

A code of conduct makes employees aware of:

- company policy on security

- the handling of software

- what to do to avoid viruses

- how to use e-mail correctly

- how to use the Internet correctly

- the legislation relevant to these points e.g. the Data Protection Act and the Computer Misuse Act

Employees who do not follow the code of conduct can expect to be disciplined, depending on the severity of their misconduct.

The British Computer Society has produced a professional code of conduct for members, setting out social, moral and ethical standards for behaviour. Most companies will add or delete sections according to their area of business. Another example, the code of conduct for the UK Web Design Association Limited (UKWDA), is shown below.

Figure 19

UKWDA Code of Conduct

7.2 Data security

Data security means keeping data safe from accidental damage or physical loss. The fact that some people might try to maliciously alter, delete or steal the data must also be considered. The methods of ensuring data privacy described above will help limit the risk of this.

Different methods can be used to ensure data security. It must be remembered that data can be threatened by both internal and external factors, and by intentional, accidental, or natural incidents.

Internal threats to data

Internal threats to data include:

- **Intentional incidents**. It is not always possible to foresee these, but steps can be taken to minimise the risks.

  Someone within a company, perhaps someone who has been sacked, could purposely delete data to cause disruption. It is important that log-ins are cancelled promptly as soon as someone leaves a company.

It has also been known for people to download information that they believe might be of use to a new company they are joining onto a disk or CD. Little can be done about this, other than ensuring that access rights are allocated to the right level and hoping that people's professionalism might stop this.

■ **Accidental incidents**. Some accidental incidents might affect the integrity of the data being held.

- The disk on the main server computer might crash, due to overload or a system error. To minimise the risk of this, it is vital to ensure regular back-ups are made and stored separately (we will look at this later in this section).
- Data might be accidentally over-written. If the data is being held on disk or tape, it is possible to write-protect the disk or tape so that this is not possible. Floppy disks have a special mechanism whereby a tab can be slid forward to make the disk write-protected. No data can then be written to the disk unless the tab is slid back. Most tapes have a central ring that can be removed to ensure the tape cannot be written to. The ring has to be re-inserted to enable you to write to the tape again.
- A user might spill a drink over the computer, causing it to short circuit and crash. A simple measure to prevent this type of accident is to ban drinks from rooms where computers are held. This is probably the rule in your centre.

■ **Natural incidents**.

- The room where the main server computer is held could have a fire. A sprinkler system could help prevent total damage.
- The room could have a flood; when installing a system, it is a good idea to choose a room above ground floor level for the main server, to minimise the risk of this.
- The electricity supply for the system might be hit by lightning. The use of circuit breakers or surge protectors could help minimise damage by cutting off the supply before the lightning reaches the system.

External threats to data

External threats to data include:

■ **Viruses.** A virus is a piece of software that is introduced to a computer illegally, which can be merely irritating or have momentous results, such as all the data on that system being deleted. It is usually designed to propagate itself without the user intending it to, and it can then infect other computer systems the user is in contact with.

Someone might load some data or a program onto the system that contains a virus. This could cause a lot of disruption or even data loss. Setting up access rights to ensure only authorised personnel are able to load things onto the system would help minimise this risk. Also, a virus checker should be installed – this is software that will check all incoming and downloaded data for viruses, and will alert the user. A virus checker is not a prevention tool but can be used to detect viruses before they are downloaded onto the system, inform the user and give different options for the course of action to take, including destroying the virus. It is important to keep the virus checker up to date, as new viruses are constantly being introduced.

Networked systems might have data sent through e-mail that contains viruses. Again, the use of a virus checker would help minimise the risk.

■ **Hackers.** These are people who intentionally break into a computer system. Most of the time, hacking is done for reputation and status and is not about intentionally damaging data held on the system. However, a hacker's intention cannot be known, and a firewall should be set up to minimise the risk of hacking.

A firewall is a combination of hardware and software that is loaded onto a system between the file server and the external network. This will prevent users on the system from connecting and communicating directly with computers not on the network, and acts as an intermediary stage of the communication link. The messages between computers are passed through the firewall, and the firewall software judges whether it is safe to let the communication link proceed. If safe, the communication will pass through the firewall onto the computer, but if it seems unsafe, the communication link can be blocked and the computers prevented from linking up.

Figure 20

Communications via a firewall

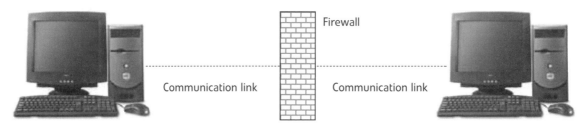

Networked computer   Networked computer

- **Physical loss of hardware, resources and data.** People have been known to steal hard drives, monitors, printers, keyboards, and other equipment from companies. To minimise the risk of this, physical security should be set up. The use of locks on doors to computer rooms so that only authorised personnel can enter is one way of doing this. Hardware can also be 'locked' onto desks through the use of bars, or through clipping mouse cables, for example, to the hard drive cables, which can deter people from trying to take them away. In many companies, security guards and security passes for staff are used.

7.3 Back-up and recovery of data

Back-up and recovery of data are the most important ways of ensuring data security. If a current back-up copy of data is kept securely, then although some data loss might occur if a disaster strikes the system, other data can be restored. Recovery procedures can be used as a part of a wider contingency plan to ensure that a system can be up and running as soon as possible following a major disaster. It must be noted that recovery procedures are different from 'data recovery' where an attempt is made to recover data from a damaged disk, for example.

Backing up data

Backing up means that files and programs held on the system are copied onto a separate source and kept in a safe place. There are different types of back-up medium, which are discussed below.

The place where the back-up is physically kept is as important as the process of backing up data. If data is backed up onto, for example, a disk, and the disk is kept in the same room as the computer system, a company will not be able to recover any data if that room is consumed by fire. Ideally, back-ups should be stored in a fire- and flood-proof location, preferably away from the site of the main system.

Different types of back-up can be performed:

- **Full or global backup**: a copy is taken of every single file that is held on the hard disk. It can be very time consuming but ensures that the maximum amount of data is available for recovery purposes. The computer system cannot be used while a full back-up is taking place, so this is normally performed overnight when the system is not in use.

- **Incremental backup**: only those files that have been updated or created since the last back-up was performed are copied. It is usual to have a labelling system of some kind, for example the date of the copied file, so that it can be clearly seen when a file was last backed up. Incremental back-ups are often carried out on a daily basis, whereas a full back-up is performed once a week. This is a quicker way of backing up, so the system can be in use for longer periods of time.

- **On-line back-up**: several copies are made at the same time, with the data being written to different disks. At least one copy is normally written to a disk that is held off-site. This is a very useful type of back-up for companies where it is important that the data is never lost, as the main system can be switched to another drive quickly if any problems occur.

How the back-up is performed will depend to an extent on the amount of data that needs to be stored. Different back-up media include:

- **Back-up tape** (usually 8mm), also known as a tape streamer – this can be used to store large amounts of data. A tape cartridge is used to store the data and can hold up to 40 gigabytes of data. The transfer rate for back-up tape is about 60–80 megabytes per second.

- **Zip disk** – this looks similar to a floppy disk, but is larger and can hold more data, up to 250 megabytes, compared to 3 megabytes on a normal floppy disk. A special zip drive is required. The computer that a zipped file is sent to or loaded onto will need to have special software in order to access the data. The transfer rate for zip disks is about 60 megabytes per minute.

- **Removable hard disk** – this is just the same as an internal, permanent hard disk, but can be easily removed to keep the data separately from the hardware. The storage capacity is constantly being upgraded by manufacturers in line with hard disks inside the computer, so they are capable of holding extremely large amounts of data.

- **CD-RW** (re-writable CDs) – these are similar to CD-ROMs but data can be written, read, deleted and overwritten. They can hold up to 650 megabytes of data.

- **DAT** (digital audio tape) – this is similar to a zip disk, and will need a special DAT drive. It is capable of storing up to 40 gigabytes of data.

- **DVD-RAM** – DVD-RAM drives are capable of reading and writing to a 2.6 gigabyte DVD-RAM disk. They can also read and write-once to a 3.9 gigabyte DVD-R disk and read a 4.7 gigabyte or 8.5 gigabyte DVD-ROM. DVD-RAM disks can be read on both DVD-R and DVD-ROM drives.

- **Jaz disk** – this similar to a zip disk but is a small, removable hard disk. It needs a special jaz drive that can also be used to install and use applications, as the computer recognises it as another hard disk. A jaz disk can store up to 4 gigabytes of data, with the use of compression, and the transfer rate is about 7 megabytes per second.

■ **RAID (redundant array of independent disks)** – this is a combination of two or more disk drives on one server. When the back-up is performed, the same data is saved simultaneously on all the disks. This means that if there is a problem with one of the disks, data from another disk can be used with minimal disruption to the business. RAID devices are usually set up on networked systems. The drives have a high capacity and are capable of storing up to 40 gigabytes of data, with a transfer rate of about 80 megabytes per second.

Recovering data

A recovery procedure is usually part of an overall contingency plan held by a company to ensure that a system can be recovered with the minimum delay and disruption should a disaster occur. The contingency plan would include other factors as well as data recovery, such as change of building should the original building become unusable, for example following a major fire. Contingency plans and disaster recovery will be looked at further if you go on to study at A2 level.

Recovery procedures should include factors such as:

■ having an alternative system available

■ having access to other communication systems

■ having a service agreement with a system provider to replace all equipment as soon as possible following the loss of a system.

Part of a recovery procedure is the back-up strategy, which determines the way in which back-up is performed and how often back-up of data is done. The back-up strategy should mean that programs and data are never totally lost. The back-up strategy will depend on the value of the data and the size of the company, and several factors need to be considered. These include:

■ How much data needs to be backed up? If there are large amounts of data then the back-up medium will need to be capable of storing all of it, for example on DAT. For smaller amounts of data, it may be that a CDRW will be sufficient.

■ How often does the data change? This may determine how often the data should be backed up. Earlier we looked at the fact that large back-ups will make the system unavailable for long periods of time. Smaller, daily back-ups or incremental back-ups may be the best solution if the data does not change very often.

■ When is the best time for back-up to be performed? If an overnight back-up is decided on because the system is not in use then, the type of back-up chosen can include a full or global back-up as the time taken will not affect business transactions.

■ What is the value of the data? If it is imperative that a company suffers no data loss at all, then it is probably important to perform a full back-up daily.

■ Can the back-ups be restored easily? Whichever back-up medium is used, it is important that data restoration can occur with the minimum delay and disruption.

■ Is back-up storage required off-site? If the data has a high value, then it would be wise for a company to invest in some off-site storage for back-ups. There are companies that offer back-up facilities on the Internet. You send the back-up data directly to them over the Internet and it can be stored anywhere in the world. Fire- and flood-proof safes are a good way to ensure back-ups remain secure, and many companies choose this option in safes that are off-site.

Other factors that will need to be considered once the back-up hardware and software has been decided on include:

▓ Are security measures set up to prevent unauthorised access to the back-up? In most companies it will be important to ensure that if the back-up copy is held on the system, it is not accidentally or maliciously accessed, thereby changing the data. Security measures can be set up to prevent this, such as encrypting the data, or password protecting the back-up file.

▓ Is there a company procedure for labelling the back-up copies? A standard procedure should be introduced to ensure that at all times, people responsible for back-up and the copies held will know which is the current copy.

▓ Who is responsible for backing up and the back-up copies? At least two people within the company need to be responsible for the back-up and recovery procedure. If one is away, the other person will still be aware of the procedure and be able to take responsibility for the back-up.

Whatever the recovery procedures, back-up strategy and overall contingency plan, the important factor for all of these is that systems can be in use again as soon as possible following loss of data for whatever reason.

Activity 10

T & S Limited is a small employment agency which specialises in providing staff for the service industry. The agency wants to computerise its data, using a networked database as the main storage facility for client records. The agency holds information on employers seeking staff and on people wishing to find work. The current system does not have any security or back-up programs installed.

T & S Limited currently employs four people in its office:

▓ two who require access to all information on the system and need to be able to add, change and delete information
▓ two who need only to be able to access some information, e.g. contact details for both employers and job seekers, job requirements from employers, experience and qualifications of job seekers.

You are an IT Consultant hired by the agency to ensure its data is being held securely, and is not breaking any laws. You need to produce the following:

▓ a questionnaire for the agency to find out its requirements for data security and privacy
▓ a brief report giving recommendations advising the agency of the type of threats, potential problems and laws it needs to be aware of
▓ an outline contingency plan, covering security, back-up and recovery procedures.

Test your knowledge

1 What is the difference between data privacy and data security?
2 What is meant by the term 'data integrity'?
3 Describe two levels of access that can be set up to ensure data privacy. For each, give an example of why this might be used.
4 Describe one possible internal and one possible external threat to data.
5 What is the difference between full back-up and incremental back-up?
6 What factors need to be considered when implementing a recovery procedure?

Exam questions

1 An Internet sales company carries out its business with the assistance of a database system running on a network of PCs. The main tasks are the processing of customer orders and the logging of payments. You have been asked to advise the company on back-up strategies and to explain their importance.

(a) Give **two** reasons why it is essential that this company has a back-up strategy. *(2 marks)*

(b) State **five** factors that should be considered in a back-up strategy, illustrating each factor with an example. *(10 marks)*

AQA Jan 2001

2 Employees can often be responsible for causing loss or damage to their company's data. Regular back-ups are taken by the company, but in order to prevent employees from causing such loss or damage, describe:

(a) **two** measures that could be incorporated into the hardware used; *(4 marks)*

(b) **two** software features that could be used; *(4 marks)*

(c) **two** other procedures that the company could introduce. *(4 marks)*

AQA Jan 2001

3 A publishing company administers its business by using a database system running on a network of PCs. The main uses are to process customer orders and to log payments. You have been asked about back-up strategies and their importance.

(a) Give **two** reasons why it is essential that this company has a workable back-up strategy.

(2 marks)

(b) State **five** factors that should be considered in a back-up strategy, illustrating each factor with an example. *(10 marks)*

(c) Despite all the precautions, some data might still be lost if there was a system failure.

Give **two** reasons why this might be the case. *(2 marks)*

AQA Specimen question

4 Passwords, entered at a keyboard, are often used as a method of protecting data against malicious access.

Give **two** other methods of preventing access to data. *(2 marks)*

AQA Jan 2002

8 Nature and types of software

This section will provide coverage of the following key areas:

- Describe the need for interfacing with peripheral storage devices, input and output devices and display devices

- Describe the need for printer and other peripheral drivers

- Describe the distinction between systems software and applications software

- Describe the purpose of operating systems

- Describe the nature of package software, generic and specific, and of bespoke software

- Describe the functionality offered by software which provides access to the Internet.

The most common meaning of **software** is a set of computer instructions that has been written for a particular task. However, software can also refer to data held in an electronic form. In this section we are concerned with the most common meaning for software.

Software can be broken down into two different types:

- systems software

- application software.

A good place to start is to look at the way in which software is held on the hard disk. The hard disk sits inside the computer and an operating system is loaded onto it.

Figure 21

The operating system is loaded onto the hard disk

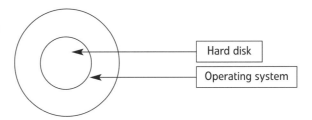

The applications software is then loaded onto the hard disk and is run and managed by the operating system.

Figure 22

All the software loaded onto the hard drive

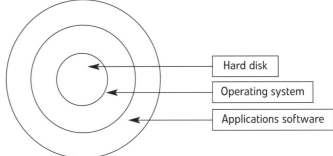

This section will look at the functions performed by an operating system, the different types of systems software available, and application software. It will also look briefly at the functionality offered by software that provides access to the Internet.

8.0 Systems software

Systems software is the software that enables the computer to function. There are two main types of systems software: **operating system** software and **utility** software. Both of these types of software are essential components when using a computer, for loading and using application software, saving documents and files, and operating the computer on any level.

Operating system software

The term 'operating system' (often abbreviated to OS) refers to the software that is responsible for linking the user with the hardware on the computer and for managing all the applications software that is loaded. It also provides standard services and supports standard operations, for example file access. Operating system software is held permanently on the hard disk of a computer. If it becomes corrupted or is deleted, the computer will not run.

All operating systems have basic functions. These include:

- **The management of the booting process.** When you first switch your computer on, an operation called **bootstrap loading** will take place, where the operating system is loaded into the computer's memory from disk. The system then runs through several diagnostic tests, which you have probably noticed appearing on screen while the system is loading. You may not have read what appears on the screen, but it is the operating system that is checking systems operation factors, such as memory capacity and checking for peripherals attached. Once these operations are complete, the user interface will appear.

- **The management of internal memory.** If more than one application program is running at one time, the opened applications are sharing the available memory. The operating system has to constantly check the memory of the computer in order to ensure that there is enough memory available for these applications to run smoothly. For example, you probably stay logged on to e-mail, a messenger service, or the Internet while you are working on an assignment in a word-processing program. This means that you are multi-tasking, and the computer is running all the applications that you have open. You may have experienced problems with the system becoming slow. This means that the memory required to run all these applications simultaneously is running out, and you will find that if you close one of the applications, the speed will increase again.

- **The management of input-output resources.** The system will allocate the order in which attached hardware devices are used. For example, if you have asked for a long document to be printed and you try to close the program the document is in before the data has been sent to the printer, a message will appear reminding you that if you close the program, some of the data will not be sent. Similarly, if you try to send another document to print before the data from the first document is loaded, a message will appear reminding you that the system is still in the process of sending data and you will have to wait. If you have an external disk drive, for example a zip drive, when you try to open a document from that drive the system will recognise that the zip drive on your system is an external piece of hardware and automatically switch to it.

■ **The management of processor use for multi-tasking systems.** If the system in use is capable of multi-tasking, it is the operating system that determines which application uses the processor first, and for how long. For example, in a company, it may be that a person in the accounts department is using a financial application and a person in the marketing department is using a DTP application at the same time, from a central server. Both these applications will require the use of the processor while they are open, but what happens if they both need to save a document at precisely the same moment? The processor must decide which command will be actioned first.

■ **The management of shared resources.** On a networked system where several computers are sharing the same resources and peripherals, the operating system has to determine the order in which requests are dealt with. For example, in the example above of the accounts department and the marketing department, they might be sharing a printer. What would happen if they both needed to print a document at the same time? It is possible on most systems to set up priorities for this. If one person was printing out a very long document on a shared printer and an urgent print run was required, the system could interrupt the long print run and send through the urgent print run, before resuming the long one.

■ **The management of error/advice messages.** When a system sends users a message to inform them of an error, or to advise them of the status of a program, this is known as **interrupt handling**. The operating system is responsible for detecting what is happening on the system, from a simple print request to a system malfunction, and informing the users.

■ **The management of user interface.** Any commands from the user, such as clicking on an icon to open a program, are actioned by the operating system. It is the operating system that loads and opens the required programs, files and documents.

■ **The management of back-up storage and file restoration.** The operating system is responsible for reloading programs from the back-up storage and carrying out file restoration where required. If you are using a word-processing program when a computer crashes, once the system is loaded again you may be sent a message asking if you want to revert to the last saved version. When the operating system detects a malfunction, it is common for it to automatically save the latest version of the document you have been working on. You will find it is only a temporary file, and will probably have a temporary file name that you do not recognise, but most of what you were working on should be there.

Different types of operating systems are available and users can interact with the operating system in two ways:

1 Using a **command-line interface** –where the commands are input to the system by the use of text-based instructions, responding to on-screen prompts. The disadvantage with using command-driven interfaces is that the user has to remember the commands required to drive the operating system.

2 Using a **GUI (graphical user interface)** – where the commands are input to the system by the use of mouse clicks, laser pen points or keyboard strokes on graphical icons. The advantage with using a GUI is that most commands will be graphical and the user needs only to be able to recognise the icons and the functions they perform. GUIs use an environment known as WIMP (windows, icons, mouse, pointer). The environment is user-friendly as the icons represent software held on the computer, so all the user needs to do to open a piece of software is to click on the icon.

The most common types of operating systems used today include:

■ **DOS** (disk operating system). The most widely used DOS system is MS-DOS (Microsoft Disk Operating System). This uses a command-driven interface. The user interacts with the operating system directly through text-based instructions. The interface is quite simple, but is not user-friendly. For example, the instruction 'dir c:' tells the operating system that you want to list the directory of files on the 'c' drive, as shown in Figure 23 below.

Another type of DOS system is Mac OS (Apple Macintosh Operating System). This uses a command-driven interface and works in the same way as MS-DOS. Mac OS is also used for the Macintosh computers that use a GUI.

Figure 23

MS-DOS command prompt screen

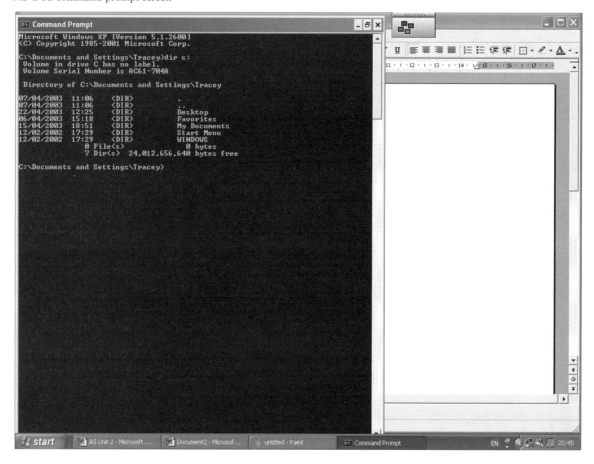

■ **Unix.** Unix is another command-driven operating system. It was designed so that several programmers can access the system at the same time and share its resources. It is a powerful system that controls all the commands from the keyboards of all the users, although users will feel as if they are the only people using the system as their work is unaffected by the others. The operating system was originally designed for mini-computers. It can also be used for mainframe and personal computers, so is very adaptable.

■ **Linux.** The Linux operating system was developed to be similar to Unix but to be used specifically for personal computers at a low cost, or even for free. Linux uses a GUI and is a system that performs very quickly and efficiently. Linux can be used for a wide variety of purposes, including software development, as well as an end-user platform.

■ **OS/2** (Operating System/2). The OS/2 was originally developed by a partnership between IBM and Microsoft to replace MS-DOS. However, the operating system had many initial problems and that, along with the development of window-based interfaces, meant that it did not become as widely used as originally intended. The technology was not wasted, however, as an OS/2 Warp version was developed which is used today by ATMs.

■ **Windows.** Windows is a Microsoft operating system that replaced MS-DOS. There have been several versions available and all have used a GUI. Some of the more widely used Windows operating systems are:

  – Windows 98 – this was the first Windows operating system to incorporate web technology as part of the user interface, along with support for USB (universal serial bus), DVD (digital versatile disk) and ACPI (advanced configuration and power interface).
  – Windows NT – this is the Windows New Technology operating system that does not use any form of DOS to operate. It is a robust, secure system that was developed for the larger business market.
  – Windows 2000 – a version of Windows NT that has been designed for small businesses, home users and professional users. It was developed further so that the larger business market also uses it as a replacement for Windows NT.
  – Windows Me – this was developed specifically for the home user as an update to Windows 98 and has added functionality for those users who are more experienced with using Windows operating systems.
  – Windows XP – the newest version of the Windows operating system has the greatest ease of desktop use to date. Windows XP is also capable of scanning images, using digital

Figure 24

An example of a Windows XP desktop with 'My Computer' window open

camera images, acquiring and running music and video files, and transferring data onto portable devices.

Utility software

Utility software is the software held on the hard disk that helps the management and use of a computer. You will almost certainly have used utility software, although probably without realising it. The purpose of utility software is to perform all the routine tasks on the system. Different types of utility software include:

- **Disk formatters.** Disk formatters are programs that enable you to format removable disks on your computer. For example, when you buy a floppy disk now it is usually pre-formatted, but a few years ago a user would have had to format a floppy disk before being able to store data on it. When using a CDR/CDRW to store data, the disk formatter enables you to label the disk, see how much memory is available and change file names or delete files.

- **Virus checkers.** Virus checkers are programs that enable the system to check incoming documents, files and programs for viruses. For example, when you are transferring data from one computer to another via floppy disk, the virus checker program will run a check on the data held on the floppy disk when it is inserted. If a virus is detected a message will appear on screen to warn the user that the data contains a virus, before allowing data to be transferred from the floppy disk to the hard disk. Users can thus prevent the transfer of viruses between computers.

- **Security programs.** The most common use of security programs is to check a user's log-in ID and password. The programs can be set up to allow a user a certain number of attempts at logging on and prompting for clues to a forgotten password, for example.

- **File management utilities.** File management utilities are used to copy, save, rename, delete and move files and documents around on the system. This software is also used for sorting and searching data on the system. For example, you may have used the 'Explore' option that is part of the utilities offered by a Microsoft Windows operating system. Within this window you can perform a full range of file management functions, for example dragging and dropping a file or document into a different area on the system.

Using and adding peripheral devices

It is the responsibility of the operating system to recognise and manage peripheral devices. It is important to users that they are able to check the status of these devices. If a document is sent to be printed and the printer does not respond, the user would not know what the problem was or how to overcome it if he or she was not able to view some information, such as a prompt from the operating system to add more paper.

It is equally important, as users become more competent with computers, to be able to add devices such as scanners, light pens, and new printers. When a new hardware device is added to the system a process must be carried out to ensure that the system has accepted and recognised it. This is known as configuration. The most commonly used configuration process is through the use of a **device driver**. A device driver is software that allows the system to communicate with the device. Usually, the correct device driver must be installed on the system in order for the device to be recognised and therefore work. The device driver contains features about the device, its capability and any control sequences that are necessary to the device to perform its function. For example, a printer driver will include:

- features that are specific to that model of printer

- information on the capabilities of the printer, for example the print speed

- the control sequences that will enable the printer to use different fonts, recognise paper layout and colour choices

- error detection capabilities to inform the operating system when problems arise, for example if the paper runs out or the wrong size of paper has been specified for that print job.

8.1 Applications software

Applications software refers to the different programs you use to perform tasks on the computer. Applications software is so called because it is applied to a particular problem and used for a specific purpose or 'application'.

Types of applications software commonly used include:

- word processing – used for creating text-based documents, although most word-processing software is also capable of some drawing functions

- desktop publishing – used for combining text and graphics, this software enables the user to lay out pages and see how the page will look once printed, resulting in high quality output of, for example, leaflets, brochures and books

- spreadsheet – used for creating and managing electronic pages split into rows and columns (known as 'worksheets') to enable the input and manipulation of data

- database – used for creating and managing electronic tables of data to enable record and transaction processing

- vector – used for design and graphical drawing, including CAD (computer-aided design)

- bitmap – used for artwork, graphics, graphical presentations and slides

- financial and accounts processing – used to manage figures for payroll, budgets, etc.

When selecting applications software, several factors need to be taken into consideration. These include:

- the platform the software will be run on

- the hardware used to run the applications software

- what the user needs the software to be able to do

- whether the user requirements will be met by generic, specific, or bespoke software.

Platform and hardware considerations

The platform the software will be run on is the hardware and the operating system. In an ideal world, applications software would be chosen before the hardware and operating system. However, in many situations a person selecting applications software will already own a computer with hardware and an operating system. Therefore, the type of applications software chosen often depends on compatibility with the existing hardware and operating system, and also on the memory available on the system.

With most modern personal computers, memory is no longer a consideration, as hard disk memory capacity is now commonly available in gigabytes instead of megabytes and kilobytes. However, for large networked systems, memory may be an important factor.

Most applications software is now developed so that it can run on all the most common types of operating system. In the past, much applications software was developed specifically for a particular type of operating system, which often caused problems for the user who required a certain application. For example, graphical design and DTP software was often developed only for use on a Mac OS, whereas today these applications are also used on Windows-based operating systems.

User needs

With so much choice and availability of applications software, different brands of the same type of applications may offer slightly different functions and features. When considering which applications software to purchase, the user must take into account the following factors:

- How much am I able to spend? The budget for purchasing applications software is a very important consideration. Even large companies need to consider this. Although applications software has become cheaper with more users purchasing different types, much of it is still expensive when compared, for instance, to the cost of the hardware. Often, a cheaper product that is capable of carrying out all the tasks the user requires will be a better purchase than a more expensive product that has many extra features and functions that are unlikely to be used. Think about the applications software you have on your own computer at home. There are probably a lot of features and functions on each piece of applications software that you have never used, and are never likely to.

- What tasks does the applications software have to carry out? It is important to think through what the software will be required to do. Larger, more complex products that have a lot of features and functions that will never be used will sit on a system and take up memory, as well as costing more for the initial purchase.

- What is the available memory on the system? As well as the computer's main memory, which needs to have sufficient space available to load and run the software, there is another type of memory for computers that is used as a temporary memory to run applications that have been opened and data in use. This type of memory is known as RAM (random access memory). It is important to check the size of RAM on a computer before purchasing applications software, as some larger applications such as graphics packages will need a high level of RAM in order to run efficiently.

Generic, specific and bespoke applications software

Once all the above factors have been taken into consideration, the decision can be made as to whether to purchase readily available software or to have software designed specifically to meet the user's needs. Applications software is generally broken down into generic, specific or bespoke.

■ **Generic applications software** – software that is readily available and is sometimes known as general purpose software. Generic applications software includes programs such as word processing, graphics, databases, spreadsheets, DTP and presentation. The applications software is designed for general use in a wide range of tasks. For example, word-processing software can be used in many different contexts: letter writing, report writing, book writing, and many others. This type of software can be purchased 'off the shelf' from a shop selling computer software.

■ **Specific applications software** – software that is designed for one specific purpose. For example, we previously listed financial and accounts processing software as a type of applications software. These software packages would be considered specific applications software as they are designed purely to run financial and accounts data. You could not, for example, write a letter using this type of software, whereas with a word-processing package you could run a basic accounting table.

■ **Bespoke applications software** – software that the user has written specifically for a required task. It is sometimes known as 'tailor-made' software. A large company might, for example, have its own stock-control system written specifically for its needs. This is usually a more expensive way of acquiring applications software than using generic or specific packages but if readily available software does not meet user requirements then it might save costs in the long run. Bespoke applications software can often be written by a programmer in-house, especially in larger companies. If staff within a company do not have the technical capability of writing the software, a software house or consultant will need to be brought in to write the software program. Acquiring bespoke applications software can also be very time consuming, as the process will involve finding out user requirements, writing the program, testing it and then loading it.

■ **Integrated software packages** – groups of applications, available for purchase as a pack. For example a word-processing application, a spreadsheet application, a database application and a graphics application may be packaged together. You have probably seen or used these; examples include Microsoft Works. Integrated packages are often cheaper to purchase than the individual components would be. Also, an integrated package makes it easier for a user to move between applications (the icons and commands are usually the same or similar), and to share data between the applications. However, the quality of each application included in the package is not always as good as if the application was purchased separately. It is common for some functions and features to be missing from some, or all, of the applications in an integrated package. A lot of applications available in Microsoft Works, for example, are watered-down versions of the applications available in Microsoft Office or those purchased individually, such as Microsoft Access. Office suites, such as Microsoft Office and Lotus SmartSuite, are fully functional packages bundled together by the same manufacturer.

8.2 Web-browser software

This software is required to view the World Wide Web on the Internet. There are two common brands of web-browser software, Netscape Navigator and Internet Explorer. Other web browsers are also available. Web browsers read the HTML (hypertext mark-up language) code for a page that the user has requested, and convert the coding to a user-friendly format that is displayed on the screen. Any HTML coding that has indicated a word or graphic should be a link to another area of information will be recognised by the web-browser software and displayed as such to the user. An example of HTML coding and how this would be displayed is given below.

Figure 25

The HTML coding for the Heinemann web page logo

```
<!DOCTYPE HTML PUBLIC "-//W3C//DTD HTML 4.01 Transitional//EN">
<html>
<head>
<meta http-equiv="Content-Type" content="text/html; charset=null">
<meta http-equiv="Content-Type" content="text/html; charset=iso-8859-1">
<title>Heinemann – inspiring generations</title>
```

Figure 26

The Heinemann web page logo as it appears

Within web-browser software, many different features and functions are available, which we will look at in more detail in Section 9.

Activity 11

T & S Limited is very satisfied with the consultancy work you have previously performed for them. They would now like you to advise them on the type of software to use for their needs. As well as having a database for employer and job seeker details, they want to be able to:

- produce leaflets and brochures to promote their company
- keep their own accounting system rather than employ an external accountancy firm
- produce word-processed documents.

You must produce the following:

- a presentation outlining the functions of an operating system and explaining how the software works with the system
- a short report recommending:
  – the type of software to install
  – any utility programs you think they require.

Justify your recommendations.

Test your knowledge

1. What is the difference between systems software and application software?
2. Describe three functions of an operating system.
3. Which interface uses WIMP? What is meant by the term WIMP?
4. Describe two different utility programs that could be used and explain why they are used.
5. What is the function of a device driver?
6. Describe the differences between generic, specific and bespoke applications software.

Exam questions

1. You have installed a new piece of applications software onto a stand-alone PC. You then find that the printer attached to the PC fails to produce what can be seen on the screen in that package.

   Explain clearly why this might happen. *(2 marks)*

   AQA Specimen question

   The following question also requires knowledge gained from sections 10 and 12:

2. A new printer is supplied with printer driver files. The files are provided both on a floppy disk and on a CD-ROM. The CD-ROM also contains sound files for use with the printer.

   (a) Describe the functions of a printer driver. *(2 marks)*
   (b) State **one** reason why the sound files are not provided on a floppy disk. *(1 mark)*
   (c) Give **one** possible use of the sound files. *(1 mark)*

   AQA May 2001

   The following question also requires knowledge gained from Section 9:

3. A small company is purchasing a new computer system and software. The new software includes an operating system, and generic package software which contains an application generator.

   (a) Give **three** tasks that are performed by an *operating system*. *(3 marks)*
   (b) State **three** characteristics of *generic package software*. Illustrate your answer with **three** different examples of the type of packages that could be chosen by the company.

   (The use of brand names will not gain credit.) *(6 marks)*

   (c) State **two** characteristics of an *application generator*. *(2 marks)*

   AQA May 2001

9 Software capabilities

This section will provide coverage of the following key areas:

- Describe the general characteristics of generic packages and the integration of objects and facilities for processing data protocols and standards

- Describe the desirable features of packages that would be appropriate to particular users and activities such as: links to other packages; search facilities; macro capabilities; application generators; editing capabilities; ability to change or extend data and record structures; short access times; data portability and upgrade paths

- Explain the technical and human implications of package change/upgrade

- Explain the difficulties of thoroughly testing complex software.

In the last section we looked at the types of generic software that are commonly available. We considered the fact that generic software is capable of performing a wide range of tasks across different applications. Generic software packages have other capabilities, apart from the purpose for which they were bought. It is important to consider factors other than tasks the software is capable of performing, such as how reliable the software is, and whether or not it can be upgraded to a newer version.

9.0 Common features of generic software packages

Generic software packages often have a range of available features that can help the user perform many other tasks apart from its original purpose. These 'extra' features will depend on the type of software that is purchased, but can include the following.

Editing capabilities

Nearly all software packages provide editing capabilities. Functions such as copy, cut, paste, delete, insert, undo, select all and find will save the user time when working on a document or file. Some software packages also provide editing features for people other than the author, for example review features such as highlighting a suggested change to a document.

Search facilities

Software packages usually include a search and/or find facility to make life easier for the user. If you choose this option from the menu, a window will be displayed that allows the user to either search for a specific word or phrase, or have the option of replacing that word or phrase once it has been found. This feature can be used to edit documents quickly and easily where necessary. For example, if a lengthy report about a new product has been produced on a word-processing package and it is then decided to change the name of the new product, instead of having to read through the document and change each name by hand, the search/find facility can be used to find the old product name and replace it with the new one. Alternatively, if someone is querying a phrase that has been used in the report, rather than call it up on screen and scroll through to find the phrase that is being discussed, the search facility can be used to find it and, if necessary, edit it.

Figure 27

Edit menu options in Microsoft Word

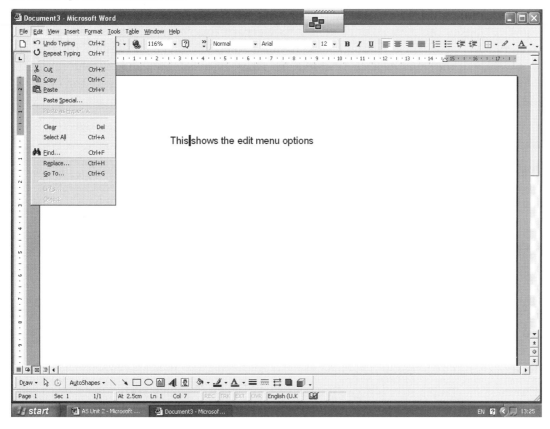

Figure 28

Find and replace window in Microsoft Word

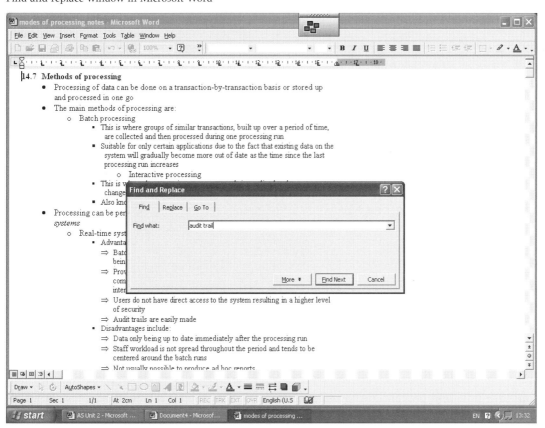

Object integration

One of the most common features available with generic software packages is the ability for the user to integrate objects into a file or document. An object is a collection of data and instructions needed to carry out a particular task, and is usually represented visually. For example, a Home button on a website is the set of data that includes the image or text shown and tells the computer where on the screen to place the button. The coding will give instructions on how to draw the button and where on the button to place the image or text.

Objects that can be integrated include graphics, text, charts and graphs, worksheets, slides, presentations, video clips and sound.

Object linking and embedding (OLE) is a way of placing objects into the current file or document, so you can still edit the object in its original software package. Linking objects and embedding objects are two different techniques that can be used, and the way in which the object is integrated will depend on its use within the destination document or file.

Linking an object means that once the object has been inserted, any editing can be carried out in the original software package from which the linked object was inserted. This is because the object is stored not in the destination document or file but in its original source file. The destination document or file stores the location where the linked object can be found, and when the document or file is opened, the object is collected from that location and displayed within the destination document or file without opening the source file. If you were to edit the object in its original software package, the next time you opened the destination document or file the changes would automatically be reflected in the object displayed.

This may sound a bit complicated, but you may have experience of linking without realising that this is the technique being used. For example, you may have inserted an image from a graphics package into a word-processing document you are working on and decided that you needed to make some changes to the image. If you double-click on the image, the original graphics package from which the image was inserted will open automatically, allowing you to edit it. This makes life easier for you, the user.

By using the 'Insert', 'Object' option within a software package, you can either insert an object that already exists in another format, or you can choose to create a new one. If you choose to create a new object, a new window containing the software package in which you are going to create your object will open, allowing you to create it and then insert it automatically into the document (see Figure 29 on the next page).

Embedding an object means that when you integrate the object in the document or file you are working on, it is then constantly present and saved within that document or file. It can often still be edited within the original software package by double-clicking on the object, but the main difference is that if you edit the object in the original software package, the changes will not show in the document or file in which you have already integrated the object.

Macro capabilities

A macro is a piece of simple programming that can be incorporated into a command or keystroke to call up some previously written data or set of instructions. The programming records the required data or instructions and stores it under a series of keys or under a command key on the keyboard. For example, shortcut keys are often used to copy and paste data (ctrl-C and ctrl-V). A macro to give the computer instructions to carry out these functions when these keys are used in the correct sequence has been developed for these shortcut keys.

Macros can save time and prevent errors, as long strings of data can be recorded into a macro. For

Figure 29

The insert object window in Microsoft Word showing some of the choices available

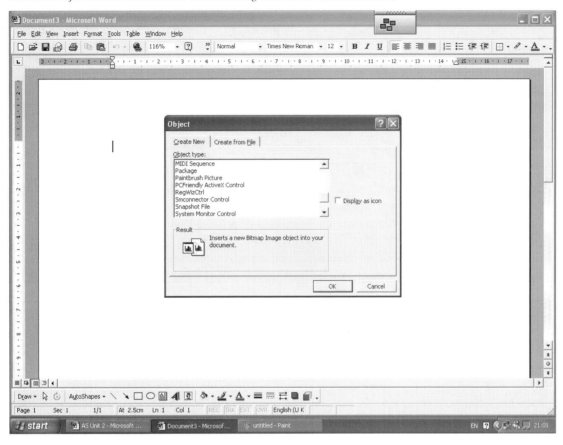

example, a law company may use a macro to produce standard paragraphs for legal documents such as house deeds.

Application generators

An application generator creates code that then produces a program, without the user having to write any program code. It uses built-in instruction sets to create the code. For example, in database development a user can create a user interface that consists of data from different files by linking them through the application generator, or create a simple input form that is more user friendly than inputting data via a table. The user can follow a set of on-screen instructions, making the relevant choices to specify the type of interface and functions required, and the behind-the-scenes programming will be completed through the application generator recognising the choices being made.

The advantages to the user of an application generator are that it is a quick way of producing an application that does what is required without having to have any specialist programming knowledge. The limitations are that the user may not be able to produce the most efficient application possible, or the application may not be able to do everything that is required by the user due to limitations of the package.

Report generators

A report generator is software that allows reports to be designed and created using data from one or more files, often existing as part of a database management system. The user inputting certain criteria selects the files or records to be used and the report is designed by the user instructing the report generator how the fields are to be displayed and laid out on the report. Once a report has been created it can be saved and the same format used again. Report generating capabilities can be an important factor in considering which database software package to use, as this can provide a flexible way to output the data.

The ability to change or extend data and record structures

This is an important factor when developing databases. The software should allow the user to make changes in the structure of an existing database in order to update or improve it. If another set of data needs to be included after the database has been designed and built, more fields will need to be added. Alternatively, if a set of data is no longer required within a database, the field will need to be deleted. It is important to ensure that this can be carried out without the loss of any required data. Modern versions of relational database management software normally have this capability, but earlier versions did not.

Short access times

Users require software to respond to commands quickly. For example, if a search/find function was very slow, it would be quicker for the user to read through the document rather than use this function. Software packages may have many different features but these are only a bonus for the user if they are quicker to use than manual methods.

Data portability

Data portability is the ability to transfer data from one software package to another, for example by copying and pasting. Having this ability could save the user time and reduce input errors, as data does not have to be input more than once even if it is required in different software packages. The ability to transfer data between different versions of the same software package is also a consideration. By using filters it is possible in some software packages to transfer data between different brands, for example Rich Text format or comma separated values to transfer text between different word-processing packages, or cell values between different spreadsheet packages.

Activity 12

Prepare a short presentation to show your understanding of:

- linking between packages
- macros
- report generators
- changing or extending data and record structures
- search facilities
- application generators
- edit functions
- data portability.

Use screen shots where necessary to emphasise your points.

9.1 Software upgradability

If your home software needs to be upgraded, it can normally be done without encountering many problems. The files and documents you need to access are held only on one hard drive and a software upgrade will not normally affect existing data held on your computer. The most important thing that you, as an end-user, would need to consider would be the ability to use all your data in the newer version of software.

Software upgrade paths

If a user decides to upgrade a software package, it is important that any existing data that has been created on the old version can still be accessed and used on the new version. Most software companies now ensure that this is possible. When you create documents in a new version of software, it is not always possible to then open and edit them in the older version. For example, if you have created a document in Microsoft Word 97 and you upgrade your system to Office 2000 with Word 2000 incorporated, you should be able to transfer across all existing Word 97 documents and be able to open and edit them in Word 2000. However, if you create a document in Word 2000 and then want to transfer it via a floppy disk to a friend's computer that runs Word 97, the document format will not be recognised and you will be unable to open it.

The term given to the ability to use older files and documents in new software is 'backwards compatibility', and one of the reasons that software is being produced with this compatibility is the standards and conventions that are now in place for software manufacturers. The term given to the ability to use data in a possible future product is 'upwards compatibility' or 'forwards compatibility'.

Software upgrade considerations

If a company decides that it requires its software to be upgraded, many other factors need consideration, especially if it is running a networked system. These could include:

- **Budget considerations.** There are many different aspects to consider when costing the upgrading of a system, or individual software packages:
  - Cost of the software – how many licences will be needed? Does the upgrade really offer value for money, i.e. are the extra features going to be so useful that it is worth investing in the upgrade?
  - Cost of training – even if the upgrade offers only a few extra features, the likelihood is that some commands and the way in which the software behaves will have altered. Staff must be trained on the new version to ensure that it is used correctly and efficiently. Another consideration would be who is to carry out the training. Is there someone within the company who can train the other staff, or will the company need to run in-house training with a trainer from outside the company, or send staff on external training days? All these will cost money, as staff will be away from their jobs during the training.
  - Cost of help facilities – if a new software version is in use, even after training staff will often encounter difficulties until they are used to the way the new software works. In-house help might require extra staff for a while. Is an expert available externally who can be contacted for help?

■ **Compatibility of existing hardware**

– Even if you are able to use older-version data on the upgrade version, it is possible that the hardware might not be compatible. The upgrade might mean that the system is running slowly, as the upgraded software might take more storage space. Also, sometimes peripherals such as scanners and printers may not be compatible with a newer version of software. All these must be taken into consideration when looking at upgrading. Cost will also be a consideration here because if the entire system requires upgrading in order to run upgraded software, this will become an extremely expensive upgrade.

■ **System unavailability**

– Whatever software is being loaded onto the system takes time, and the system will not usually be able to run while this is taking place. The importance of the system being available for use will need to be taken into account, along with how much money the company might lose if the system has to be down for a period of time. This problem can be overcome if the software upgrade is being performed on a centralised network, as the software is loaded directly onto the central server and can then be accessed by users connected to the central server. Upgrades on a centralised network would normally take place overnight or over a weekend, when the system is likely to be less busy.

■ **Compatibility with other organisations**

– Even though a software, and possibly hardware, upgrade might be expensive and inconvenient, it could be that it is the only way for a company to survive in the marketplace. Companies often communicate with suppliers or customers using EDI or exchanging documents through e-mail attachments. If the recipients of these documents use a newer version of software, an upgrade will become essential for commercial reasons – the company may lose customers and have to switch suppliers if they cannot use the same communication methods.

9.2 Software reliability

When looking at software reliability, we are looking at how smoothly the software will run; in other words, how many errors might occur while using it. It must also be able to do what it was designed to do – for example, if it is a word-processing package, can you type in it? This is an obvious example, but there are times when testing the functions of software is vital, for example the software used in air-traffic control.

It is important for software manufacturers to have a good reputation, so they need to ensure that each piece of software is as error free as possible. It is impossible to make software completely error free, as a manufacturer can never predict all the possible problems that might occur. However, with good design and thorough testing, the manufacturer can ensure that the software is reliable and robust. Robustness means that if an error does occur, the software is capable of dealing with it by informing the user that an error has occurred and suggesting what the user can do to correct it, or how the user can ensure that data is not lost due to the software crashing.

There are several tests that manufacturers can perform on software before it is released to the general public. These will be discussed in depth on the A2 course. Most software manufacturers perform testing both internally and externally.

■ Internal testing includes white-box testing and black-box testing. **White-box** testing is carried out to ensure that the correct paths exist within the software program, so it is a way of testing the physical structure of the software. **Black-box** testing is carried out to ensure that the software does what it is supposed to do – it is a way of testing the functions of the software. This is also known as **alpha testing**.

■ External testing is where end-users are provided with a copy of the software and test it by using it for the purpose it was designed for. For example, if a new computer game were at the testing stage, once the white-box and black-box testing had been completed, the game would be given to people who play computer games frequently. They would play the game for an agreed number of hours, and report to the manufacturer any problems they encountered. This is also known as **beta testing**.

Test your knowledge

1 Describe three common features of generic software packages.
2 Explain the terms 'backwards compatibility' and 'upwards compatibility'.
3 Describe two factors that need to be considered when upgrading software.
4 Explain the terms 'alpha testing' and 'beta testing'.

Exam questions

1 State **two** editing facilities that are offered by word-processing software. *(2 marks)*
AQA Jan 2001

2 A spreadsheet package has macro capabilities.

(a) Describe what is meant by the term *macro*. *(2 marks)*
(b) Give **two** examples of situations where the use of macros would be appropriate. *(2 marks)*
AQA Jan 2001

3 Why does commercially available software not always function correctly when installed onto a computer system? *(2 marks)*
AQA Specimen question

4 There is now a wide range of software tools available to increase the productivity of the end-user. Two such software tools are application generators and report generators.

(a) Explain what is meant by an application generator. *(2 marks)*
(b) Explain what is meant by a report generator. *(2 marks)*
(c) Give an example of when it might be sensible to use each one. *(2 marks)*
AQA Specimen question

10 Hardware

This section will provide coverage of the following key area:

■ Describe the broad characteristics, capabilities and limitations of processing devices and output devices and identify appropriate contexts for their use.

Hardware is the physical components of computer systems. The main hardware components of a system are:

■ input devices
■ communications devices
■ output devices.
■ storage devices
■ processing devices

We have looked at input devices in Section 1 and storage devices in Section 7, and will be looking at communications devices in Section 11. We will now look at the other hardware components.

10.0 Processing devices

In Section 4 we looked at the way in which data is processed. A processing device is the piece of hardware that will perform the instructions sent by a program held in the computer's memory. This is often referred to as the CPU (central processing unit). The processor interacts with the main memory of the system, auxiliary storage devices, input devices and output devices. It is the central part of the system, without which the system cannot be used for its intended purpose: to input, process and output data.

Figure 30

The function of the CPU in a computer system

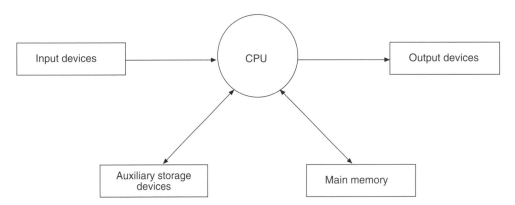

The processing device inside the computer is usually a computer chip, and most computers will have one processor. However, larger systems may use two processing chips to ensure that if a long process is being run another processor is available, meaning other processing work can still be performed.

The speed at which a computer runs depends on the processor, so the quicker the processor speed, the quicker the work can be completed. Most PCs on sale in 2003 work at between 1 and 3 gigahertz, although higher-specification models are rapidly being introduced.

10.1 **Output devices**

Section 6 looked at the format in which data and information can be output and at the importance of remembering the target audience for the output. An output device is the hardware component that enables data and information to be seen by the user and others.

There are many different ways to output data and information. A few will be looked at in detail below.

Visual display screen

A visual display screen is a computer screen used to display the output. The screen is also called a monitor or VDU (visual display unit).

Figure 31

Display properties window showing different options available

These devices have different settings that can ensure the end-user is able to view the data or information in the way that suits him or her best. By accessing the display properties from the control panel of the computer, a user can set a theme for the display, choose a background image, choose a screen saver, decide on a colour scheme for the appearance of folders, text etc., and select settings such as the colour profile.

Activity 13

An end-user wants to change his display settings, but does not know what can be changed and how to do this.

Investigate the display properties than can be altered. Write a short report for the end-user detailing your findings. In the report, explain what each display property does, the options available for each, and how to change them.

Printer

A printer is an output device that takes data output from a computer and transfers it to a paper-based format. Printers can be very different in their speed, cost and size and all of these should be considered when purchasing. Also, printers require print cartridges or ribbons – the part that contains the ink. These can prove to be expensive to replace when the ink runs out. When looking at printer specifications, the things to consider are:

- Colour – a colour printer will cost more to maintain, as it will use several print cartridges. It can also be slower than monochrome printers (printers that use black ink only).

- Speed – different printers operate at different speeds, and for some users who print large documents this may be an important consideration.

- Memory – printers have their own memory, usually quite a small amount. The amount of available memory can affect the speed of print. Extra memory can be added to some printers to speed up the printing process.

- Resolution – the resolution is the quality of the print and is measured in dots per inch (dpi). The better the quality required, the higher the resolution that will be needed.

As with software, it is not necessarily the printer with the best features that will be suitable for a user's needs. Top-end printers are very expensive. There are three main types of printer:

- Dot matrix – this uses ink dots to produce the image on paper. The print head consists of wire-pins that are punched against a ribbon onto the paper as it is fed through. It is the combination of wire-pins that are punched each time that produce the shape output onto the paper. Dot-matrix print output quality depends on the number of wire-pins in the print head. A 9-pin print head will output a lower quality of print than a 24-pin print head. A dot-matrix printer is an impact printer; the image is made by the impact of the wire-pins against the ribbon and the paper, similar to the way in which a typewriter works. Impact printers can be adapted for use with blind people and are called Braille printers. Dot-matrix printers are also used in many commercial situations. For example, most till receipts are printed using dot-matrix technology, as are credit/debit card receipts. The speed of a dot-matrix printer is normally expressed in terms of characters per second.

Figure 32

The letter A as represented as a dot matrix character

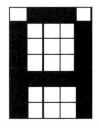

- Ink jet – this sprays tiny dots of ink, in a matrix formation, from a nozzle to produce the data characters on paper. These printers are capable of producing high-resolution print quality. Because of the way in which the print is produced, documents output from ink-jet printers often have wet ink on them and must be left to dry before being handled. An ink-jet printer is a non-impact printer.

- Laser – this uses technology similar to that of a photocopier. When the print command is initiated, a laser beam draws the document onto a drum within the printer through an electrical charge. Once this has been completed, the drum is rolled in print toner which sticks to the electrically charged sections of the drum and is then transferred to the paper through the use of heat and pressure. Once the document has been printed, the drum is cleared of electrical charge ready for the next print run. Laser printers usually have a high speed of print, expressed as pages per minutes, and a high resolution.

Graph plotters

A graph plotter is different from a printer. It uses ink pens that follow instructions to draw images onto a paper-based output. The ink pens can be raised, lowered and moved over a sheet of paper so that lines and curves can be drawn using a combination of vertical and horizontal movements. Most plotters use vector graphics to make the image.

Speakers

Speakers are now a common output device for computer users. Some computers have speakers as an external part of the computer hardware. Other computers have speakers built into the hardware of the computer. In order to have sound output, not only speakers are required, but also a sound card.

Group activity

As a group, research the different printers currently available, looking specifically at:

- cost of purchase
- cost of print cartridges or ribbons
- speed of print
- resolution of print.

Following your research, state what type of printer you think would be best for the following users:

- a home user who prints one or two pages a month from the Internet but otherwise uses a printer for letter printing
- a home user who prints photographs that have been taken with a digital camera
- a small publishing company
- a mail order company.

Test your knowledge

1 What is a processing device?
2 What is the main difference in the way a dot-matrix printer works compared to a laser printer?
3 Describe two other output devices, giving an example for each of when they would be used.

Exam questions

The following question also requires knowledge gained from Section 7:

1 The head of a company's IT services department is to give a presentation on data security to all computer users within the company.

   (a) Give **three** methods of ensuring data security that she should include in the content of her presentation. *(3 marks)*

   (b) She decides to develop a computer-based presentation to be displayed using an LCD projector rather than creating overhead projector transparencies.

       (i) State **three** functions of presentation software that are only available for use with an LCD projector. *(3 marks)*

       (ii) Describe **two** design considerations that she needs to take into account in order to develop an effective presentation. *(4 marks)*

AQA May 2001

The following question also requires knowledge gained from sections 1 and 12:

2 A company has offices on five different sites, each office with between 10 and 20 members of staff working in it. Internal e-mail is used as a means of communicating between the staff. It has been suggested that speech recognition input and voice output might be used for the e-mail system.

(a) State the extra input and output devices each PC would need to support speech recognition input and voice output. *(2 marks)*

(b) State **two** advantages to the staff of using a speech recognition system. *(2 marks)*

(c) State **three** reasons why the speech recognition system may not be effective. *(3 marks)*

(d) State **two** disadvantages of the voice input system. *(2 marks)*

AQA Jan 2002

11 Network environments

This section will provide coverage of the following key areas:

- Describe the broad characteristics, capabilities and limitations of communications devices

- Describe the characteristics and relative advantages of network and stand-alone environments

- Describe the difference between a local area and a wide area network

- Describe the elements of network environments.

A network is a system that allows people to share information with each other. It can be a simple two-way communication network or a computer network between millions of people. Simple two-way communication networks can be anything from toy walkie-talkies to two computers side by side, linked through a cable. In this section, we will be looking at computer network environments, the ways in which computers can be linked together, and the components required to build the computer network.

When you work at home, the probability is that you are working on what is known as a 'standalone' computer. This means that your computer does not use any components, software or files from other computers. Everything you need is contained on your computer, from the hard drive with the operating system through to the software packages you have installed. When you work at your centre, you will probably use a networked computer. Most resources and files will be held on a central computer and accessed from workstations that are networked to it. For example, if you save some work onto the computer at the centre, you will probably be saving to a designated space on the central computer, not saving onto the hard drive of the computer you are working at.

11.0 Why use a networked computer system?

There are many advantages in using a networked computer system rather than standalone computers, especially in an organisational context. Networking the system will mean that organisations can ensure communications are efficient and effective. Advantages of a networked system include:

- Resources and files can be shared between many people. A drive can be set up which is accessible from individual workstations for everyone in the organisation. It is often cheaper to purchase one copy of a piece of software along with a multi-user licence than to purchase individual copies and install it on all the required computers. The organisation can save money and standardise the software used throughout the business. Resources can also include peripherals, such as printers and scanners. Sharing the use of these means that the organisation does not have to invest as much money in purchasing individual peripherals for each person.

- Internal communication can be improved through the use of a company intranet and user groups, such as e-mail and newsgroups. The intranet could contain company policies and regulations, for example, along with standard documentation, all of which would be easily accessible through the use of bookmarks and links. E-mail would enable staff to communicate quickly and efficiently, sending messages and attachments with ease.

- External communication can be improved through the use of EDI, e-mail, a company website and externally accessible newsgroups. The organisation could set up a company website to attract new customers and keep existing customers informed of, for example, new products.

- Access to external websites may help staff within the organisation carry out research, check on competitors and keep abreast of any new legislation that may affect the organisation.

There are also disadvantages to consider. These include:

- Information may need to be accessed only by certain members of staff within the organisation. For example, if personal records were held on the networked system it would be a breach of the Data Protection Act if the organisation allowed all members of staff access to this information. Security measures can be set up to ensure that only authorised staff gain access to certain areas of the shared drive. One way to do this is to set up password access. The system can be programmed individually for different password entries. For example, a sales director may be able to access confidential files concerning the development of a new product, but a receptionist may not be able to. This practice is known as access rights. See Section 7 to remind yourself of the different access rights that might be used.

- Some departments may need access to specialist software that is not required by other members of the organisation. It would be not be cost effective for the organisation to purchase enough licences for every member of the organisation, but if only a certain number of licences were purchased and a greater number of people were to access the software, the organisation would be breaking the law. Again, the software a user is allowed to access and use could be restricted by access rights.

- The hardware used to set up the network might not be adequate for its use. If a large organisation did not use adequate hardware, this could cause the system to run very slowly, and even crash if it became overloaded. Users would become very frustrated and the organisation might lose money through time and data lost, or from lack of ability to perform financial transactions with customers.

- Security could become a problem if not taken into consideration before the network is designed and installed. As well as the need to adhere to legislation, other security issues would include hackers, unauthorised users, viruses, loss of data, and physical aspects such as components being stolen. We have looked at ways to address these issues in Section 7.

11.1 Network groupings

There are different ways of networking computers, but the most important difference is whether the network is set up as a local area network (LAN) or a wide area network (WAN).

What is a local area network (LAN)?

A local area network is where computers are connected across a small geographical area. Two computers in the same room connected to each other would be a LAN connection.

Figure 33

A simple LAN connection

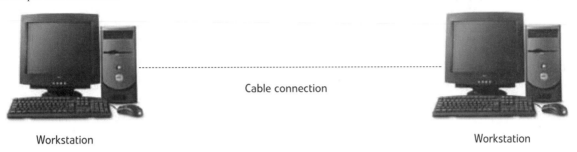

Cable connection

Workstation · Workstation

What is a wide area network (WAN)?

A wide area network is where computers are connected across a large geographical area. For example, an organisation might have offices in more than one location in the country. Let us say they have an office in London and an office in Birmingham. Because of the distance between these two offices, it would not be possible to connect computers by using a simple cable connection. The organisation would need to use other types of connection, for example a telephone line, to connect the computers.

Figure 34

A simple WAN connection

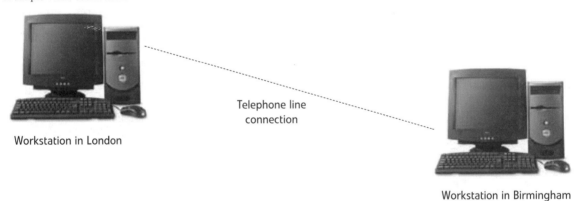

Telephone line connection

Workstation in London

Workstation in Birmingham

In both LAN and WAN connections, the workstations are usually connected to a server that holds the hardware, software, information and resources that the computers can share.

What does this mean?
Server: The name given to a central computer that stores the hardware, software and data on a network. The server then 'serves' any other users, known as 'clients', with any resources needed
Client: The name given to a workstation connected to a server. It is also the name given to software that has been designed specifically to work with a server application. For example, web-browser software is client software. It is made to work with web servers, like the Internet

11.2 Types of networks

Organisations use two basic types of local area network:

- client-server
- thin client.

Client-server network

A client-server network is where one computer acts as a server for one or more clients. This means that one computer holds most of the information, resources and software. Other computers that are networked to it can access what is needed without having the software or hardware installed on their hard disk.

Think about how you access documents and software on your school or college computers. It is likely that you use a computer in the classroom that you have to log onto. Once you have logged onto the computer, you will be able to access work that you have stored on the hard disk in your own work area. You will not able to access work that a friend has stored on the hard disk in their area. This is because you are not accessing the hard disk of the computer you are using, but the hard disk of the server computer.

The computer you are using does have its own hard disk. This can be used to store data temporarily during the lesson, to install software that is needed only within that classroom, or to process information you are working with.

The important thing to remember is that when you save something during your lesson, you are not saving it to the computer you are working on, but to the main, server computer.

Figure 35

Client-server network

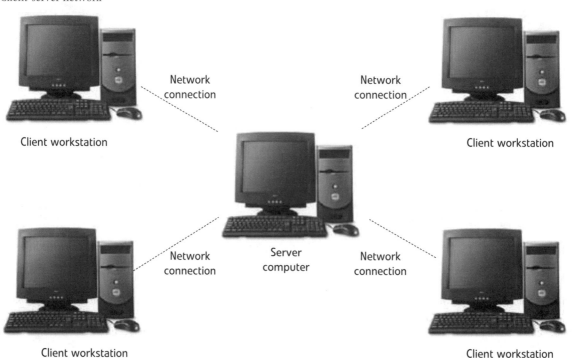

Thin client network

A thin client network is where computers are connected to a network, but each workstation does not need to have its own hard disk. There will usually be a server within the network of computers that stores all hardware, software and information that is needed. The individual workstations will not usually store any software, but will temporarily download software from the server as and when it is required.

Figure 36

Thin client network

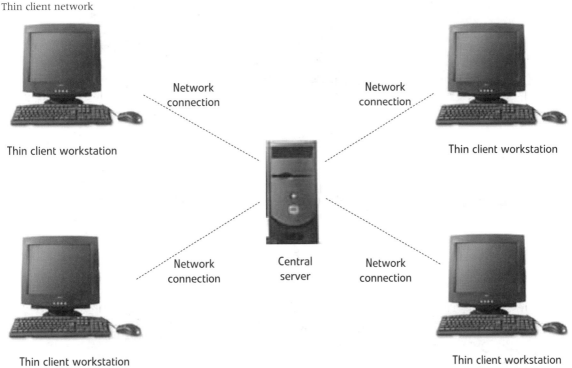

Network connection   Network connection

Thin client workstation   Thin client workstation

Network connection   Central server   Network connection

Thin client workstation   Thin client workstation

11.3 Network topologies

There are many different network topologies. A topology is the term given to the arrangement, or shape, of the different connected pieces, or **nodes.** Nodes include PCs, servers, printers, scanners and other hardware connected to the network. The most common topologies that organisations use are known as bus, star and ring.

Bus topology

This topology has been given the name 'bus' because it works in a similar way to a bus following its route on the road. All the nodes are connected to a central cable. When data is sent from one computer it is carried by the 'bus', visiting each node in turn until it reaches the correct destination. The central cable is not joined up, so the 'bus' has to travel backwards and forwards along the length of the cable to let data on and off the bus. The central cable has T connectors, sometimes called T-pins, which terminate the signal at either end. The connectors, shaped like the letter T, have three connectors; two ensure a continued signal along the cable, and one connects to the workstation. At either end of the cabling, one of the connectors on the T-pin needs to be blocked off with a small plastic or metal cap to terminate the system. These are then known as terminators rather than connectors.

Figure 37

A bus network

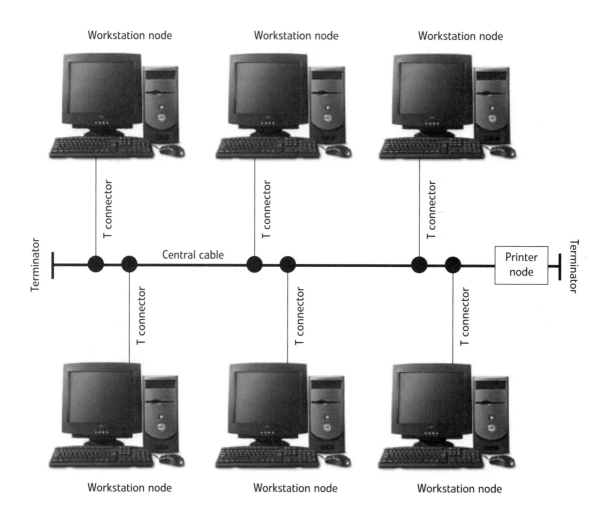

With a bus topology, there is no main computer as it is easy to connect all nodes to the central cable. There is no level of priority between the nodes; all nodes have equal status for transmitting data. For this reason, if the central cable is busy elsewhere, other transmissions have to wait their turn.

The main problem with a bus topology is that only one node at a time can send or receive data. For this reason, bus topologies are normally used for small LANs, where not many workstations are connected to the network. If more workstations are added to the network as the organisation grows, the network topology may need to be changed. If too many workstations are connected to a bus topology, the system will become very slow and the work rate will not be efficient.

The main advantage of a bus topology is that it is easy to set up, it is a reliable network connection and, because only one main cable is required, it is not as complicated to set up as other network topologies.

Star topology

This topology has been given the name 'star' because it consists of a central controlling computer, connected to nodes by individual cables. Each workstation can send and receive data from the central computer when needed, without having to wait for a turn. This means that it is a faster network than the bus topology.

The central computer is sometimes known as a hub node, as it is responsible for controlling the flow of data between the other nodes.

Figure 38

A star topology

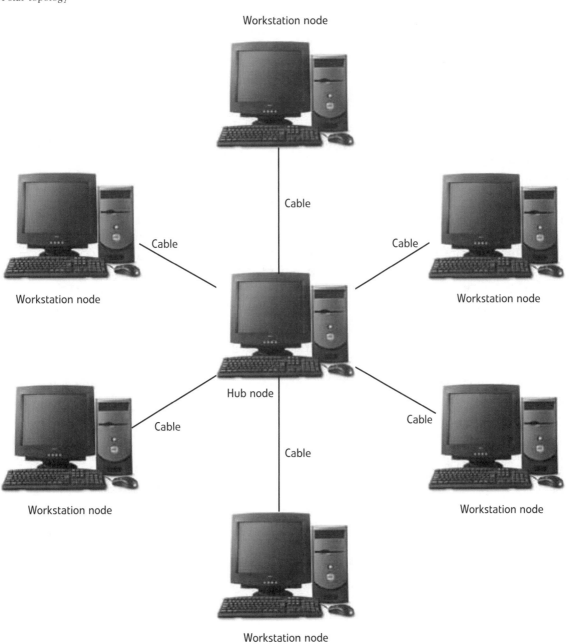

Workstation node

Cable

Cable

Cable

Workstation node

Workstation node

Hub node

Cable

Cable

Cable

Workstation node

Workstation node

Workstation node

One of the main problems with a star topology is that if the hub node has a problem or crashes, the entire network will be affected. It is likely that no one will be able to work. However, as each node is connected by its own cable, if one of the nodes has a problem then the rest of the network will be unaffected. A client-server network is normally arranged in a star topology.

There are several advantages of choosing a star topology for a network, including the following:

- Applications are held in one place, so only need installing or updating in one place.

- All data and files are held centrally, so there is more security. Back-ups can be performed centrally and access rights can be better controlled.

- If one node breaks down, it does not affect any other node in the network.

- Non-compatible computers, on different platforms, can be attached to the same star network, as all communication is through the central hub. This means that protocol differences are not an issue.

Ring topology

This topology has been given the name 'ring' because all the nodes are connected together in a circle in what is known as a 'closed loop'. Each device, whether it is a workstation or a printer, for example, is connected directly to two other devices either side of it. There is no controlling computer, and all workstations have equal status.

The way in which data is transmitted in a ring topology is by using 'tokens'. Tokens travel around the ring and a node has to have the use of a token before it can send a message. The node waits for the token to reach it, captures the token and then sends its message. Messages can be divided between more than one token. The tokens then passes around the ring, holding the message, until the correct destination is reached. The node that has been sent the message then downloads it from each token in turn, and releases the token so that it can continue passing around the ring waiting to be used again. Once all parts of the message have been received, the destination node can action that message.

The main problem with a ring topology is that if one node has a problem this affects the whole network. Another problem is that if nodes need to be added or removed, or new hardware or software put onto the network, the whole network cannot be used while this is being done.

The main advantage with using a ring topology is that because all nodes have equal status and can use a token as it passes around the ring, there should not be any situation where one user is holding up the other users.

Figure 39

A ring topology

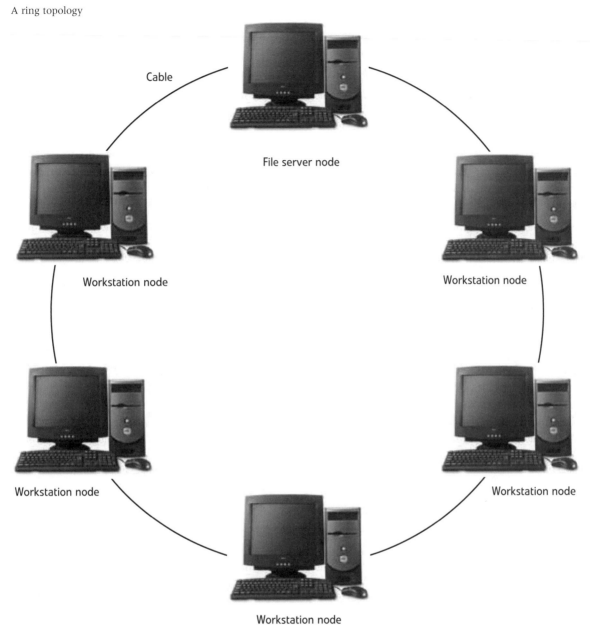

Cable

File server node

Workstation node

Workstation node

Workstation node

Workstation node

Workstation node

11.4 Hardware for local area networks

Some hardware components for LANs will be needed no matter which type of network is set up on the system. We will look at the different hardware components used in LANs, see what their objective on the network system is, and how they work.

Just as in any type of computer system, the main hardware components required will be the hard disk, monitor and keyboard. There may be other types of data capture devices on the system, depending on the nature of the organisation. Supermarkets, for example, will normally have a bar-code scanner as an input device, as well as a type of keyboard known as a concept keyboard. The computer system that you work on at school or college is likely to have a mouse as an additional data-capture component along with the keyboard.

Some types of network will not require all their workstations to have individual hard drives, but other types of networks use both the server and individual hard disks for each workstation.

To be able to access the network, each workstation will require a network adaptor (often referred to as a network card). This will be installed into an expansion slot inside the computer and acts as an interface for connection to the network. The type of network card used will depend on the network topology being used.

Once these basic components are present, other kinds of hardware will be required to connect the workstations to the network. Different types of cables and wires are required, again depending on the type of network that is being set up. The main type of cable used for networking is made of copper wire. The cable can be different types. The most common are:

- **Coaxial cable** – this is similar to the cable used for television aerials.

- **Unshielded twisted pair cable (UTP cable)** – this is a cable where the wires are twisted together in pairs and held together by a plastic covering.

- **Fibre optic cable** – this is a cable which is made up of glass or plastic fibres and carries a digital signal through a laser light. Because there is no conversion from analogue to digital, it is a much faster way of transmitting data.

Depending on the type of network being installed, you may also need a hub. This is a type of electronic switching box, and its purpose is to control the traffic flow around the network. It can also give workstations some independence from the other connected workstations. This is useful if, for example, one computer on the network develops a problem. Using a hub will mean that the other workstations can carry on working normally.

If peripherals are to be a shared resource on the network, then these items of hardware will also need to be taken into account.

Other hardware components that can be used in networks include:

- **Repeaters** – these are electronic devices that boost signals when received, before sending them on along the network. They are also used to connect two cables together in a LAN if the cable needs extending.

- **Bridges** – these are used to extend a network by linking two LANs together.

11.5 Wireless networks

Networks today do not have to be physically linked by cables. It is possible to set up a network using a wireless link through the following technologies:

- **Satellite communication** – this uses a two-way transmission beam via a satellite.

- **Infra-red communication** – this uses infra-red waves to transmit and receive data. Infra-red waves are longer than light waves, but shorter than radio waves.

- **Microwave communication** – this uses short wavelength electromagnetic radio transmission, operating at high frequencies. It can be used only over quite short distances, a few kilometres at most, as both the 'sender' and 'receiver' components must be able to 'see' each other.

You will no doubt be aware of wireless technology, even if you do not know that this is what it is called. Mobile telephones use wireless technology.

One of the main problems with wireless technology is that the connection is not as fast at the moment as when using cabling. Also, wireless connections are not as reliable as cabled connections.

However, the use of wireless connection for LANs is becoming more popular. This is because a wireless connection is easier to install; cables do not need to be laid. This can often make it a cheaper alternative for a network connection too as little building work is involved.

An example of a LAN that uses wireless technology is when stock checks are being carried out in supermarkets. You may have seen people carrying portable devices with keypads. These are terminals that have a wireless link to a central computer. When they are out on the shop floor, the stock checkers can enter codes and quantities of products into the terminal and the information is then sent through to the central computer. Many supermarkets use this method to check the prices showing on the shelves are correct, to record how many of each item is out on display so that shelf stackers can be alerted to restock, and also to enable automatic stock orders to be made if the stock level is low.

11.6 Wide area network technologies

WANs have to be connected in a different way from LANs because of the problems (or sometimes impossibilities) of connecting nodes through a simple cabling system. Wide area communication technologies that are available include the following.

Voice-band PSTN (Public Switched Telephone Network)

Voice-band PSTN is a type of modem. Modems are looked at in more detail later in this section (see page 171). It was one of the first types of modem and became available in the late 1950s. Voice-band modems work by transmitting data through the public telephone network, along the usual telephone communication line that a landline telephone uses.

There are advantages and disadvantages to using a voice-band PSTN connection.

One of the main advantages is that the telephone lines needed to connect the network are normally already available. Many standalone home PCs are connected to the Internet. While some use newer technology, there are still many that use either an internal or external modem, connected to an ordinary telephone line, which in turn will dial a number for an Internet connection. For this reason, it is often a cheap way of setting up a WAN.

One of the main disadvantages, however, is that the ordinary telephone line is what is known as an 'analogue' transmitter. We will look at the difference between analogue and digital signals on page 171, but what this basically means is that the data being transmitted has to go through two conversions in its format to get from one computer to another. This means that the transmission rate is often very slow in comparison with other connection methods.

Leased lines

Leased lines are a permanent or switched connection which links a user's computer to a service provider WAN. The line is usually leased on the basis of how often and for how long the user connects to the WAN. The user will normally pay a monthly or annual fee for the use of the line, and will probably pay extra each time they connect to the WAN. Leased lines usually use the same number to connect to the Internet as the home or business telephone.

An example of a switched connection leased line is the situation we looked at above, where an ordinary telephone line is used to connect. By using an adaptor, you can connect both a telephone and a modem to the same line. When you want to use the Internet, the modem will connect to the telephone line, and when the modem is not connected, the line can be used for the telephone.

The main disadvantage of this is that you cannot use both the telephone and the modem at the same time. So, if you are on the Internet for long periods of time, people will not be able to reach you on that telephone number. You can buy gadgets nowadays that will let you know if someone is trying to telephone you when you have your modem connected, so that you can still take your telephone calls without having to pay for an extra line to be installed.

Dedicated lines

Dedicated lines are those where a permanent connection to a WAN is set up through a different line from that of the normal telephone. In other words, a dedicated line uses a different number to connect to the Internet, not the same number as the home/business telephone. They are usually still leased lines as the user pays to be able to use the dedicated line.

The biggest advantage of using a dedicated line is that it is much quicker than using a switched line, as you do not have to wait for the line to become free in order to connect, nor do you have to wait so long for the dial-up and connection process. Your telephone will never be engaged just because you are using, for example, the Internet.

The most common domestic example of a dedicated line is the use of broadband technology, available from many telecommunications companies.

Satellite technology

Satellite communication technology uses satellites in the earth's orbit to receive and retransmit data. The signal being transmitted is known as an 'uplink'. Once the satellite has read the destination address, it can be sent back to the correct location. This retransmission of the data is known as the 'downlink'.

Because the satellite is above the earth, the transmission can be made over many thousands of miles, as there is always a line of sight between the sender and receiver.

The main disadvantage of using satellite communications is that because the data has to travel to the earth's orbit and then back again, the connection is not always reliable and there is normally an appreciable time delay.

Microwave technology

Microwave transmissions use a short wavelength electromagnetic radio transmission that operates at a high frequency.

One problem with using microwave technology for networking is that data can only be sent over fairly small distances, up to about 50km. This is because the nodes require lines of sight to be able to transmit to each other, and the earth's curvature can affect the line of sight.

Cellular radio technology

Cellular radio transmission works through a dedicated radio channel being allocated to a single transmission. While this is an efficient way of transmitting lengthy and continuous data, it can prove a waste of the dedicated bandwidth. Once a bandwidth has been allocated for a transmission, if the transmission is sent in bursts of data, the bandwidth will remain unused during other times.

Digital and analogue lines

Digital and analogue are two different types of transmission systems. Data cannot be sent directly between them unless an analogue-digital converter is used.

Analogue signals are a continuously varying set of electromagnetic waves. An example of an analogue signal would be the data sent along a telephone landline.

Digital signals are discrete voltage pulses, measured in bits per second. An example of a digital signal would be the data sent into a television via a digital cable.

Computers cannot deal with analogue signals, and some types of cabling cannot deal with digital signals. For this reason, when a node is transmitting data via an analogue line, it is converted from digital to analogue before travelling along that line. However, the user's computer at the other end of the network would not be able to read the analogue signal, so the analogue has to be converted back to digital again before entering the computer system.

Digital technology is therefore quicker and more reliable than analogue technology. This is why digital technology is one of the fastest-growing areas within the communication sector.

Modems

When using analogue transmission, a process known as 'modulation' carries out the conversion process. In order to do this, a modem is involved.

The word 'modem' comes from the two processes involved in this conversion: modulation and demodulation. When the digital signal is leaving the computer, the conversion into analogue is known as the modulation process. When the analogue signal is being converted back into a digital signal, the process is known as demodulation.

Modems can process asynchronous and synchronous transmissions.

- Asynchronous transmissions are where the data is sent at irregular intervals. So that the receiver knows when a transmission starts and stops, asynchronous transmission uses what are referred to as 'start bits' and 'stop bits'. These extra bits are added to the beginning and end of the data being transmitted.

- Synchronous transmissions are where the computer sending the data and the computer receiving the data can keep up with each other during the transmission. The data transmission is one continuous flow of data, with no irregularities. This is a quicker and more reliable method of transmission than using asynchronous transmission.

Broadband technologies

Broadband technology is a general name given to any communication method that has a faster transmission rate than that of the fastest telephone line.

Broadband is becoming more popular as a network connection, as it usually provides a permanent connection. Most broadband technologies work through a digital signal, so it is also a fast way of connecting to a network as no conversion process is required for data. Broadband technologies are capable of using a wider bandwidth than other connection technologies.

The most commonly available broadband technologies are:

- **ASDL** (Asymmetric Digital Subscriber Line). This is a high bandwidth digital service that is normally offered by telephone companies, although some ISPs (Internet service providers) can supply an ASDL. Depending on the service provided, these can supply an extremely high transmission rate.

- **ISDN** (Integrated Services Digital Network). This is a digital connection that can be set up using existing copper telephone cables. Until the introduction of ASDL, ISDN was one of the most advanced communication technologies to be introduced. ISDN has a lower transmission rate than ASDL.

- **Fibre optic cables**. These are cables consisting of glass or plastic fibres. They carry a digital signal and can have a very high transmission rate. They are also one of the most secure ways of networking. Fibre optic cables do not give off any electromagnetic radiation, so remote sensing equipment cannot detect them.

11.7 Issues concerning wide area network technology

When considering using WAN technology, some of the issues that need to be taken into account include the following.

What are data rates?

Data rates are the speed of the transmission over the network. The data transfer rate is calculated on the basis of its transmission through a channel per second. The advantages a broadband connection can give in relation to data rates have been referred to above.

Factors that determine data rates include:

- **Bandwidth**. This refers to the capacity of an information channel, i.e. how much data can be carried at one time. Analogue transmissions are measured in cycles per second; digital transmissions are measured in bits per second (bps). Modems typically work at 128 Kbps, although older versions may work at 56 Kbps. Domestic broadband works at 256 Kbps, 512 Kbps or even 1024 Kbps. Commercial links can be even faster.

■ **Delays**. These can affect the speed of a system. Delays are caused by many different things on the network. Some of the most common causes of delay are:

– the distance that the transmission has to travel
– errors occurring during transmission, and error recovery programs running to deal with errors
– the amount of 'traffic' on a network, i.e. the congestion factor, where the more connections and the more messages, the slower the transfer time of each message
– the processing capabilities of the systems involved in the transmission.

■ **Throughput**. This refers to the amount of work done by a system. In a network situation it means taking into account possible delays and then measuring system performance including delays.

 Activity 14

A small marketing company has decided that it needs to network its computers. The company currently has two offices, one in Birmingham and one in Belfast. It employs 35 people, most of whom need access to information that could be held on the network. This information is currently held on each standalone computer. Factors the company has already considered are:

■ They do not want to spend a lot of money on setting up their network system but are aware that they need to ensure they have the correct set-up for the network from the beginning.
■ They are willing to purchase a central controlling computer if this is necessary.
■ It is important that the system is never out of use for more than a few hours.
■ Most of their work is done on the computers:
– customers are contacted by telephone, but customer details are called up from a large database in order for the staff to do this
– mailshots are sent out on a regular basis to a mailing list held on a computer
– leaflets and questionnaires are designed in-house to be sent in mailshots
– administration tasks are performed on computer, such as the payroll.

You have been asked to prepare a report, which can be in presentation format or a written report, to recommend a network system for the company.

Compare the different technologies available for the connection of WANs and produce a table to show the following:

■ different technologies currently available
■ a basic explanation of how each technology works
■ any advantages or disadvantages of using each technology.

Give a recommendation for a network system that you think would best suit the company's needs, and justify your recommendation.

Test your knowledge

1 Describe one possible advantage and one possible disadvantage of using a networked computer system.
2 What is the difference between a wide area network and a local area network?
3 Explain what is meant by the term 'thin client network'.
4 Compare two network topologies, giving examples of when each could be used.
5 Describe two wide area communication technologies, giving examples of when each could be used.
6 What is the function of a modem?

Exam questions

1 Describe **two** differences between a local area network (LAN) and a wide area network (WAN).

(4 marks)
AQA Jan 2001

2 In a solicitor's practice there are 10 employees working in three offices. Each employee has a stand-alone computer system and there is a shared printer in each office. The head of the practice has been advised that it would be more efficient if the 10 computers were formed into a server-based network.

(a) State **three** benefits that the practice would gain from networking their computer systems.

(3 marks)

(b) Give **two** reasons for choosing a server-based system rather than a peer-to-peer system.

(2 marks)

(c) State **two** items of hardware that will be needed to connect these 10 computers as a server-based network. State why each item is required. *(4 marks)*
AQA May 2001

3 At the central office of a landscape gardening company there are six employees. Each employee has a stand-alone computer system and printer. The company director has commissioned a business survey which indicated that it would be more efficient if the six PCs were formed into a peer-to-peer network.

(a) State **three** benefits that the company would gain from networking their computer systems as a peer-to peer-system rather than a server-based system. *(3 marks)*
(b) What additional hardware would be needed to connect the six stand-alone computer systems as a peer-to-peer network system? State why each item is required. *(4 marks)*
AQA Specimen question

4 A small company is installing a computer network. Employees are to be issued with a handbook to help them to understand the networking terms.

Provide an explanation of the following terms for the handbook:

(a) *local area network* and *wide area network*; *(5 marks)*
(b) *server* and *peer-to-peer*. *(5 marks)*
AQA Jan 2002

12 Human/computer interaction (HCI)

This section will provide coverage of the following key areas:

- Understand the need to facilitate an effective dialogue between humans and machines
- Explain the need to design systems which are appropriate to users at all levels and in different environments, and the impact of clarity of structure and layout
- Describe how the user-interface can be designed for effective communication with the user
- Describe the advantages of common user interfaces between different generic application packages
- Describe the advantages and limitations of a natural language interface.

HCI means the interaction between a human (the user) and a computer. The interface provides the means by which the user tells the computer what to do and the computer produces a response, thus creating an interaction between them.

12.0 Importance of good interface design

Interfaces determine the ease with which the computer can be used. There are now many different interfaces through which a user can input data into the computer, which we looked at in Section 8.

The study of the human/computer interface can lead to improvements in productivity and job satisfaction, make the interface user-friendly, and make sure that work practices are safe.

Humans receive information from the outside world via the five senses:

- taste
- sight
- hearing.
- touch
- smell

In an ideal world, interfaces would incorporate as many as of these as is possible. Multimedia and virtual reality applications are good examples of this. The absolute ideal will be when interfaces become so user-friendly that communications between computers and users are like humans interacting with other humans. Although we are a long way from that, new operating systems and applications software are continually making interfaces easier to use.

12.1 Designing useable systems

Designers of interfaces have to take many issues into consideration, such as:

- Who will use the system?
- What is the computer environment like?
- What tasks is the computer performing?
- What technology is feasible?

Clarity of structure and layout is important if an interface is to be easy to learn and use. Guidelines for interface design include:

■ reduction in mouse movements

■ use of pull-down menus

■ design of pull-down menus so that the selections used most frequently are situated at the top of the menu

■ inclusion of a facility to select which icons are displayed.

Interfaces for the disabled must ensure that they are designed so that the senses unaffected by a disability are utilised. Factors that should be considered include the following.

■ A visually impaired person cannot see the screen and is not always aware when a mistake has been made – special software can be used that converts text or commands into speech. This is known as 'speech synthesis' software.

■ Some disabled users may have problems pressing individual keys – special software can be used that converts a user's spoken word into text or commands. This is known as 'speech recognition' software.

12.2 Interface styles

Interface styles were looked at in Section 8. The common interface styles include the following:

■ **Command-line/command-driven interfaces:** the user has to learn a command language similar to a specialist programming language. Examples of these are MS-DOS and UNIX. Refer back to Section 8, page 138 for an example of a command-driven interface.

■ **Menus:** full-screen menus take up the whole screen and remain in view until the user makes a selection. Pop-up menus are usually brought up by clicking the right-hand button of the mouse, and the user can then select from a list. Pull-down menus are shown only if the user clicks on a particular item in the menu.

Figure 40

An example of a screen menu and a pop-up menu in Microsoft Word

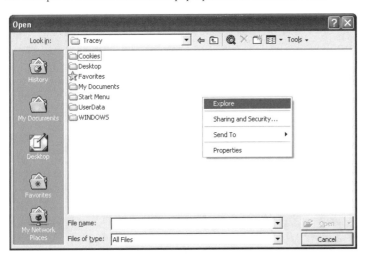

■ **Natural language:** a system whereby users can input commands or data into computers in the same way as they would talk to a person. The computer has to be able to understand what the user wants without requiring specially structured commands or data names in a particular order. The system needs to be able to cope with different ways of saying things, misspelled words, bad grammar, slang, dialect, etc. The foundation of the research into a natural language for common use is the area of artificial intelligence.

Figure 41

An example of a natural language interface from Brainhat

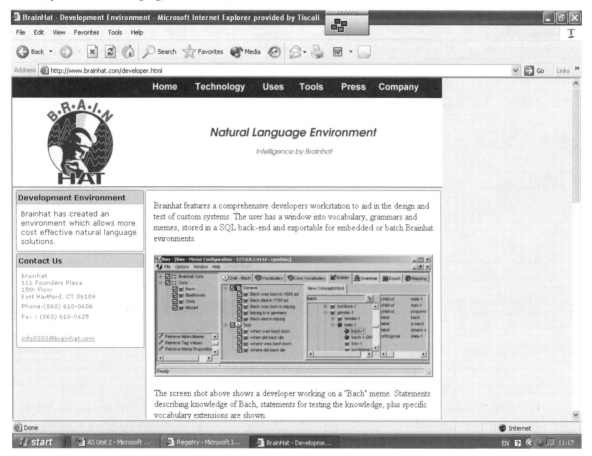

■ **Forms and dialogue boxes:** forms on a screen enable data to be entered into a system in a pre-determined and structured way. Forms usually guide the user by clearly naming each data box, and can have buttons and pick lists that give the user a drop-down list of options to choose from. Checkboxes can also be used.

Figure 42

An example of an on-line form with drop-down boxes from the Google advanced search page

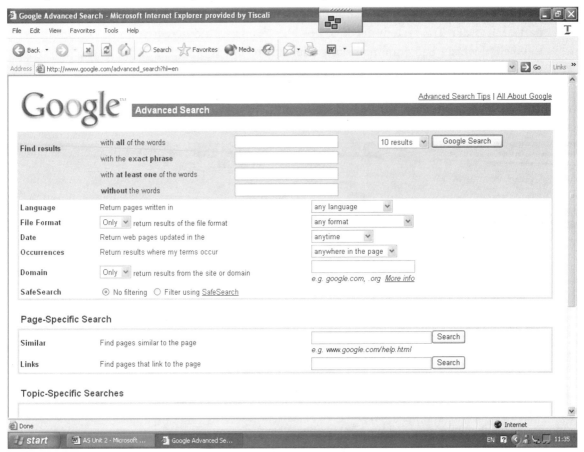

- **GUIs (graphical user interfaces):** all the memory and file management activities are taken care of by the operating system. On these interfaces users can multi-task. A mouse is used to navigate around the screen and the mouse buttons are used to make selections from icons and buttons. (Refer to Figure 24 on page 139 for an example of a GUI interface.) Dialogue boxes and pull-down menus are incorporated into the interface, with the work area usually being located in the centre of the screen. The GUI environment is referred to as a WIMP interface – windows, icon, mouse and pointer. GUIs can be used by the person programming them to influence the way the user interacts with a program, allowing the programmer to standardise the way a program works, and making it easier for users to transfer skills from one application to another. The main features of GUIs are:
  - a mouse is used as the main input device
  - overlapping windows are used
  - there are many graphics features
  - pointer-based interfaces work by using a pen-like stylus or pointer to interact with the computer (special software called handwriting recognition software is required)
  - a graphics tablet or pad can be used, where the user points to certain shapes or commands with the stylus (touch-sensitive screens which detect the pressure of a user's finger are another form of this type of interface)

– keyboards, the most usual type of interface when coupled with a screen. Dedicated keys, which are used for only one purpose and cannot be altered, use short-cuts to give commands, e.g. the page up/page down keys. Soft keys can be used for different things by different packages, e.g. the F1 to F12 keys.

12.3 Common user interfaces

There are many advantages to users having the same operating system, not only because it is easier to switch between different computers and still know how to work them, but also because generic packages will work in similar ways.

■ Common commands mean that the same combination of keys can perform the same task, whoever manufactured the software.

■ There is increased speed of learning for users as the same operational basics of one application can easily be applied to other applications.

■ There is also consistency in toolbars, menus and dialogue boxes, and customisable and operational features are similar.

■ On-line help is provided in each application in a similar way.

It is important to companies to adopt a common user interface to avoid unnecessary calls to the help line in order to sort out problems caused by changed settings. Many companies make use of a network where the software is stored on the server. When a user logs onto the system he or she is presented with the same interface and will be able to customise this for particular needs.

12.4 Speech input (voice recognition)

Speech input allows humans to communicate directly with the system, and is currently most commonly used for word-processing packages. The main advantages are that there is no longer any need to learn commands or complex procedures, and it avoids any need for devices that are difficult for those with hand-movement disabilities, such as a mouse and keyboard. Speech input is useful in preventing RSI (repetitive strain injury) and enables blind people to use computers without having to acquire specialist Braille keyboards.

However, there are problems with using speech input, including:

■ complex speech recognition software is required in order to understand what the user means, translate this into a machine command and execute it

■ different kinds of voices and different accents need to be understood

■ background noise has to be dealt with.

Speech input is most useful when using the Internet, especially for searches where an intelligent agent can search for what the user requires. Sometimes speech recognition will not be suitable and you need to bear in mind that at times another form of input could be required, e.g. if preparing a confidential letter.

Activity 15

Carry out some research into how the use of HCI is making computers user-friendly.

Prepare a short presentation to show your understanding of the meaning of HCI and make recommendations for:

- factors that should be considered when designing a user interface
- software and/or hardware adaptations for at least two people who have different disabilities
- the selection of a suitable interface style for a child aged 10.

Justify your recommendations.

Test your knowledge

1 Why is it important to ensure that computers are user-friendly?
2 What factors need to be considered to ensure clarity of structure and layout for an interface?
3 What is meant by the term 'GUI'?
4 Describe two other interface styles, giving an example for each of when they could be used.

Exam questions

1 All the staff in a small office use the same word-processing, spreadsheet and database packages. These packages all have a common user interface.

   (a) Give **four** advantages of having a common user interface. *(4 marks)*
   (b) State **four** specific features of a user interface which would benefit from being common between the packages. *(4 marks)*
   AQA Jan 2001

2 Most modern PCs make use of a GUI (graphic user interface) and have a WYSIWYG (what you see is what you get) word-processing package.

   (a) State **four** characteristics of a GUI. *(4 marks)*
   (b) Describe **three** advantages to the user of a WYSIWYG word-processing package. *(6 marks)*
   AQA May 2001

3 Speech recognition systems for personal computers are now becoming more affordable and useable.

   (a) State **two** advantages to a PC user of a speech recognition system. *(2 marks)*
   (b) Give **two** different tasks for which a PC user could take advantage of speech recognition. *(2 marks)*
   (c) Speech recognition systems sometimes fail to be 100% effective in practice. Give **three** reasons why this is so. *(3 marks)*
   AQA Specimen question

4 An Internet search engine is said to have a *natural language interface*.

   (a) Explain, using examples, **two** advantages to the user of the natural language interface. *(4 marks)*
   (b) Explain, using examples, **two** limitations of a natural language interface. *(4 marks)*
   AQA Jan 2002

UNIT 3 – COURSEWORK:
THE USE OF GENERIC APPLICATION SOFTWARE FOR TASK SOLUTION

This unit will help to support you in the selection, development, design and implementation of a suitable project using generic application software.

The unit is divided into a number of key sections covering the following issues:

- project considerations
- process skills - review of applications software packages
- specification
- implementation and testing
- evaluation
- documentation – user guide.

For this project you are required to undertake a 'task-related problem which will have a limited scope and will be self-contained'.

The value of each of the project areas is as follows:

Specification	13 marks	Implementation	20 marks
User testing	12 marks	Evaluation	6 marks
User documentation	9 marks		

1 Project considerations

There are a number of factors to consider when taking on a project and working within a project environment. Some of these have been identified in Figure 1 below.

Figure 1

Project considerations

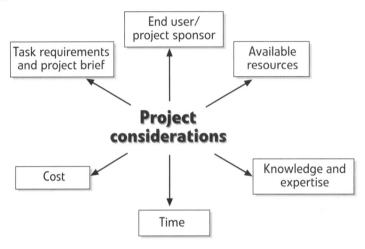

- **End user/project sponsor:** this can be a single person, a department or an entire organisation. The end user/project sponsor will commission the project. They will provide a project brief identifying:

  1 Background to the problem
  2 Project requirements
  3 Proposals for overcoming the problems identified
  4 Information on the users and resources the project will impact upon
  5 Project constraints, e.g. time or money.

  You are accountable to the end user/project sponsor; you will need to ensure that you fulfil the requirements of the project brief and possibly report back at key stages on progress made.

  For your project, the end user can be defined as your teacher, or a real end user, e.g. an employer.

- **Task requirements and project brief:** this will outline the requirements of the project and the expectations of the people undertaking the project.

- **Available resources:** in order to meet the requirements of a given project, certain resources may be required. These can include:

  – hardware
  – software
  – money
  – time
  – people.

■ **Cost:** this is a major consideration and constraint for the majority of projects. How much will it cost to complete? If you have been allocated a certain budget you must ensure that all factors impacting upon the development and implementation of the project have been accounted for within the budget.

■ **Knowledge and expertise:** people who have a certain set of skills or expertise will undertake certain projects. A project team may consist of a number of different people who each contribute individual skills and expertise.

■ **Time:** This is a major issue, especially when a project has to be completed within a certain period. Time is also important when linked with cost, because 'time is money'. The longer it takes to complete the project, the more delay is caused to operations and procedures. This could cost an end user hundreds or even thousands of pounds.

All projects will follow a life-cycle that extends from the initial investigation through to the final evaluation. Depending upon the nature of your project, some stages are more important than others. A traditional project life-cycle model is shown in Figure 2.

Figure 2

Project life-cycle model

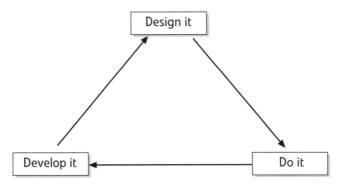

■ **Design it:** identify needs and wants, analyse, propose, justify and agree

■ **Do it:** gather necessary resources, carry out activities, implementation and testing

■ **Develop it:** review and evaluation.

When you are working on your own task-based solution, it may help to set up a framework that you can follow to ensure you have covered each step. Some of the stages such as investigation, analysis, design and testing are quite prescriptive in that you would need to ensure these are completed in order to succeed with your solution. Other stages, such as review and evaluation, will help you to assess why your project has been a success or failure.

Documentation forms an integral part of the project life-cycle, and although it is not highlighted in the model it is assumed that documentation will be provided to support each stage of the cycle.

2 Process skills – review of applications software

In order to meet the requirements of the project, you are expected to use applications software tools:

'The solution is very likely to be based on the facilities of one piece of generic software but candidates are encouraged to use other software tools and objects as appropriate to complete the solution.'

To assist you in your choice of applications software a review of some of the more generic packages will be given in this section. The software to be reviewed includes:

- word-processing and desk-top publishing
- database
- presentation
- spreadsheet
- graphics
- multimedia.

Although you may use only one piece of generic software, other software tools may be selected and integrated into the project; for example, word-processing tools may be used to assist in the preparation of user guides and user documentation.

Each area below includes a list of acceptable advanced features which would show more than just a layperson's knowledge of the package. The use of a variety of these features will earn you an improved mark.

2.0 Word-processing

Word-processing software is commonly used because of its simplicity and the types of multi-functioning tasks it can perform.

For this task-based project, word-processing software can support you in the preparation and writing of any documentation. Depending upon the nature of the task, it can also be used in the following activities:

- producing standard templates
- producing logos and letterheads
- mail-merging documents
- producing documents that require specific formats, e.g. tables or columns
- basic desk-top publishing.

Examples of these can be seen in Figure 3.

Figure 3
Uses of word-processing software

Producing standard templates: Reports

IT DEPARTMENT
PROJECT REPORT

PROPOSALS FOR IMPROVING EFFICIENCY IN IT DEPT

Richard G. Wright

24 January 2003

PROPOSALS FOR IMPROVING EFFICIENCY IN IT DEPT

1 Introduction

The introduction should provide a short summary of the overall focus and content of the report.

2 Procedures

Identification of any procedures used to collect, collate, analyse and present information.

3 Main findings

The main findings section is where the bulk of the report content should be placed. The section should be broken down into task, action or research areas. Each area of the findings section should put forward arguments or statements supported by research and analysis. The main findings section can be broken down further into sub-sections, for example:

3.1	Feasibility study
3.1.1	Fact-finding techniques
3.1.2	Requirements analysis
3.1.3	User analysis.

4 Conclusions

The conclusion section should bring together all of the items discussed within the main findings section and provide a summary of the key areas identified.

5 Recommendations

This section is solution based, providing the subjects of the report with proposals as to how they can move forward with the report objective.

References

This section should identify and give credit for all information sources used, including books, magazines or journals, other documents or reports, the Internet, etc.

Appendices

This section will provide supporting documentation. Appendices could include lists of facts and figures, leaflets, downloaded information, etc.

Logos and letterheads

For all your building needs

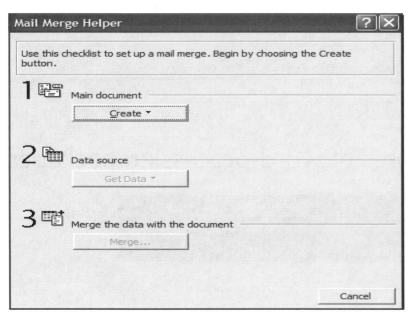

Mail-merging

Table

TEST PLAN	passed	not passed
Can enter data formats	✓	
Validates data formats	✓	
Produces a report		✗

- *Table: Testing criteria for applications software project*

Basic desk-top publishing

Advanced features of word-processing packages

Tables	Columns	Merging text and lists
Graphics	Watermarks	Templates
Indexing	Table of contents	Links/hyperlinks

2.1 Spreadsheet

Spreadsheets are a common project-development and support tool. They are used to:

- produce and display numerical, graphical and statistical data, such as:
  - sales forecasts
  - profit and loss accounts
  - general expenditure
  - wage and salary information
  - distribution facts
- forecast information
- calculate information
- analyse information
- automate procedures.

Figure 4

Sample spreadsheet to calculate and forecast information

Microsoft Excel - Sales forecast example

File Edit View Insert Format Tools Data Window Help

Arial 12 B I U

SUM X ✓ = =SUM(B5:B14)

	A	B	C	D	E	F	G	H	I	J
1	**Sales forecast spreadsheet January-June 2003**									
2										
3		January	February	March	April	May	June	July		
4		£	£	£	£	£	£	£		
5	Part A	12,000	5,600	4,800	4,700	5,000	11,900	11,200		
6	Part B	3,400	3,900	1,200	3,400	4,678	6,900	2,578		
7	Part C	4,900	6,765	4,500	3,900	9,555	5,372	8,900		
8	Part D	6,100	10,970	9,230	4,776	1,345	3,400	7,200		
9	Part E	7,200	4,390	8,900	9,444	10,670	11,900	4,877		
10	Part F	3,900	2,300	5,670	1,455	4,899	3,800	9,300		
11	Part G	6,890	3,100	2,400	3,299	4,777	4,378	2,355		
12	Part H	7,970	6,000	1,900	7,900	6,488	8,944	3,788		
13										
14										
15	Total	=SUM(B5:B14)								
16										

Advanced features of spreadsheet packages

Charts and graphs	Filtering/sorting	Pivot tables
Functions	Exporting/importing	OLE
Macros	Input forms/mechanisms	Ranges
Formulae	Multi-sheet workings	Auto start-up and close
Formatting	Locking and protection	

2.2 Database

Database software can certainly be used as an ICT solution for a task-based problem, but databases are quite complex to design properly – especially if the intention is to link information, build data structure relationships and fully integrate the tables and forms with a reporting or menu system.

In order to get the optimum benefit from a database it is also recommended that validation controls, queries and integrity constraints are used. These features may be too advanced to learn and apply at this level.

If a database route is desired, however, a number of projects can be developed using this software. These include:

- referencing and recording systems (cataloguing books, CDs, videos or DVDs)

- storage systems (stock control, financial data, insurance claims records, etc.)

- booking and reservation systems (hotels, holidays, flights, etc.)

- contact information (accessing and updating customer records, supplier details, membership records, etc.)

Sample input, output and query screens are reproduced in the figures below for guidance.

Figure 5

Producing tables

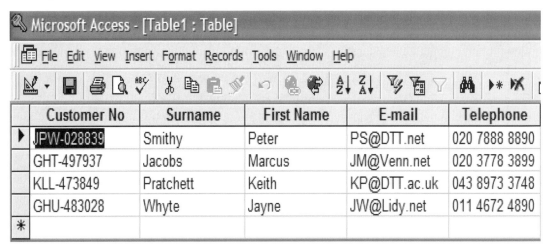

Figure 6

Producing forms

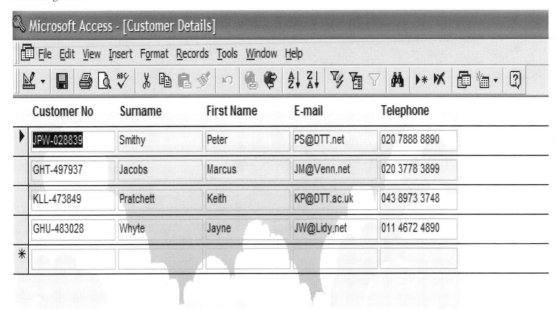

Figure 7

Producing reports

Customer report

Customer No	JPW-028839
Surname	Smithy
E-mail	PS@DTT.net
Customer No	GHT-497937
Surname	Jacobs
E-mail	JM@Venn.net
Customer No	KLL-473849
Surname	Pratchett
E-mail	KP@DTT.ac.uk
Customer No	GHU-483028
Surname	Whyte
E-mail	JW@Lidy.net

Figure 8

Using queries

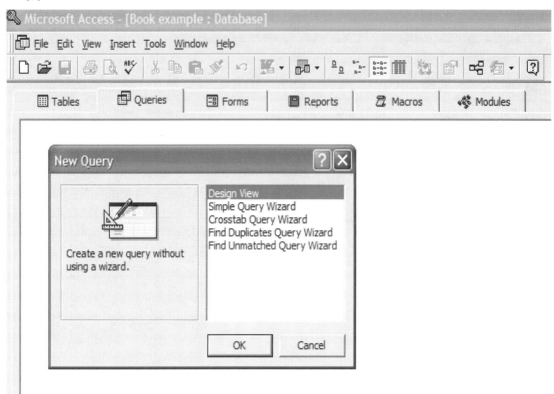

Figure 9

Using macros

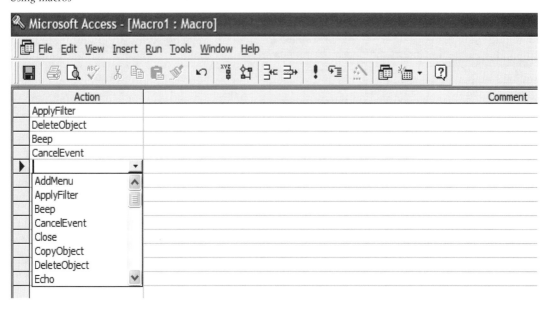

Advanced features of database packages

Import and export	Queries and reports from queries	Form design expert
Querying multiple tables	Forms designer	Report designer
Mailing labels	Custom reports	List boxes/combo boxes
Calculating values	Customising forms	Macros
Importing data	Customising menus and icons	VBA programming (limited)
Switchboards	Adding a graph	Mail merge
Menu builder	Relational database referential integrity	Primary and foreign key usage
Dynamic data interchange	Database administration	OLE
	Application integration	Creating a runtime application

2.3 Graphics

The use of graphics and graphical tools will vary depending upon the nature of your project. Projects that will require heavy graphical use include:

- architectural projects – designing houses or housing developments
- engineering projects – designing vehicles and motorised products
- technical projects – designing specialist electronic products
- scientific projects – designing medical, government or military products.

2.4 Presentation

You may want to use presentation software as a way of delivering certain aspects of your project. This could be done verbally – by presenting your findings to the end user – or in a written format by enclosing presentation slides with your final report and documentation.

Figure 10 Presentation slide examples

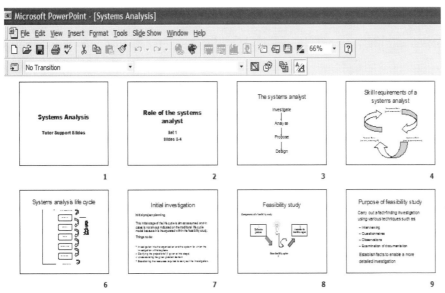

2.5 Multimedia

Multimedia software includes the use of sound, graphics and images or moving images. The most widely recognised source of multimedia elements is the Internet, as it incorporates each of these elements.

Within your project the Internet may be used to:

- research information
- download sound
- download graphics
- download images and photographs.

Remember

You may need permission from copyright holders to download text, sound, graphics, images or photographs.

Using the Internet may enhance your project because you can include more detailed facts, figures and analysis taken from a global resource, as opposed to a local resource such as your library.

To illustrate how the Internet can be used, let us use an example. If your project brief is to 'design and implement a new bookings and reservation system for a hotel', the Internet could be used in the following ways:

1 Investigate how on-line reservations systems work by looking at hotel websites that have this facility.
2 Carry out searches on the Internet to find information about electronic reservation systems.
3 Download examples of on-line reservation systems (if permitted).
4 Investigate the costs and resources that would be needed to set up an on-line bookings and reservations system for a hotel in conjunction with a more conventional electronic bookings system.

Figure 11

Sample reservations system

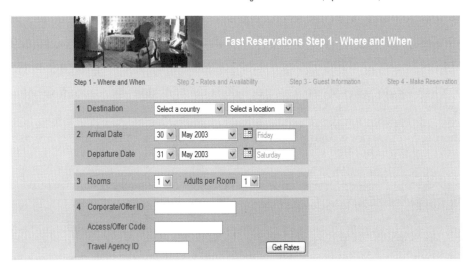

Advanced features of graphics packages, presentation packages and multimedia

Much depends on the actual task and the actual package. Many advanced features are the same as the relevant ones listed for word-processing above (page 188), especially if the project is paper based. However, these projects tend to be designed to be shown 'live'.

Graphics projects need to show both manipulation and design of images and layout. If using the Internet, then HTML programming needs to be shown (this does not have to be wholly original, as long as the source of the original code is acknowledged for copyright purposes). Some Java code may also be necessary. The same rules apply as for HTML code – it is not expected that ICT students should produce Java code from scratch.

For presentation software, the advanced features are:

Slide transition	Slide animation	Automatic timing
Use of images	Use of OLE	Real-time links out e.g. hyperlinks to the Internet
Slide templates and master layouts	Charts and images	Printer-friendly version

3 Specification

In order to generate a solution that demonstrates a thorough understanding of both the user's needs and the applications software, consideration should be given to the following factors:

- Has the problem domain been fully investigated?

- Has adequate time been allocated to each stage of the project?

- Are adequate resources available to produce a detailed and complex solution specification?

- Have alternative solutions been considered, and on what grounds have they been rejected in favour of the working solution?

- Is there adequate documentation about decisions made during the solution specification process?

The specification section carries a total of 13 marks. The criteria for gaining marks are as shown below:

Maximum marks	Allocation of marks
11–13	■ A detailed requirements specification has been produced for the identified problem, which matches the needs of the stated end user(s) ■ The input, processing and output needs, which match the requirements specification, are clearly stated ■ Effective designs have been completed which would enable an independent third party to implement the solution ■ An appropriate test strategy has been determined. An effective test and full testing plans have been devised. The testing plan includes the test data and expected outcomes and directly relates to the requirements specification
8–10	■ A detailed requirements specification has been produced for the identified problem, which matches the needs of the stated end user(s) ■ The input, processing and output needs, which match the requirements specification, are stated ■ Designs have been completed but lack detail, thereby preventing an independent third party implementation of the solution, or are inefficient in relation to the problem stated ■ A test strategy has been determined and testing plans have been devised but are limited in scope or do not relate to the requirements specification stated
4–7	■ A requirements specification has been produced for the identified problem, but does not fully match the needs of the stated end user(s), or lacks detail and clarity ■ The input, processing and output needs are stated but do not fully match the requirements specification or are unclear ■ Design work has been attempted but is incomplete and does not reflect an efficient solution to the problem stated

Maximum marks	Allocation of marks
	■ A test strategy has been determined but is either incomplete or does not relate to the requirements specification stated. The testing plan is either vague or has been omitted
1–3	■ The requirements specification is vague or has been omitted ■ The input, processing and output needs are only vaguely considered or have been omitted ■ There is little or no effort on design ■ The test strategy and testing plan are vague or missing
0	■ The candidate has produced no work

Interpretation of specification requirements

Marks / Criteria	11–13	8–10	4–7	1–3
Requirements specification				
Level of detail	Detailed	Detailed	Has been produced	Vague or missing
Matches end user needs	Yes	Yes	Not fully	Not stated
Input, processing and output				
Match requirements specification	Yes	Yes	Do not fully match	Vaguely considered or absent
Stated	Yes, clearly	Yes	Yes	Vague or absent
Designs				
Status and completion	Effective designs that are complete	Complete but lack detail	Attempted designs but incomplete	Little or no design effort
Enable third party implementation of the solution	Yes	No, or is inefficient for the problem stated	Does not reflect an efficient solution	No
Test strategies and test plans				
Test strategy determined	Yes	Yes	Incomplete	Vague or missing
Effective testing and full test plans	Yes	Limited scope	Vague or missing	Not stated
Presence of test data	Yes	Not stated	Not stated	Not stated
Expected outcomes relate to requirements spec.	Yes	Do not necessarily relate	Does not relate to the specification	Not stated

197

3.0 Requirements specification

The requirements specification should outline the deliverables of the project in terms of:

- aims and objectives
- investigation (fact-finding) methods
- analysis of the problem domain
- proposals specification:
  - input, processing and output needs
  - design tools and techniques
- implementation and test strategies.

3.1 Aims and objectives

The task-related problem can be structured around aims and objectives – identifying what you want to achieve and how you are going to achieve it. These can provide a framework that sets out targets both short-term (for each stage of the project) and long-term (for the life of the project).

3.2 Investigation and fact-finding

The task-related problem could originate from one of two sources:

- virtual end user, e.g. teacher/lecturer
- real end user, e.g. an organisation.

Whatever the source of the problem, a thorough investigation should take place to ensure that all the necessary information has been gathered to aid the project design.

A number of established investigative techniques aid data collection. These are sometimes referred to as *fact-finding techniques*. These techniques include the ones shown in Figure 12.

Figure 12
Fact-finding techniques

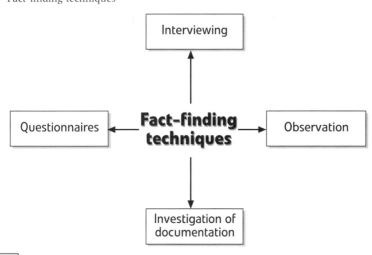

3.3 Interviewing

Interviewing end users is in some cases the best way to gather information about your task-related problem. Ask questions such as:

- Can you clearly outline the problem?

- How many and what type of user does the problem impact upon?

- Does the problem impact upon other systems or tasks?

- What solutions do you have to overcome the problem?

- Are there any constraints that could impact upon any proposals given?

Answers to these will provide you with a detailed overview of the environment and issues relating to the task. Interviewing may also give you the opportunity to prioritise what needs to be done, and when.

The objectives of interviewing include the ones shown in Figure 13.

Figure 13
Interview objectives

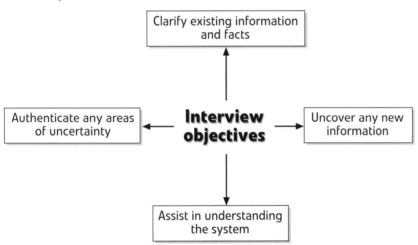

By interviewing users, you can ensure that the information already received is correct. Furthermore, interviewing might allow new information to be uncovered, and give you an opportunity to understand the system through the eyes of the user.

A number of factors need to be considered when interviewing users. These include the ones shown in Figure 14.

Figure 14
Interview considerations

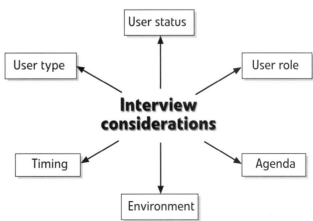

- **User type** – senior management, head of a department, team leader, data entry clerk, administration staff, etc.

- **User status** – the higher the position in the hierarchy of the organisation, the more limited their time might be to assist with an interview.

- **User role** – the position they have within the organisation and the impact they have on the system investigation.

- **Agenda** – users within the system might have their own reservations about changes to their system and may therefore be biased in their answers. It is your job to detect this, which can be achieved by validating information with another user or third party.

- **Environment** – users will feel more comfortable in certain environments in which they feel safe and are sure that they can talk in privacy.

- **Timing** – if the interviewee is prepared, and has made an effort to set time aside for questioning without interruptions, the information given will be of a better quality and more detailed.

3.4 Questionnaires

Questionnaires are sometimes a more convenient way of collecting information, because it can be difficult to pin down an end user for questioning.

The benefits of using a questionnaire include:

- you have a documentary record of wants and needs

- it is flexible and convenient

- it can be given to a number of users simultaneously

- it is a mass data collection tool.

Questionnaires are an excellent way of gathering and also consolidating information provided that the following conditions are met:

✓ The questionnaire is structured appropriately.

✓ A control mechanism is in place for gathering up the questionnaires.

✓ The correct user group has been targeted.

The questionnaire should be set out clearly to provide opportunities for both short answers based on facts and figures, and descriptive answers. A balance of questions will ensure that you collect all of the information required to continue with your investigation.

It is always best to provide a time limit for the return of questionnaires, such as 'please return within three working days'. Another way to ensure that the questionnaire is returned is to ask users to fill them in and then collect them yourself.

When designing a questionnaire a vital factor to consider is who the questionnaire is aimed at. The target audience is very important, because users can interpret a question very differently depending on their status and the role they play within the system.

Figure 15

Sample questionnaire template

ID number: *001*		System objective: **Upgrade computers in the Finance and IT departments**	
Name: *Daniel Browne*	Department: *Networking*		Job title: *IT Support Administrator*

Tasks undertaken each day:

- Remove back-up disks and take them off-site
- Set up new users on the system
- Set up security on the file systems
- Produce system documentation and procedures manuals
- First line support – help desk
- Assist with installations and upgrades

Communicates with: *Network manager, other IT support staff in the department, users at all levels, software and hardware manufacturers*

Documents used:

- new user set-up forms
- Internet access forms
- back-up schedules
- support call log

Constraints and problems:	User solutions:
1 Too much documentation 2 Users sometimes have to make multiple requests for passwords because there is no tracking system of who applied when, and sometimes the set-up forms are mislaid	*Make the support call log automated, using a database* *Better storage system and introduce a tracking system*

Please tick the following if you agree:

Problems exist with the following

Network ☐   Operating system ☐   Other software ☐   Inexperienced users ☐

Please identify how the above have contributed to problems with the IT system:

Any other information:

User complaints about the time it takes to attend a call-out. Network keeps crashing especially between 8:00 and 9:00 in the morning.

3.5 Observation

For some task-related problems that are quite dynamic it may be more convenient to observe the end user performing his or her actual role. Observation will enable you to see first-hand what is going on, the issues and the type of environment and conditions under which a new system would need to operate.

3.6 Investigation of documentation

Depending upon your end user/project sponsor, you may find that you are given a range of documentation to help you plan your project. This may be especially true if you have a real, organisational-based end user.

If for example you were carrying out an investigation on a specific functional department within an organisation, such as finance, suggesting ways of increasing efficiency in the payroll system in the finance department, documentation that you may be given could include:

- an organisational chart
- a breakdown of personnel within the department
- job roles of finance personnel
- sample forms used in the payroll system
- lists of procedures that are carried out on a daily basis by finance personnel.

Investigation of the documentation in this case would give you an overall picture of what is done, how it is done and by whom. You may indeed have to use other fact-finding methods to collect more detailed information, but at least you would have a starting point to direct your investigation.

3.7 Analysis of the problem domain

Once the fact-finding investigation has been carried out, the next stage in the project development would be to analyse the information that has been collected. Depending upon how much information you have, you could present the analysis in a written format – outlining your findings step by step and documenting stages of your investigation. An alternative would be to present the analysis in a visual form – illustrating the relationship between end users, task dependencies and the overall systems environment.

The use of diagrams to illustrate any problems in the existing system can have a number of advantages over a written analysis. These include:

- no need to write large volumes of notes
- clearer overview of what is happening with the entire system
- easy to identify key elements within the system such as:

- information types
- information flows
- storage mechanisms
- users

▨ easier to identify relationships and working patterns within the system.

One set of tools that could be used to illustrate what is happening within the system is a model referred to as **systems analysis**.

Systems analysis looks at the life-cycle of a system, and follows the development of the system from initially investigating the problems through to analysing, designing, implementing and testing a new system proposal. This is very similar to your own task-based project life-cycle.

Although the tools that are used in systems analysis would be appropriate to your own analysis and possibly design stages, application is not a requirement of the specifications.

3.8 Proposals – solution specification

In order to put forward feasible solutions to the problem, a number of factors need to be taken into consideration, including:

1 how the overall system is going to look and perform based on given input, processing and output needs

2 what design tools and techniques are going to be applied.

There might be a very obvious solution to the problem, but this may not be the best solution for the end user. Therefore to ensure that all proposals and solutions put forward do meet end user requirements, these considerations need to be addressed.

3.9 Input, processing and output needs

A system can be broken down into three component parts:

▨ input(s)

▨ processing

▨ output(s)

Figure 16

Basic systems model

Inputs are resources that trigger the system. They initiate the process and make things happen. Inputs could include:

- data and information
- people
- technology
- capital
- research and development
- a thought or idea
- raw materials or ingredients.

Processing enables the inputs to be modelled into a workable solution. For example, to make wine, fermentation would need to take place:

The system **output** would reflect the end result or what is expected from the processing activity.

When designing a system to meet the needs of a user, importance should be placed on all three aspects, from the input stage through to output. A checklist as shown below could be used to address this.

Input/s	Considered ✓
What type of data or information does the user work with?	
Is the data in a particular format?	
Does the data have to remain in this format?	
At what level is the end user in terms of working with a computerised application-based system?	
Processing	
Is the user familiar with the applications software chosen?	
Does the user know how to access, manipulate, update and store the data in the newly proposed system?	
Can the user take advantage of the range of processing tools available within the application at a simple and complex level?	
Output/s	
Will the information be presented in a format that the user requires?	
Can the user output the information easily?	
Can the user change the output mechanism if required?	

Within the requirements specification, the input, processing and output needs should be acknowledged and the system should be designed around these areas.

3.10 Example of designs for a database system project

If you were using database software, the design areas that would need to be considered include the following:

1 What entities are present?

2 How do these entities link together (what is the relationship between them)?

3 How can each entity be identified (entity/data descriptions)?

4 How do these entities fit into a database design?

5 How do they link together within a database?

6 What is the best way to input the data?

7 Can the data be easily manipulated?

8 Can the data be easily output?

9 Are any consistency, validation or testing mechanisms set up?

All of these questions can be incorporated into a checklist similar to the one above.

What are entities and entity relationship diagrams?

Entity relationship diagrams use a set of tools and associated textual descriptions to represent the links between certain data sets within a given system.

The diagrammatic aspect of entity relationship diagrams has four main components:

1 entities
2 relationships
3 degree
4 optionality.

Entities

Typical entity types

Relationships

Relationship identified by a
linked line between entities

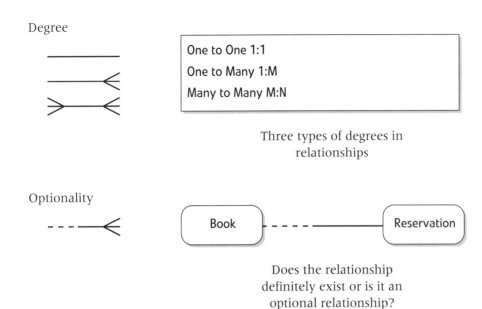

Degree

One to One 1:1
One to Many 1:M
Many to Many M:N

Three types of degrees in
relationships

Optionality

Book - - - - - - - - Reservation

Does the relationship
definitely exist or is it an
optional relationship?

Entities

Entities are the source, recipient and storage mechanism for information that is held on the system. For example, here are typical entities for the following systems:

Library system

Entities: book
              lender
              reservation
              issue
              edition

Hotel system

Entities: booking
              guest
              room
              tab
              enquiry

Airline system

Entities: flight
              ticket
              seat
              booking
              destination

Each entity will have a set of attributes that make up the information occurrences, for example:

Entity: book
Attributes: ISBN number
              title
              author
              publisher
              publication date

Each set of attributes within that entity should have a unique field that provides easy identification. In the case of the entity type 'book', the unique key field is that of ISBN number. The unique field or **primary key** will ensure that although two books may have the same title or author, no two books will have the same ISBN number.

Relationships

To illustrate how information is used within the system, entities need to be linked together to form a relationship. The relationship between two entities could be misinterpreted; therefore labels are attached at the beginning and at the end of the relationship link to inform parties of the exact nature of the relationship. For example, if you had two entities linked as below,

the nature of the relationship could be any of the following:

- an author can write a book, therefore the book is written by the author
- an author can refer to a book, therefore the book is referenced by the author
- an author can buy a book, therefore the book is purchased by the author
- an author can review a book, therefore the book is reviewed by the author.

The relationship that exists in this case is that an author reviews a book, therefore the book has been reviewed by an author.

Degree

There are three possible degrees of any entity relationship.

One to one 1:1   This denotes that only one occurrence of each entity is used by the adjoining entity.

A single author writes a single book

One to many 1:M   This denotes that a single occurrence of one entity is linked to more than one occurrence of the adjoining entity.

A single author writes a number of books

Many to many M:N   This denotes that many occurrences of one entity are linked to more than one occurrence of the adjoining entity.

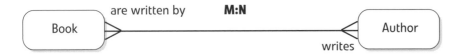

An author can write a number of books and books can have more than one author

Although M:N relationships are common, the notation linking two entities directly is adjusted and a link entity is used to connect the two.

In this scenario a customer can make a number of bookings and each of those bookings are made by a customer.

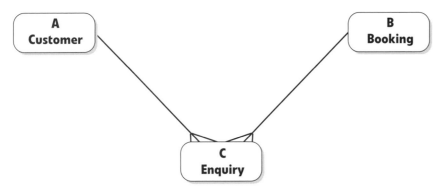

In this scenario a customer can make a number of enquiries which lead to a booking and bookings result from a number of enquiries made by customers.

Optionality

Two status types are given to a relationship – firstly those that definitely happen or exist, and secondly those that may happen or exist. This second status is referred to as 'optional'.

A dashed rather than a solid link represents optionality in a relationship.

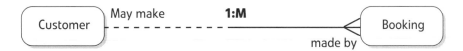

In this scenario a customer may or may not decide to make a booking. If he or she does, the booking will definitely belong to or be made by a customer.

Entity relationship documentation

The second component of entity relationship diagrams is the documentation that supports the data structures. The documentation that can be used includes:

- entity descriptions
- attribute lists.

Every entity should have an associated **entity description**, which details items such as:

- entity name and description
- attributes
- relationship types and links.

Every entity has a set of attributes. If a large system is being investigated, a number of entities and their associated attributes will need to be defined, therefore an **attribute list** can be prepared.

Attribute lists identify all of the attributes and a description of the attributes. The primary key attribute is normally made up of numerical data, for example a supplier number, National Insurance number, examination number. This is referred to first, followed by the remainder of the attribute items.

3.11 Solution specification considerations

Considerations	Feasible Y/N
1 Has all of the appropriate information that can impact upon the proposal been gathered from the initial investigation?	
2 Have any constraints been imposed upon the task solution?	
3 Do I have to work to a certain deadline?	
4 Has the end user given me a solution to work with or design?	
5 Am I restricted to using certain hardware or software?	
6 Does the solution have to be designed and implemented in a certain way?	
7 Are any other limitations or constraints imposed upon the project?	
8 Do I have adequate knowledge and skills to develop the project solution?	

If the answer is yes to questions 2-7, you have to ensure that you work within these boundaries. If you have been asked to design a system using specific spreadsheet software within a two-week period and produce a written user guide, there will be no point in designing a system that cannot be completed in time using a database with no user guide.

If your project brief does not specify how the new system needs to be designed and implemented, you have more flexibility.

3.12 Design tools and techniques

A number of tools and techniques can be used to support your system analysis and design decisions. These tools include a range of planning, costing and feasibility criteria to aid your choice, such as:

- Gantt charts
- impact analysis
- cost-benefit analysis
- SWOT analysis.

Although other more advanced tools can be used, the ones mentioned will provide a good level of justification as to why you have designed your system in a certain way.

Gantt chart

Gantt charts provide a diagrammatic overview of the sequence and timing of events. They predict when activities will start and end, and also examine the ordering of tasks.

A sample Gantt chart can be seen in Figure 17.

Figure 17

Gantt chart

	May				June				July	
Week no.	1	2	3	4	5	6	7	8	9	10
Activity:										
Do research	▓									
Examine requirements		▓								
Generate proposals			▓	▓						
Present proposals				▓						
Plan designs				▓	▓					
Implement designs						▓	▓	▓		
Test designs							▓	▓	▓	
Evaluation										▓

Cost-benefit analysis

A cost-benefit analysis can be used to justify the cost of your proposal by offsetting this against the benefits. Regardless of whether you have a virtual or real end user, costs need to be considered.

A cost-benefit analysis provides an overview of the costs involved in a certain project, and maps these against the attributed benefits.

In theory every cost listed should have one or more benefits marked against it in order to justify the expense. The costs can be broken down into two areas:

1 tangible costs

2 intangible costs.

Tangible costs can be assigned to physical items such as new hardware, software, or additional office equipment. **Intangible costs** are non-physical items such as installation of the hardware, or training to use the new software, and can be hard to measure.

To produce a cost-benefit analysis, draw up a matrix similar to the one shown in Figure 18.

Figure 18

Cost-benefit analysis

Tangible costs	£	Intangible costs		Benefits
Three new PCs	4,700.00	Installation of PCs	Disruption to users and the working environment	Wider access to the system by users Reduction in processing activities Improved customer service due to faster response time
New desk-top publishing software	400.00	Training in use of the software	Time taken to train	Ability to create company documents in-house, such as letterheads and logos Saving of £650.00 per quarter by producing promotional material in-house and not via a marketing agency
	5,100.00			

Impact analysis

An impact analysis examines the impact of a proposal on the system's environment. The degree of the impact is then quantified in terms of being positive or negative. The aim of carrying out an impact analysis is to ensure your proposal has a majority of positive aspects and minimal negative ones. It would be unrealistic to expect to design a new system proposal with no negative impacts, because of the constraints imposed (for example costs, limited time and resources). A change to the existing system could always be seen as a negative impact initially for some users, who are familiar with current processing activities and cannot see the advantages of change.

To carry out an impact analysis, a number of areas should be examined, as shown in Figure 19, and the impact on each considered. A table can then be drawn up as shown in Figure 20, identifying the subject of the analysis (for example a user of the system, a customer or a specific processing activity) and the degree of the impact in terms of whether it is positive, negative or both.

Figure 19

Areas to be considered in an impact analysis

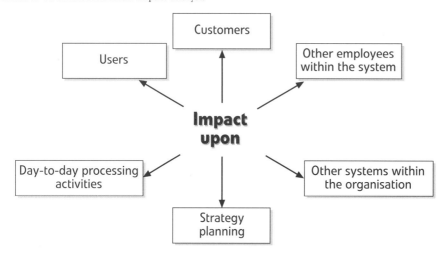

Figure 20

Example of an impact analysis table

Introduction of a new stock control system in warehousing		
Areas examined	**Impact positive or negative**	**Rationale**
Customers	+ve	More items in stock Improved information on availability
Users (stock checkers, warehouse manager)	+ve −ve	Easy access to stock information Time taken to become familiar with new system
Other employees within the system	+ve	Shared and better communication Information readily available
Day-to-day processing activities	+ve	Reduced stock paperwork Automatic reordering
Other systems	+ve	Compatibility with other systems, such as automatic links to point of sale
Strategy planning	+ve	More competitive for the future

SWOT analysis

A SWOT analysis examines the strengths, weaknesses, opportunities and threats of a given issue. The strengths and weaknesses are examined from an internal point of view, and the opportunities and threats are examined from an external point of view – how influences outside your system boundary can impact upon it.

An example of a SWOT analysis can be seen in Figure 21.

Figure 21

SWOT analysis for the upgrade of a stock-control system in the warehouse department

Strengths	Weaknesses
▪ Reduction in the amount of paperwork ▪ Automatic stock ordering ▪ Automatic tracking of the stock distribution in the warehouse ▪ Information can be accessed by all warehouse personnel ▪ Reduction in overheads of 5%	▪ Initial financial outlay ▪ Training needed for all warehouse personnel
Opportunities	**Threats**
▪ Stock system can be integrated into other department systems ▪ Access to stock information can be given to all store personnel ▪ Links into supplier systems	▪ Incompatibility with existing systems in the store

For a proposal to be viable, the strengths should outweigh the weaknesses and the opportunities should exceed the threats.

3.13 Design

Taking the work from the specification, you should now produce the designs from which you will work. That is, a design for every screen (input and output); a design for every printed report; a data dictionary showing all data fields to be used, their type and length, any default values and any validation that is required; and a written description of all processing and calculations that will be required.

Somewhere in the specification there should be an indication of the hardware and software available for the implementation of the solution. This needs to be taken into account when designing – if the monitor available is black and white, then avoid use of colour for differentiation. Remember that some fonts take up more space than others, so if the processor is slower than some, or the memory or storage space is limited, allow for this.

Obviously, what these sections contain depends in a large part on which software package is being used. However, a rule of thumb is that screen and report designs should be either hand-drawn or drawn up in a different package to that being used for the solution.

Screen design

The first thing that must be done is to decide on a 'look' for the screens – this is the user interface, so consistency and professionalism are required.

- Choose a standard layout, showing company name and logo, system name and function (screen) title, date, and screen reference, using the same colours and fonts to indicate the same type of field or element.

- If you are using buttons, decide on the shape, size and colour to be used. For any function buttons, e.g. navigation or calculation functions that will be part of the screen, make sure there is a standard place and icon/button for each one.

If you are hand drawing the screens, make sure they are to scale. As for all design work, another person should be able to take your designs and produce exactly the same screen that you would have done.

A sample screen design (produced in a spreadsheet package for a project that is to be implemented in a database package) is shown in Figure 22.

Figure 22 Sample screen design

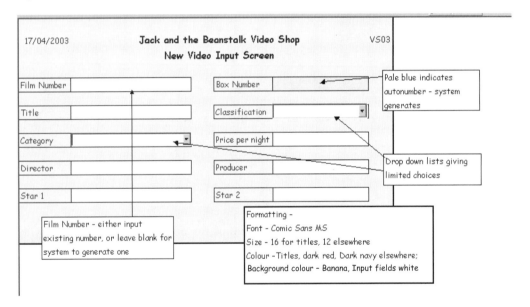

Printed report designs

In a similar way to screen designs, report designs should have a standard look for the systems and the company.

There should be an indication of how big the paper is (for example, a receipt would not necessarily be designed for A4 paper); the number of lines that can be shown per page for long reports; and so on.

If you know it, the relevant printer can be allowed for – if you know there is a colour printer, you may wish to design colour into the report to differentiate or highlight data.

Figure 23 shows a list report which is likely to be more than one page long. The main processing steps are included in this design.

Figure 23

Design for list report

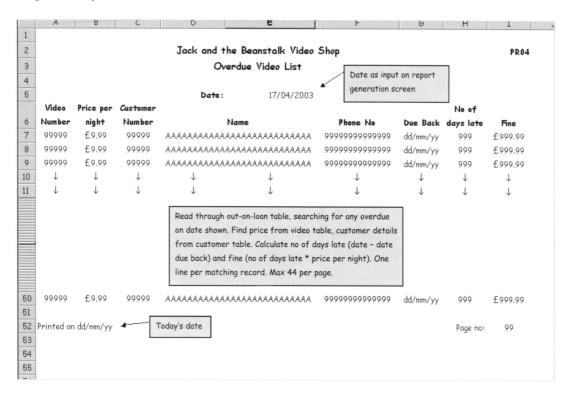

Data dictionary

This is simply a list of all the data fields that will be used. Take the list of entities and attributes identified in the analysis phase of the specification, and tabulate them showing names, types, lengths, default values, validation to be applied, etc. See the example below.

CUSTOMER

Field name	Type	Length	Default	Validation
Cust_Title	Alphanumeric	6	Mr	Drop-down list – Mr, Mrs, Ms, Miss, Master, Dr
Cust_Sname	Alphanumeric	20		Must be present
Cust_Fname	Alphanumeric	10		Must be present
Cust_Pcode	Alphanumeric	8		Look-up on postcode table
Cust_House	Alphanumeric	4		Must be present
Cust_AddChk	Boolean	1	N	
Cust_Tel1	Alphanumeric	13		Must be present
Cust_Tel2	Alphanumeric	13		
Cust_O18	Boolean	1	N	
Cust_DOB	Date	8		If Cust_018 = N, must be present

Processing and calculations

All processing must be written down in some way – you could use diagrams or flowcharts, step-by-step English instructions, or more formal pseudocode. It depends on the project and the software.

For example, many packages allow the recording of macros. The steps for each macro need to be written down, so that another developer could create the macro you envisaged during design, and attach it to the button you designed. The name of each macro must also be decided upon, for the same reason.

3.14 Test strategy and plan

Once the proposals you have put forward have been deemed feasible and realistic, the end user should agree your solution specification. It is important to include the end user and ensure he or she agrees the design prior to the build. Once the solution specification has been agreed, you can start to consider the physical design aspects of how the new system will look and function.

The test strategy should take into consideration the following issues.

- When testing is to take place – at interval stages during the design and/or at the end of the design.

- Which areas of the system are to be tested, and how.

- How much involvement the user will have during the testing phase.

- How the tested information will be recorded.

Testing will be addressed in more detail in Section 4.

4 Implementation and testing

4.0 Implementation

Whatever software you decide to use as part of your ICT system solution, procedures need to be put in place to ensure that the design meets the end user's expectations. Therefore good, systematic implementation procedures have to be carried out.

The implementation section carries a total of 20 marks. The criteria for gaining marks are as shown below:

Maximum marks	Allocation of marks
16–20	■ An effective solution has been developed which is operable in the proposed environment by the intended end user ■ Appropriate data capture and validation procedures, data organisation methods, output contents and formats and user interface(s) have been used ■ Generic and package-specific skills have been fully employed in an effective and appropriate manner ■ The selection of the chosen hardware and software facilities have been fully justified in relation to the solution developed
11–15	■ A solution has been developed which is operable in the proposed environment by the intended end user, but has some inefficiencies ■ There is evidence of the use of some appropriate data capture and validation procedures, data organisation methods, output contents and formats and user interface(s). ■ Generic and package-specific skills have been fully employed but not always in an effective and appropriate manner ■ The selection of some of the chosen hardware and software facilities have been justified in relation to the solution developed
6–10	■ A partial solution has been developed, but those aspects completed are useable by the intended end user ■ There is some evidence of the use of some data capture and validation procedures, data organisation methods, output contents and formats and user interface(s) ■ Generic and package-specific skills have been employed, but not always in an effective and appropriate manner ■ The selection of some of the chosen hardware and software facilities has been only vaguely justified in relation to the solution developed
1–5	■ A solution has been developed which is very limited and is not practically operable in the proposed environment by the intended end user

Maximum marks	Allocation of marks
	■ Few, if any, data capture and validation procedures, data organisation methods, output contents and formats and user interface(s) have been used ■ The generic and package-specific skills used are simplistic and/or were not always applied appropriately ■ The selections of the chosen hardware and software facilities are not justified in relation to the solution developed
0	The candidate has not implemented the system

Interpretation of implementation requirements

Marks / Criteria	16–20	11–15	6–10	1–5
Solution developed				
Solution status	Effective solution that is operable	Developed and operable but with some inefficiencies	Partially developed, completed aspects are useable	Limited solution developed, not practically operable
Data capture and validation procedures				
Appropriate procedures used	Yes	Some evidence of use	Some evidence of use	Few, if any, used
Generic and package skills				
Have been employed	Fully and effectively	Fully but not always effective	Employed but not always effective	Simplistic and/or not always applied appropriately
Justification of hardware and software				
Justified	Yes, fully	Yes	Vaguely	No

Depending upon the type of software used, the implementation of the system may be phased in to ensure that everything is fully integrated and working efficiently. With a database solution, for example, checks may be carried out to see if the input screens are laid out appropriately, followed by validation checks and procedures to see whether links and relationships are working, and accessible by a fully activated menu system.

In the implementation and testing stages, consideration should be given to the following criteria, as shown in Figure 24:

- data capture

- validation procedures

- data organisation methods and operational procedures

- output content and formats

- user interface.

Figure 24

Implementation considerations

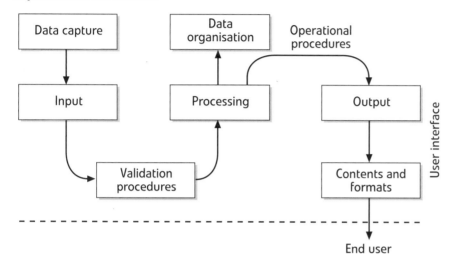

These considerations can be addressed in terms of:

- how the data is fed into the system

- control mechanisms of the system

- how data is processed and organised

- what the system looks like.

Depending upon the type of software used, a number of tests can be carried out to ensure that these considerations are addressed.

Data capture

Data capture involves the collection and inputting of data into a system in order for it to be processed. Data capture can be done manually or electronically, by using a data capture tool. Examples of electronic data capture tools include:

- bar codes and readers

- optical mark recognition (OMR)

- optical character recognition (OCR)

- magnetic ink character recognition (MICR)

- punched cards

- magnetic stripe cards

- keyboard

- sensors.

All of these tools reflect different ways in which data and information can be input into a system. These different ways should be assessed in terms of:

1 How much data is to be input and processed.

2 How easy the data capture tool will be to use.

3 How appropriate the selected tool is in relation to the system specification.

4 How fast the data capture tool needs to be.

5 What conditions or system environment the data capture tool will be used in.

When these factors have all been addressed, a decision can be made as to the type of data capture tool to use.

Validation procedures

Validation checks should be carried during these stages to ensure that any data entered and processed within the system is complete. A number of checks can be carried out, including the ones shown below:

Check	Purpose
Presence check	To ensure that certain fields of information have been entered, e.g. hospital number for a patient being admitted for surgery
Field/format/ picture check	To ensure that the information that has been input is in the correct format and combination (if applicable), e.g. the surgery procedure has an assigned code made up of two letters and six numeric digits – DH245639
Range check	To ensure that any values entered fall within the boundaries of a certain range, e.g. the surgery code is only valid for a four-week period (1–4), therefore any number over 4 in this field would be rejected
Look-up check	To ensure that data entered is of an acceptable value, e.g. types of surgery can only be accepted from the list 'orthopaedic, ENT (ears, nose and throat) or minor'
Cross-field check	To ensure that information stored in two fields matches up, e.g. if the surgeon's initials are DH on the surgery code they cannot represent the surgeon Mary Timbers, only Donald Hill
Check digit check	To ensure that any code number entered is valid by adding a digit that has some relationship to the original code
Batch header checks	To ensure that records in a batch, e.g. number of surgeries carried out over a set period, match the number stored in the batch header

Data organisation methods and operational procedures

Data organisation methods look at how the data and information in the current system is managed, and the methods used to get it into a meaningful data set. Operational procedures look at how the data set is managed.

During the implementation and testing stages, the following areas will need to be considered:

- What existing methods and procedures are in place?

- Does the end user require you to adapt these methods and procedures, or recommend more appropriate ones?

- Is the data organised in a suitable format, e.g. does the data need filtering or sorting prior to a new system design?

- Do the current operational procedures fit into the new system design, or will they have to be modified? If so, is the end user happy for you to do this?

Output content and format

Output content and format examines what the user is able to get out of the system following processing. The output requirements may change between different users, for example:

- a report

- graphics – charts and graphs

- summary document.

Consideration should also be given to how complex a breakdown is required from the output information. In the case of developing a sales forecast system, the end user may require an output screen with a month-by-month report, with supporting graphs to illustrate which product performed the best and the worst.

User interface

The user interface is of vital importance to any system design. How the user will interact with the system is of prime consideration throughout the development stages. Factors that should be taken into consideration include the following:

- At what level is the user in terms of knowledge, understanding and use of a computerised system?

- How easy is the system in terms of inputting, processing and outputting information?

- Are the screen designs (if applicable) clear and simple?

- Will the user be able to navigate around the system easily?

- Are there any integrated help/support features – menus, documentation, etc.?

If the user interface has not been designed around the needs of the user, it may well be too difficult or impractical to use.

4.1 Testing

Testing is required to ensure that the overall system and each of the component parts of the system work. Testing also ensures that everything is working in accordance with the requirements of the end user.

The testing section carries a total of 12 marks. The criteria for gaining marks are as shown below:

Maximum marks	Allocation of marks
9–12	■ The test strategy and test plan previously devised have now been followed in a systematic manner, using typical, erroneous and extreme (boundary) data ■ The results of testing are fully documented, with outputs cross-referenced to the original plan ■ Corrective action taken due to test results is clearly documented
5–8	■ The test strategy and plan devised have been followed in a systematic manner but using only normal data ■ The results of testing are partially documented with some evidence of outputs cross-referenced to the original plan ■ There is some evidence of corrective action taken in response to test results
1–4	■ The test strategy and plan devised have been followed in a limited manner using only normal data ■ There is little or no documentation of the results of testing ■ There is little or no indication of corrective action required due to test results
0	■ There is no evidence of testing

Interpretation of testing requirements

Marks / Criteria	9–12	5–8	1–4
Test strategy and plan			
Followed	Systematically using typical, erroneous and extreme data	Yes, using only normal data	In a limited manner using only normal data
Results of testing			
Results documented	Fully, with outputs cross-referenced to the original plan	Partially, with some evidence of outputs being cross-referenced	Little or no documentation
Corrective action			
Action taken	Taken and clearly documented	Some evidence of action taken	Little or no indication of action being taken

Testing can be applied to each stage of system development and is indeed recommended, especially as certain parts of the system may be dependent upon others being operational.

In terms of software testing, this checking at regular intervals or stages can be referred to as **module testing**. Module testing should be carried out to ensure that a variety of test data has been examined under a range of conditions.

Following the completion of each module, overall software testing can be carried out to ensure that each component of the application design or program is fully functional.

Test plan

Test data sets should have been prepared during the specification stage of the project. If not, they must be done before testing commences, as knowing the expected result makes performing the test much faster.

The test plan and test log provide documentary evidence that testing has been carried out. They should take into account the following points:

- version control – which test number/ version you are on
- what has been tested
- at what stage in the development
- the purpose of the test
- the results of the test
- comments – did the test run as expected?

Each time a test is carried out the test plan and log should be updated and used as a working document that can be integrated into the final evaluation.

An example test plan can be seen in Figure 25, and a test log in Figure 26.

Systems Test Plan

Test date: .... Performed by: ....

Stage in the systems development:

....

....

Test version: (e.g. V1.0) ....

What is being tested:

Software used:

Test/s carried out: Successful: Yes   No

1

2

3

4

5

Changes to be made:

Recommendations:

Figure 25

Sample test plan

Figure 26

Test log

Version number	Test	How	Test data used	Expected results	Date	Actual results	Action taken
1.0	Width of fields in customer table	Enter test data onto data entry screen	Graham Jarvis Henderson	All field sizes should be acceptable	24/03/03	Surname field is too small for longest name	Increase size of surname field
2.0	Width of fields in customer table	Enter test data onto data entry screen	Didcott Jefferson Hamble	All field sizes should be acceptable	26/03/03	Surname field is correct length	None

5 Evaluation

The evaluation section carries a total of 6 marks. The criteria for gaining marks are as shown below:

Maximum marks	Allocation of marks
4–6	■ The effectiveness of the solution in meeting the detailed requirements specification has been fully addressed, with the candidate showing full awareness of the criteria for a successful information technology solution ■ The limitations of the solution have been clearly identified
1–3	■ The effectiveness of the solution in meeting the original requirements specifications has been partly assessed with the candidate showing only partial awareness of the criteria for a successful information technology solution ■ The limitations of the solution are vague or have been omitted
0	■ There is no evidence of evaluation

Interpretation of evaluation requirements

Marks / Criteria	4–6	1–3
Effectiveness of solution		
Addressed	Fully	Partly
Awareness of the criteria	Full awareness shown	Partial awareness shown
Solution limitations		
Identified	Clearly	Vague or missing

The evaluation section of your project can be broken down into two key areas:

- ■ individual progress evaluations
- ■ overall project evaluation.

Individual progress evaluations are required to ensure that each stage of the project has been examined and analysed. There may be problems that occur with a particular stage in the project that could have been avoided, or a stage in the development that went particularly well. These failures or problems should be evaluated to identify:

- ■ the cause of the problem
- ■ inadequacy of certain skills, knowledge or resources
- ■ inaccuracies and inefficiencies in the data collection, analysis or design phases

■ poor investigative skills in collecting system and user information about the problem domain and/or expectations from the new system.

Stages of the project that went well should also be evaluated, to identify:

1 What contributed to the success in terms of:

- ■ thorough data collection methods

- ■ good understanding of the problem domain

- ■ ability to listen to the end user's needs

- ■ a clear and logical structure to the project development process

- ■ working within given boundaries and constraints.

2 The measures and tools used to assist in the project development, and how they contributed to the success.

If you evaluate each stage of the development it will be much easier to reflect on what has been done for the **overall project evaluation**.

A reference back to the user requirements is an important part of evaluation – make sure that the solution you have provided meets these requests at the start.

6 Documentation – user guide

The user documentation section carries a total of 9 marks. The criteria for gaining marks are as shown below:

Maximum marks	Allocation of marks
7–9	■ There is extensive user documentation for the solution which covers all relevant aspects, including normal operation and common problems, and is appropriate to the needs of the end user
4–6	■ A user guide is included, which describes the functionality of the solution and is appropriate to the needs of the end user
1–3	■ A limited user guide is included which describes only the basic functionality of the solution
0	■ There is no evidence of user documentation

Interpretation of user documentation requirements

Marks / Criteria	7–9	4–6	1–3
User documentation/guide			
Status	Extensive user documentation	User guide is present	Limited user guide
Contents	Covers all relevant aspects, operation and common problems	Describes the functionality of the solution	Describes the basic functionality of the system

It must be remembered that the user does not need to know how to use the software package, merely the new system that has been produced.

A user guide will help to support the end user in the use and understanding of the system that has been developed. The guide should be set out to reflect the knowledge level of the user, for example a non-technical document for entry-level users who have little or no experience of working with computerised systems. For a more advanced user, a more technical guide could be produced, outlining some of the more advanced features of the package you have used.

In all cases the use of jargon should be avoided, and pictures and screen shots should be included to make the guide as user-friendly as possible.

7 Documentation required to present evidence

All documentation, including draft copies of screen designs, should be included in your final submission as it illustrates the rationale you have applied at each stage of systems design.

All documentation should be clearly labelled and presented in a professional format such as a report.

Documentation forms a critical part of any project. For this coursework task, documentation should be used to:

- support users in understanding how to use the new system's hardware/software

- provide evidence for each stage of the project life-cycle

- demonstrate how the new system works

- justify the way the system has been designed and implemented.

Examples of the type of documentation that can be used are identified in Figure 27.

Figure 27

Possible documentation requirements

Documents	Use
Interview question sheet Questionnaire	Gather information on the task-related problem
User catalogue Requirements catalogue	Recording the wants and needs of users in respect of the new system
Draft plans Designs Screen shots	Demonstrating project development and the generation of ideas and proposals
Implementation plans Test logs	To check that the system meets user requirements and works to agreed standards
User guide Training booklet	Support end users by providing help and advice

REVISION

This revision unit looks at topics covered in AS modules 1 and 2 and, using past papers and mark schemes, addresses how the knowledge gained in these modules can be applied to the examination questions.

Reading and understanding the question is half the battle for marks. If you just glance at the question, see a technical term, and – feeling relieved to recognise something – simply write everything you know about that term, you will be disappointed when the results are published.

Specifically, this unit covers:

■ Examination vocabulary: what the words mean and what they are asking you to do

■ Examination technique: how to read the question and interpret what is required

■ Frequently asked definitions: technical vocabulary

■ Contrasts and differences: some common misunderstandings

■ Lists of features, etc., to use for quick topic revision.

1 Examination vocabulary

One of the most important factors in exam success is learning to read the question paper. You need to be familiar with the vocabulary used. Most questions on the AS papers are formatted so that there is a question stem, giving some form of context to the information required. This may set the context in, for example, a shop or particular office or school.

This stem is followed by one or more questions that normally start with a key word and give the number of items required. The items must be correct for the context given, so be careful to read the stem properly.

Key word(s)	Normal mark allocation per point	Comments
State *or* name	1	Answer with one word or a short phrase for each point.
Give	1	As above, but sometimes more than a single word is needed to make the meaning clear.
Define	1 or 2	This is normally asked of a technical term, and a sentence would usually be enough.
Describe	2	This normally needs you to name something, plus give a description for 2 marks; sometimes the question says 'name and describe'.
Explain	2	Similar to *describe*, this doesn't come up so often in the AS papers. Remember to keep the context in mind and watch out for the number of marks per point made.
Using an example	1	This will normally add 1 mark to each *describe* or *explain* answer.
With the aid of an example	perhaps 1	This quite often means that 1 of the 2 marks of a *describe* or an *explain* question is specifically for the example.

Sample questions

The key words described above are used in the following ways:

- **Give** three characteristics needed by an ICT professional.
- **Define** the term *interactive processing.*
- **Name** four validation checks.
- **Describe, with the aid of an example**, three ways in which a user interface can be designed for effective communication with the user.
- **Explain** two effects of software package change or upgrade.

2 Examination technique

First, make sure you have at least two blue or black pens and a pencil when you go into the examination room.

The examinations are 1 hour 30 minutes long. This is plenty of time for most people to answer all the questions carefully; it gives enough time for you to read through the paper before you start. Once you have answered the first couple of questions, you should begin to feel more relaxed.

Examiners prefer the questions to be attempted in the order they are set out on the paper. There are normally around 10 questions, the first one or two of which are always very straightforward, to ease you into the paper – they tend to ask for short definitions. Look over past papers to familiarise yourself with the styles of questions.

An answer booklet is provided, normally with plenty of pages – only those with large writing will need to use a continuation sheet. You can therefore afford to spread out the answers. Leave space at the end of every question, in case you want to add anything later. Preferably, start each question on a new page.

Make sure you read the stem of each question carefully at least once, so that you fully understand the context. Next, look at the question word (as described above) and the number of marks allocated, and plan the answer accordingly – if there are three points for each answer, there need to be three parts to the answer. See the examples below.

2.0 Some points to remember

- Make sure an example is included if specifically asked for.
- If two marks are available, find two phrases to write (extend your first thoughts and be more explicit); if there are three marks, then find three phrases.
- Keep referring back to the stem and keep your answer within the context given, if there is one – writing about supermarkets when the given context is a corner shop will mean you lose marks.
- Don't just write down all the information you can remember about a topic – if four items are requested and the first four you write down do not get the marks, the examiner may not read any further in a long list.
- Don't write a paragraph if the question word is *state* or *give* – it is a waste of time and energy and does not gain any more marks.
- Don't write a single word or phrase if the question word is *describe* or *explain*.

2.1 Sample answers

Here are some sample answers using the guidelines above. Note the differences in answer style where more marks are on offer for each point made.

Question:
Give **four** advantages of databases over flat files. *(4 marks)*

Answer:
1 Control over redundancy
2 Program data independence
3 Improved consistency of data
4 Improved security.

Question:
Describe **four** advantages of databases over flat files. *(8 marks)*

Answer:
1 Control over redundancy as there is no, or little, repeating data in a database which has been normalised.
2 Program data independence, so if the field sizes change or extra fields are added to a table structure, it is done centrally and the programs just pick up the data they require.
3 Improved consistency of data, as most data can be held only in one place. When there are changes these only need to be entered once, as all applications see the same data.
4 Improved security, as the database management system can be used to set access levels and read-write permissions on all data.

Question:
State **three** validation checks. *(3 marks)*

Answer:
1 Range check
2 Presence check
3 Format check.

Question:
Describe a validation check for **three** of the fields on the booking form above, saying why it is a suitable check. [An example of a booking form would be shown.] *(9 marks)*

Answer:
1 A range check would be suitable for the age field, as it has to be over 18.
2 The name field has to be filled in, therefore a presence check would be suitable.
3 A format check would be suitable validation for the event date field, as it would ensure it was in dd/mm/yy format.

3 **Technical vocabulary**

Some questions come up time after time on the AS papers, requiring basic definitions of terms. These are easy marks to earn, so make sure you learn and understand the necessary terms. Knowing these should enable you to reach the pass (E) grade – further application of knowledge and understanding separates the Es, Cs and As.

3.0 ICT 1

Term	Acceptable definition
Computer Misuse Act	Legislation that describes three levels of illegal activity: unauthorised access to computer material; unauthorised access with intent to commit or facilitate commission of further offences; unauthorised modification of computer material. (These might be described as 'look at it', 'look at it and touch it', and 'look, touch and change it'.)
Data	Raw facts or figures with no meaning, e.g. 23–1–7–44–8.
Data access	The ability to log on and look at/amend data held in an information system.
Data encoding	Taking raw data and translating into codes for putting into an information system. For example, a criterion for encoding might be 'If age >20 and <=25, then encode as age-band=3'. This sometimes reduces the precision of the data.
Data Protection Act	Legislation protecting personal data held in electronic systems. The first act was passed in 1984, and updated in 1998. It was originally set up because of a European Council requirement.
Data searching	The enquiry process. Search facilities are only as good as the criteria used. The simple 'Find' function is used in generic software; database searching is carried out using a special user interface, e.g. access query function. A more sophisticated use of searching is in program language searches.
Data source	The person/place where data originates.
Data subject	Under the Data Protection Act, the person who is the subject of the data kept.
Direct capture	Capturing data from an original source, not changed or manipulated or encoded, possibly without human intervention – e.g. bar-code data captured by a scanner.
E-mail	Electronic mail – messages are addressed to another e-mail address and stored in an electronic post-box for collection by the recipient.
External threat	Dangers and threats from outside the organisation, e.g. hackers attempting to gain access to an information system.
Fax	An electronic copy of a document sent down a phone line. This can be a physical document manually input into a fax machine, or an electronic document sent using the fax software on a computer.

Term	Acceptable definition
Feedback	Information coming out of an information system (e.g. from a search function on a large database). The processing time between input of query and receipt of useful information – the response speed – is vital.
Global communications	Any communication system that potentially spans the world.
Health and safety legislation	The 1992 Display Screen Equipment Regulations form part of the 1974 Health & Safety at Work Act. They cover everything to do with workstations – space, lighting, adjustable seating, footrests, anti-glare filters and tilting screens, regular breaks, regular eyesight tests, etc. The regulations apply only to office workers, not to students.
Indirect capture	Capturing data as a by-product or output of another system, or data collected for a different purpose, and using the result as input.
Information	Organised facts and figures – data that has been processed and given a context.
Information Commissioner	An independent official appointed to enforce data protection legislation. All systems that hold and process personal data must be registered with the Commissioner.
Information value	A commercial value is associated with information – e.g. in cases of industrial espionage, and on a more mundane level the name-and-address lists that are often sold to interested parties, especially if they have been classified into, say, income groups.
Internal threat	Dangers or threats from inside the company or organisation, e.g. a disgruntled employee, or malicious attempts at accessing restricted data, such as other employees' rates of pay.
Internet	A global network/framework where people and organisations post information and data for others to use and share. Many companies now run their businesses using the Internet, with ordering and other business activities taking place on-line. Internet technologies are also used to set up private intranets.
Internet censorship	This is purely voluntary, as there is no legislation or official censorship. Many Internet service providers allow users to set filters, e.g. the parental controls available with AOL.
Internet ethics	There are various Internet Codes of Practice on how sites should be set up and monitored, e.g. making sure that they are safe to visit, not passing on viruses or worms. The maintenance and policing of the Internet are a collective responsibility. For more information, look up the topic using a search engine.
Internet security	There are always those who attempt to view or use restricted information – security systems such as firewalls can be put in place to prevent unwanted access.
Knowledge	If sets of rules and expertise are applied to information, the result is a knowledge base.
Personal data	Any personal information about a living human being.

Term	Acceptable definition
Remote databases	Data held on another site. Most of the information on the Internet is classified as remote data, and libraries of information could be available via a company intranet.
Search engine	Used on the Internet to look for websites or pages that match the user's criteria. It works using key words.
Software copyright	The legislation is the same as for books and other publications – the Copyright, Designs and Patents Act 1988. Software is licensed for use. FAST (Federation Against Software Theft) has been set up to police this act.
Teleconferencing	Using telephone technology to conduct meetings with several participants across the world, by phoning into a special number.
Telephone	A device to transmit voices or data between separate points.
Teletext	A text-based information system available via television or computerised access.
Value judgement	Information that is an opinion and not a fact – e.g. someone's view of the best colour for a product.
Videoconferencing	Setting up and linking computers so that they can capture real-time video and sound, allowing users in different locations to see and hear the other participants. Video cameras are attached to the computer, and microphones capture sound. Videoconferencing is used extensively in multi-national businesses. It is better than teleconferencing in that participants can see each other's facial expressions and body language.
Viewdata	Similar to Teletext, but interactive (Teletext is not).

3.1 ICT 2

Term	Acceptable definition
Application generator	With input from the user, who specifies the interface and the functions required, this automatically generates the code to produce the customised application. No programming knowledge is needed.
Application package	Any self-contained piece of software that is developed for a specific purpose, or to act as a general purpose package. Sage is an accounts package, with one purpose; Word is a general-purpose word-processing package. As these are normally pre-written, other systems may have to change to interface with them.
Backbone	The cabling/connections used in a building to connect all of the computing power into a network.
Batch processing	Similar transactions are gathered together over a period of time (in batches) and processed together at a set time (e.g. the end of the day) without the need for human intervention. Verification is often used in connection with key-to-disk systems. Validation is often part of batch input, producing error reports for rejected transactions. An example is a

Term	Acceptable definition
	banking system, where transactions that have taken place during the day are collected and fed through in one batch to update the master file overnight, so that reports can be made on the day's business.
Bespoke software	Software written for a specific purpose for a particular company, and to do a particular job. For example, it may be used to collect quality inspection results for a breakfast cereal manufacturer. It is usually written to fit in with other systems within the company.
Bridge	A hardware combination device that allows information to be passed between two similar networks, normally LANs. A buffer in the bridge allows communication between LANs of different speeds.
Command-driven system	A system where command words drive the operations, e.g. MS-DOS where the command *Copy a, b* will copy the contents of file a into file b.
Common user interface	A selection of packages, normally produced by the same manufacturer, which look, feel and act in similar ways. WIMP (windows, icons, menus, pointers) features will be in the same place and look the same (the same icon for the spell checker, etc.).
Communications device	Any piece of hardware that allows computers and other devices to communicate e.g. modem, cable, satellite, bridge, gateway, etc.
(Relational) database	A collection of tables of information which can be linked by the use of primary and foreign keys (see page 98 for the advantages of this), managed using a RDMS – Relational Database Management System.
Data format/data type	How data is held or looked at, e.g. text (alphanumeric), numeric (binary, currency data, integer, real), sound, code/program, Boolean, picture/image/graphical/video.
Firewall	A virtual machine that prevents dangerous, malicious or unwanted communications passing through onto a PC or LAN or company intranet. It is software based.
Flat file	The accepted term for a collection of related data that has no automated links to any other data. Any combining of data has to be manually programmed. This is still in use for transaction file data, but most master data is now held on a database or a set of databases, known as a data warehouse.
Gateway	A hardware/software combination that allows information to be passed between networks of dissimilar types – e.g. a LAN to a WAN. They translate the different protocols and enable communication.
Generic software package	An applications package that is appropriate to many areas of day-to-day business operations, e.g. a spreadsheet used in the accounts department for working out profit/loss, in the payroll department for working out tax returns, and in the MIS department for producing graphs for management reports. The usual examples given are word-processing, spreadsheets and database management systems. Desk-top publishers are normally an alternative to WP. (If you use integrated packages as an example, you will earn only one mark where three might be available.)

Term	Acceptable definition
Graphical user interface (GUI)	An interface with Windows, Icons, Menus and a Pointing device (WIMP). It is simple for non-experts, intuitive (a picture of a printer means click the button to print), easy to learn, and skills are transferable. The most widely used is MS Windows.
Hub/concentrator	A hardware device that handles the cabling requirements of linking LANs together and linking them to WANs.
Human/computer interface	The way in which a computer user communicates with the operating system of the computer he or she is using. Types include command-driven, menu-driven, and graphical user interface.
Input device	Any hardware device that allows data to be input to the system, e.g. mouse, keyboard, scanner.
Integrated package	A package of generic software from a manufacturer that normally contains cut-down versions of their main generic software. The advantages are it is less complex to learn, data can easily be transferred across constituent parts, it is generally cheaper than buying full-blown versions, and the interface looks the same. An example is MS Works. The disadvantages are that it is not as powerful as full-blown packages, has less functionality, and may be harder to export to customers if they are not using the same software.
Interactive processing	A dialogue between the user and the system. The system responds to each input straight away (as distinct from *processes* straight away).
Intranet	Shareable information that uses Internet/web technology, where access is restricted to within a company.
Local area network (LAN)	A collection of computers (normally PCs) and other devices connected together locally – normally in one building or on one site, usually within a one-mile radius, and often using physical data transmission media (e.g. coaxial or fibre optic cable) although infra-red/wireless connections are also possible. There are different types (server-based, peer-to-peer) and topologies (star, ring, bus).
Macro	A small program. It consists of a programmed or recorded series of actions/commands that can be activated either by a single keystroke, or at the click of a button, and can be performed as many times as required. Macros are often used in spreadsheets to perform repetitive calculations or for printing out a report in a particular format, such as a receipt.
Menu-driven system	A system where a hierarchy of menus is used. Each level narrows the options until the correct process is chosen. They could be pull-down menus, pop-up menus, choices (e.g. a list of items, numbered, with an input field to enter the number) or programmed buttons.
Mode of processing	How processing is undertaken for a computer system. The two main modes are batch processing and transaction processing. Transaction processing is further broken down into real-time, pseudo-real-time and interactive processing.

Term	Acceptable definition
Modem	MOdulator-DEModulator – a device that converts analogue signals into digital signals and vice versa. Analogue signals travel over telephone wires or cables (sound waves) and digital signals are what the computer understands (0s and 1s).
Natural language interface	This is an interface where the user can simply type in a normal sentence, e.g. a question such as 'How do I find out about my family tree?', and the interface will assimilate the key words and apply some logic to provide the desired response. This is the opposite of a command-driven interface, where special words are used.
Network topology	The shape of the network – can be bus, ring or star.
Office suite	A collection of fully functional generic application packages sold together with some extra bits and pieces, produced by the same manufacturer, which fully interact with each other. Examples are MS Office 2000 (or XP) and Lotus Smartsuite. An example of an extra for MS Office is MS Query.
OLE (Object linking and embedding)	The mechanism that enables, say, a table of figures or a graph produced in a spreadsheet to be included in a word-processed document. Embedding is similar to copy and paste. Linking the object means that if the original changes, so does the copy in the WP document. This is achieved by copy and paste link.
Operating system	A piece of systems software that controls all events in a computer system. See page 245 for its functions.
Output device	Any piece of hardware that is used by the computer system to produce an output, either on paper or other hard copy (such as microfiche), output media (e.g. CDs by a CD-rewriter) or sound.
Peer-to-peer network	A network set-up where all stations are essentially equal in stature. Software, files and data can be seen by all, access levels permitting. Data transfer and communications are easier and peripheral sharing is improved. If one node goes down, the network normally fails, although this depends on linking – it may mean only that information on that node cannot be seen, but the rest of the network still works.
Printer driver	The interface between the operating system and the printer. It translates formatting information for the printer; stores set-up/configuration information; translates fonts, bit maps and size control for the printer; and controls printer error messaging.
Processing device	The 'chip' or the computer system's engine that performs all arithmetic and logic operations. In a PC, this is normally taken to include the CPU, the motherboard, the video and disk drive controller boards, input and output ports, plus possibly a maths co-processor (used typically for CAD/graphics systems).

Term	Acceptable definition
Program	A set of instructions that, when executed, perform a particular task. Different programming languages suit different applications. Whatever the programmer produces is normally translated or compiled into machine-readable format.
Pseudo-real-time processing	A processing system where things appear to happen instantly – a good example of this is a booking system where each transaction takes its turn in updating the master file. It may seem as if many bookings take place all at once, but in reality they are done one by one. In banking systems, Lloyds-TSB is still the only bank to use this type of processing – where your master account is updated as you take the money from the ATM. All other banks work with copies of the master files as a starting point and record transactions during the day. The batch processing at night updates the master files.
Real-time processing	Where output (from a sensor) affects input. This is used in life-and-death situations (such as heart monitors), fly-by-wire aeroplane systems, and nuclear reactors. Most business systems are not this critical!
Repeater	A hardware device used on a network to boost the data signal every so often, to stop the signal fading out.
Report generator	A piece of software that allows the user to specify the data and format required for a report, with how the data should be grouped. The RG will generate the code to produce the customised report.
Router	A combination of hardware and software that makes sure a packet of data is sent along the backbone in the fastest way.
Server-based network	A central server (on a star-shaped network) that has central control over security, back-up, and monitoring of network activity. Each node (PC or peripheral device) has direct access to the server, so can be faster than peer-to-peer. Also, it can have different (non-compatible) device types as these have direct links.
Storage device	Any hardware device that can hold data.
Transaction processing	Where each item of data is dealt with as it is submitted, and each transaction is completed before the next is begun. For example, if you call the Index mail-order company, they check each item is in stock and confirm the order before asking for your next item number. Their competitors GUS, on the other hand, check a screenful of items at a time, so their 'transaction' is bigger.
Transmission medium	Any material across which data can be transmitted. It can be metal (twisted-pair wires, coaxial cable), non-metal physical (fibre optic cable) or waves (radio-waves, infra-red waves, microwaves). Each has limitations.
Validation	Where a program/software check is made to see if data entered into a field conforms to the rules. There are many types (see page 244 below).

Term	Acceptable definition
Verification	There are two types – one is a sight check of the accuracy of data on screen or paper; the other is an automatic data preparation/key-to-disk system check, where items are keyed from the source document and stored, then keyed on 'verify' a second time again from the source document, and compared with the stored data. This checks that the details on the source document have been accurately transferred to computer.
Wide area network (WAN)	Connected hardware spread over a wide geographical area (anything from 2 km to world-wide) and making use of third-party telecommunications equipment (e.g. telephone lines, satellite communications). Examples include the Internet, but also any large national or multi-national organisation's network, e.g. big banks, car manufacturers, and government departments.

4 **Contrasts and differences**

Examination questions often ask for a comparison between two related terms, aspects or characteristics. Here are some of the more obvious pairings. Along with definitions, the question quite often asks for examples, so be prepared to give an example in each case.

Verification and validation

Verification is a second check to make sure that data has been transcribed properly from the source document (this can be a sight check or a machine-based check on a key-to-disk system). Validation is where a software program checks that the data is in valid formats or that each field holds valid data.

Accuracy and validity of data/information

Validity of data means that the data in a field is acceptable to the program; accuracy means that the data is true or correct. For example, WA15 6QF is a valid post code, but it is not accurate for an address in London.

LANs and WANs

A LAN is normally located on one site and connected physically using cable or line-of-sight infra-red wireless signal, whereas a WAN can be world-wide, but certainly over a distance of more than 2 km, connected using a telecommunication line such as telephone or satellite.

Peer-to-peer and server-based networks

Peer-to-peer networks, generally set out as a ring, use the same type of computer, and pass the data packet from machine to machine, with equal status on the network. If one machine fails, the network may stop working. Server-based networks are generally of the star type, and keep shared applications and data on the network server. Each station has direct communication with the server (which is therefore faster), central control of security, back-up and monitoring. Different types of station are possible (such as PC and Mac), and if one fails, it does not affect the network (only the server failing does that).

Security and privacy

Security is ensured by making people aware of their responsibilities to the company for which they work, being wary of how they deal with company data/information: using passwords/log-in procedures, signing a non-disclosure agreement, complying with codes of conduct/practice, and generally taking care of company property in day-to-day activities. Privacy is to do with personal data, and is covered under the Data Protection Act.

Security and safety

Security of data means using measures to prevent unauthorised persons, e.g. hackers, from accessing the data. Methods of security include encryption. Safety of data involves measures to prevent malicious or accidental damage to data. Methods include staff vetting, training, backing up, etc.

Batch and transaction processing

Batch processing is used in large-volume systems, e.g. utility billing, where it is not urgent to process the data. Transaction processing is used where it is important for the smooth running of a business for transactions to be processed as they occur, e.g. in seat-booking systems.

Whenever advantages and disadvantages are requested in a comparison, make sure that an advantage for one is not repeated as the disadvantage for another – it will not be credited twice. For example, do not say, 'an advantage of peer-to-peer networks is that there is no central reliance on a server', then 'a disadvantage for a client-server is that it relies on a single machine (the server)'.

5 Quick topic revision

Sometimes it is useful to recap what is included in a topic area, especially in those areas where exam questions often ask for lists or descriptions, such as 'Describe four' or 'Give three'.

The lists below can act as an aide-memoire. They could be used for testing yourself or working with a friend to test each other; they could also be used as a class exercise during the revision period, with the teacher asking for items or for explanations of items. Alternatively, they could be used as a basis for a team quiz, where the same questions are asked of all.

5.0 ICT 1 topics

- **Benefits of ICT:**
  - volume
  - accuracy
  - repetitive tasks are catered for
  - complexity of processing is catered for
  - speed of processing, of searching, etc.
- **Limitations of ICT:**
  - technical or hardware limitations
  - software limitations
  - inaccurate database design
  - communication systems limitations
  - inappropriate data modelling
  - inadequate data-control mechanisms.
- **Personal qualities/characteristics of ICT team member:**
  - inter-personal skills
  - strong technical competence
  - self-motivated
  - fast learner
  - flexible
  - good verbal communication skills
  - good written communication skills
  - team-working skills
  - thoroughness, attention to detail and reliability.
- **Principles of the Data Protection Act. Data should be:**
  - obtained and processed fairly and lawfully
  - held only for lawful purposes, those described in the register entry
  - used or disclosed only for those purposes
  - adequate, relevant and not excessive in relation to purpose
  - accurate and up to date
  - held no longer than necessary
  - surrounded by proper security
  - provided on request to the individual concerned, who has the right if appropriate to have the information erased or corrected.

5.1 ICT 2 topics

■ **Types of validation checks:**
- ■ Range check – input must be between/over/under certain values
- ■ Type check – input must be numeric only/alpha only
- ■ Length check – input must be exactly/no more than *nn* characters
- ■ Format check – input follows a certain pattern, e.g. *dd/mm/yy* for a date or *LL00 0LL* for a postcode
- ■ Presence check – input must be present
- ■ List/look-up check – input must be one of a list
- ■ Cross-field check – input must be *x* if other field is *y*
- ■ Look-up/existence check – input must match something on a file in the system.

■ **Advantages of relational databases over flat file systems:**
- ■ independence of data
- ■ less redundant or duplicated data
- ■ better consistency of data
- ■ improved quality of management information
- ■ single input principle – less time wasted on updating same data many times
- ■ ad-hoc reports easier to produce because of linked information – increased productivity
- ■ different access rights are possible to different parts of the database, giving increased control over data security.

■ **Data capture methods/devices:**
- ■ speech recognition
- ■ optical-character recognition
- ■ magnetic ink character recognition
- ■ optical-mark recognition
- ■ bar-code reading
- ■ keyboard
- ■ key-to-disk
- ■ mouse
- ■ magnetic-strip reading
- ■ touch-tone telephones
- ■ sensors to capture data.

■ **Output devices:**
- ■ dot-matrix printers
- ■ ink-jet printers
- ■ laser printers
- ■ graph plotters (pen or flat-bed)
- ■ monitors (VDUs).

■ **Storage devices:**
- ■ floppy disks
- ■ hard drives
- ■ zip drives
- ■ jaz drives (similar to zip, larger 2GB capacity)
- ■ RAID (redundant array of independent disks)

- DVD (digital versatile disk) drives
- DAT (digital audio tape) drives (2–40GB)
- DLT (digital linear tape) drives (70GB)
- CD-ROM drives (700MB)
- CD-R and CD-RW drives
- ditto drives (2GB capacity, tape in removable cartridge, data transfer 10MB/minute)
- optical drives (used for long-term data storage, e.g. in banking systems, where data must be held for seven years minimum).

Functions of an operating system:
- manages all other programs in a computer
- manages user communication with the computer
- handles input/output from attached hardware devices/peripheral control
- resource allocation and scheduling
- memory management
- backing storage management
- management of multi-tasking
- interrupt handling
- boot/re-boot/boot-strap loading/loading user interface.

Editing facilities of word-processing packages:
- cut/copy and paste
- drag and drop
- find and replace
- insert/insert file/insert graphic
- delete letter/line/word/paragraph
- spell check/grammar check.

Steps in batch processing:
- large volumes of like data are collected together over a set period of time or into batches of a fixed amount, e.g. 50, to be processed in one computer run at a specified time, without any human intervention.

Security measures:
- security procedures such as not leaving terminals logged on, password security
- staffing issues – vetting/training/discipline
- back-up procedures
- use of encryption
- virus checking
- permitted access levels
- use of passwords
- firewalls
- use of software for monitoring terminal activity.

Back-up procedures:
- selection of hardware/storage medium e.g. DAT tape, RAID
- selection of software
- decision on what will be copied
- decision on frequency
- decision on number of copies/generations held
- recovery procedures

- location/security of back-up copies, e.g. offsite, in fireproof safe, etc.
- job responsibilities for back-up/recovery
- prevention of access to back-up – e.g. encryption, password protection
- organisation of back-ups, e.g. labelling
- timing of back-up operation, e.g. at night.

Implications of package change/upgrade:
- upwards compatibility (no downwards compatibility)
- training needs of users
- lost productive time
- increased use (and cost) of help desks
- possible hardware incompatibility
- possible systems/other software incompatibility
- installation problems
- learning curve for users (loss of productivity).

Error types and handling:
- Transcription errors when transferring data from one place to another, e.g. from a source document or from a telephone conversation via a keyboard. Usually caused by mixing like letters/numbers from bad handwriting, e.g. o and 0, or S and 5; or a person's speech not being clear; or simple typing mistakes. For many transcription errors, using a form of verification is the only way to trap the error.
- Transposition errors where numbers, especially, are transposed. The most common way of trapping these mistakes is by using a check digit (used extensively in banking for bank account numbers, credit card numbers, etc., and also in ISBN numbers on books).

Causes of problems installing/running complex software:
- may not have been tested on the same platform as the one on which it is being installed
- may still have bugs
- may be Alpha or Beta version (a pre-release version)
- may be incompatible with systems software or other software on computer
- hardware may not be big/fast enough to run it
- may not have been tested for the amount of data being used (lack of volume testing)
- all paths may not have been tested properly
- may have been rushed to market (perhaps to beat a competitor's product).

INDEX